BRITISH MUSIC VIDEOS, 1966–2016

Music and the Moving Image

Series Editors
Kevin J. Donnelly, University of Wales Aberystwyth and Beth Carroll, University of Southampton

Titles in the series include:

Film's Musical Moments
by Ian Conrich and Estella Tincknell (eds)

Music and the Moving Image: A Reader
by Kevin Donnelly (ed.)

Music, Sound and Multimedia
by Jamie Sexton (ed.)

Music Video and the Politics of Representation
by Diane Railton and Paul Watson

Contemporary Musical Film
by Kevin J. Donnelly and Beth Carroll (eds)

British Music Videos, 1966–2016: Genre, Authenticity and Art
by Emily Caston

www.edinburghuniversitypress.com/series/mami

BRITISH MUSIC VIDEOS, 1966–2016

Genre, Authenticity and Art

Emily Caston

EDINBURGH
University Press

Edinburgh University Press is one of the leading university presses in the UK. We publish academic books and journals in our selected subject areas across the humanities and social sciences, combining cutting-edge scholarship with high editorial and production values to produce academic works of lasting importance. For more information visit our website: edinburghuniversitypress.com.

© Emily Caston, 2020, 2022

Edinburgh University Press Ltd
The Tun – Holyrood Road
12(2f) Jackson's Entry
Edinburgh EH8 8PJ

First published in hardback by Edinburgh University Press 2020

Typeset in 10/12.5 Adobe Sabon by
IDSUK (DataConnection) Ltd
A CIP record for this book is available from the British Library

ISBN 978 1 4744 3532 1 (hardback)
ISBN 978 1 4744 3535 2 (paperback)
ISBN 978 1 4744 3533 8 (webready PDF)
ISBN 978 1 4744 3534 5 (epub)

The right of Emily Caston to be identified as the author of this work has been asserted in accordance with the Copyright, Designs and Patents Act 1988, and the Copyright and Related Rights Regulations 2003 (SI No. 2498).

CONTENTS

Acknowledgements   vii

1	A Commercial Film Art	1
2	Genre	18
3	Editing	39
4	Movement and Dance	55
5	Gender	72
6	Authorship	88
7	Distribution	105
8	Art, Commerce and America	123
9	Conclusion	142

Appendices

I.	Primary Sources	158
II.	Listing and Film Credits for Landmark Special Edition Boxset	163

Bibliography   179
Index   212

ACKNOWLEDGEMENTS

The research undertaken for this book was initially made possible by a research grant from the Arts and Humanities Research Council. Enormous thanks are due to the University of West London for supporting the very substantial additional research that was necessary, as well as to my colleagues Justin Smith and Richard Paterson. Thanks to my research assistants Mimi Haddon, Alex Wilson, Marc Evans and project administrator Jennifer Roberts. Credit is also due to our project partners at the British Film Institute (in particular Dylan Cave and Will Fowler) and the British Library (Andy Linehan), to the team at Thunderbird who distributed the accompanying DVD, and to our academic steering committee Paula Hearsum, Dave Laing, Rob Dickens, Pete Dyson, Marketa Uhlirova, Diane Railton, Holly Rogers, Keith Negus and Duncan White. Thanks also to the series editor, Kevin Donnelly.

But the greatest of thanks go to everyone in the British music video industry, particularly Liz Kessler, without whose hugely intelligent contributions and corporate-savvy interventions neither this book nor the boxset would have been possible: Aaron Sillis, Adam Dunlop, Aiden Farrell, Amanda James, Andy Morahan, Angus Cameron, Anna Brunoro, Aoife McCardle, Arlene Philips, Art Jones, Astrid Edwards, Ben Totty, Bernard Rose, Brian Grant, Carole Burton-Fairbrother, Carrie Sutton, Cindy Burnay, Cynthia Lole, Dan Curwin, Daniel Wolfe, David Knight, David Mallet, David Wilson, Dawn Shadforth, Dilly Gent, Dom & Nic, Dom Leung, Don Cameron, Don Letts, Don Searll, Dougal Wilson, Fiz Oliver, Fran Broadhurst, Ged Doherty, Hannah Turnbull-Water, Helen Langridge, Henry Scholfield, Holly Blakey,

Huse Monfaradi, Jake Nava, Jake Polonsky, James Hackett, Jamie Thraves, Joe Guest, John Crome, John Hardwick, John Hassay, John Mathieson, John Moule, John Stewart, Jon Madsen, Julia Clancey, Julia Knight, Julien Temple, Juliette Larthe, Kai Hsiung, Kevin Godley, Kris P. Taylor, Lana Topham, Litza Bixler, Luke Losey, Luke Tierney, Maria Manton, Maria Mochnacz, Marissa Garner, Martin Roker, Mat Kirkby, Matt Forrest, Matthew Fone, Max Giwa, Michael Lindsay-Hogg, Mike O'Keefe, Natricia Bernard, Neil Grigson, Nick Egan, Nick Goldsmith, Nigel Dick, Nigel Talamo, Niven Howie, Paul Roberts, Pedro Romhanyi, Peter Care, Peter Whitehead, Phil Tidy, Piers Bedford, Rich Skinner, Richard Barnett, Richard Heslop, Ringan Ledwidge, Rob Dickens, Robbie Ryan, Robin Dean, Russell Curtis, Russell Mulcahy, Sarah Chatfield, Sasha Nixon, Scott Millaney, Shynola, Sophie Muller, Steve Barron, Steve Beckett, Steve Chivers, Svana Gisladottir, Tareq Kubaisi, Tim Hope, Tim Nash, Tim Pope, Tom Jobbins, Tom Lindsay, Tom Russell, Tony Kearns, Trudy Bellinger, Vaugh Arnell, Vince Landay, WIZ. All went beyond and above their duty on our official 'industry panel' to act as historical consultants in the supply of much additional information and valued reflections on the themes the project set out to explore. A full list of everyone involved in the project is given in Appendix I.

When people ask, 'Oh, why was that such a great video?' I always say there are so many reasons not to have a great video. But sometimes all the stars align and every little bit is put into place for that right thing. It rarely happens, but when it does it's just magic. Right song, right artist, right director, right time.

Andy Morahan
2016

1 A COMMERCIAL FILM ART

Between 1966 and 2016, the British music and screen industries produced tens of thousands of music videos which have been viewed and celebrated across the world. Today many of these music videos can be seen on the internet amongst a seemingly infinite stream of official videos, archive videos, lyric videos and mash-ups. But no one has yet written a history of all that content. Credits are hard to come by. Little is known about the filmmakers, still less about the companies that made them. When most people think about a music video, they rarely wonder in which country it's been produced. People regard music videos as one of the most universal of media because they are films without dialogue: essentially silent films which speak a universal language that transcends national boundaries. Even within the industry, people think about music video as a global industry made by international teams of creatives, and not as a domestic product like a feature film.

The primary objective of this book is to present evidence about the British experience of music videos from 1966 to 2016 which has been obscured, especially in the pre-digital era, by an excessive focus on the USA. The book challenges the widespread assumption that music video emerged in the 1980s as a result of the launch of MTV in New York, and that British audiences were 'Americanised' by MTV in the 1980s. Throughout the '80s and '90s the USA was seen as the champion of music video. With the exception of interest in Chris Cunningham (e.g. Leggott 2016, Lockwood 2017, Korsgaard 2017), most scholarship focuses on US 'auteurs' such as Hype Williams and Spike Jonze, and on US platforms and broadcast channels. As such this book constitutes part of a larger body of recent work in film, television and music studies correcting a past tendency to focus on the so-called Americanisation of British culture (e.g. Glancy 2014) construing Britain as a victim of US cultural imperialism inflicted through MTV. Miller (2000), for example, has convincingly argued that much US television was in fact British in origin, influenced by such imports as *Monty Python's Flying Circus* (BBC 1969–74) and *The Avengers* (ABC / Thames 1961–9). Contrary to what was suggested by Goodwin, writing in the early 1990s as he relocated from the UK to the USA (1994), British audiences were not voluminous consumers of MTV. In Britain throughout the 1990s, as British record labels and filmmakers knew all too well, music videos were not watched by most audiences on MTV – instead they were seen on terrestrial TV shows such as *Top of the Pops* (*TOTP*) (BBC 1964–2006) and *The Chart Show* (C4 1986–9, ITV 1989–98).

Two British videos routinely cited in the literature as marking the 'birth' of the music video were made before MTV was even launched: Queen's '*Bohemian Rhapsody*' (1975), which is routinely identified as the first music video ever made, and the Buggles' '*Video Killed the Radio Star*' (1979), the first video to have been broadcast on MTV (in 1981). Both videos were shot in Britain and directed and produced by British filmmakers for British recording artists, through British production companies and British record labels. These two videos are only the tip of an iceberg of tens of thousands of music videos made by a British industry that grew in the back streets of Soho from the late 1970s onwards, with aesthetic roots in the promo clips of the so-called 'British Invasion' (1964–6). This book is offered as an accompaniment to John Mundy's work on British musicals because, despite the fact that between 1944 and 1946, Britain produced more musicals than any other genre, few of those made it onto American cinema screens or into the history books on the film musical (Mundy 2007: 3); although British music videos did make it onto US television, they haven't paralleled the hegemony of American music videos.

But a secondary objective of this British analysis is to re-examine some of the main strands of thought about music videos in a different light. Today, with the publication of Burns and Hawkins' edited collection on music video (2019) and Arnold et al.'s edited collection on music video (2017), as well as publications by Railton and Watson (2011), Korsgaard (2017), Keazor and Wübbena (2010) and the considerable volume of work published by Carol Vernallis, 'music video studies' has become almost a viable term describing a *sui generis* discipline of study. Far from initiating the death of music videos, as predicted by some in the early years of the twenty-first century, smartphones and the internet seem to have breathed a new era of creativity into this medium, and music videos are attracting an increasing amount of scholarship. But through the '80s and '90s they were deemed either television fillers or postmodern flow, and generally languished at the bottom of what I have called a 'hierarchy of screen arts' in film and television studies (Caston 2019b). In those earlier years, work on music video fell into a parent discipline such as cultural studies, popular music studies, film and television studies or dance studies. In order to write this book, I have therefore had to familiarise myself with the literature within all of those paradigms, as well as this new music video studies. If this means that for some scholars amongst my readers, my interpretation of theoretical issues is not as refined as they would like, I apologise in advance. But, as Hoesterey put it when embarking upon her commendable study of pastiche, 'drawing upon the scholarly traditions of several disciplines often means sacrificing depth for breadth' (2001: xii).

The core premise of this book is that music video is a type of *commercial film art* located within the paraphernalia of selling music developed by record labels in the twentieth century. When interviewed for this project, Steve Beckett, founder and managing director of Warp Records, described music video as 'a piece of art with a purpose'. Warp has been a creative leader in music video since the '80s, pioneering the release of a dedicated compilation VHS tape for the *Artificial Intelligence II* (1994) project and a DVD compilation of the label's videos *Warp Vision 1989–2004* (2004) a decade later. What does he mean by 'purpose'? He means that it's not made in complete freedom: the filmmakers will be given, if not a brief, then a track and some technical requirements to do with synchronisation and delivery. For a creative entrepreneur like Beckett, a creative work can be simultaneously artistic and commercial. A successful video has the peer acclaim of one and the impact of the other. For Beckett art and commerce are happy partners. It's a view that finds more of a home in the USA than in the UK, where art and commerce have tended to be seen as mutually exclusive. That, in part, is what this book is about.

In the chapters that follow I will argue that, as well as being a commercial film art, music video is an art that only succeeds when it is authenticated by its core and primary target audience of fans. In marketing terms, this primary target audience is an artist's existing fanbase – often those fans who supported the artist through the first gigs, propelled them into getting their first label contract and buy their tickets on tour. A label Chief Executive Officer (CEO) or marketing department in the old days would use a music video to break through to a new secondary or tertiary market – such as an audience in a new territory, like the USA. The really challenging problem, in using a music video as a marketing tool, is that of finding a language, style and content that will attract a new audience whilst retaining the engagement and loyalty of existing fans. This process of authentication is highly specialised, and it is why not just any accomplished film director, commissioner or executive can make music videos: the whole filmmaking team needs expert specialist knowledge of musical traditions, music communities and visual culture.

To locate music videos within a longer history is not new. It is *de rigueur* to announce the existence of a list of precursors to the music video, foremost amongst these the Soundies of the early 1940s, and the later US Snader Telescriptions, musical performances shot and edited on 35mm and sold in the early 1950s to TV stations to fill gaps in their programming. Also significant were the Scopitones, created by a French division of Philips, the Italian and British Cinebox, and the American Colorsonics (Herzog 2004, Lukow 1991). But to locate music videos within the history of British film and television is less common. Mundy has drawn our attention to British musical shorts such as the *Musical Film Revue* (1933) series, the 1935 *Equality Musical Revue* series and, from 1936, the *British Lion Varieties* series. Developed during the transition from silent film to synchronised-sound film at the end of the 1920s, these musical shorts continued to be important for British film production under the quota system in the 1930s, and remained a presence in British cinema until the advent of single-feature programming. Like music videos, shorts enabled audiences to see bands and singers whilst their popularity was at its height and songs were current.

Why does the book begin in 1966? This was a landmark year in which bands like The Kinks progressed from providing TV shows with clips of pre-recorded live performances recorded on earlier TV shows when they couldn't perform in person to providing the TV shows with specific 'filmed inserts' which they had shot on location and edited independently. The work flow therefore severed its ties with television production and moved into the realm of *independent film production*: directors, owning their own kit, and with funding either from their own pocket or artist management, would shoot and edit their films at home or through an independent production company. Between 1966 and 1976 there was a ten-year period of haphazard independent production with no institutionalised procedures or trade agreements whilst artists and filmmakers made these clips. From 1976 to 1986 there was a period of conflict between music video filmmakers and established powers in the film and television industries – notably the BBC, the Musicians' Union (MU 1893–) and the Association of Cinematograph, Television and Allied Technicians (ACTT 1956–91). Then, by the late 1980s, a standardised set of procedures fell into place for the commissioning, funding, production, post-production, distribution and exhibition of music videos, which reigned until another period of transition (2001–3), when television distribution virtually collapsed. Internet distribution took over, but it was not for another period of at least ten years – until 2014 – that a viable funding model emerged as a result of advertising revenue.

Between 1966 and 1968, British artists and their labels commissioned and created a hugely impressive corpus of music videos from this emerging independent sector. These 1960s promos differed from Britain's 1930s musical shorts in a crucial way: they drew attention to the medium of film itself and to the authorship of the filmmaker. Where the 1930s musical shorts were 'unpretentious affairs, concerned to showcase the talent with little aspiration to cinematic innovation or, on some occasions, competence' (Mundy 2007: 97), the early promos were full of disjunctive edits and fancy effects. Directors such as Peter Whitehead, who shot pioneering clips for The Animals and Pink Floyd and directed a semi-documentary, *Tonite Let's All Make Love in London* (1967), about the 'swinging London' scene of the 1960s, were the new superstars of counter-culture in Britain. The '60s promos were influenced by the 16mm cinematography and location shooting of the French New Wave. The music industry was willing and able to fund this work because it had a vested interest and funds. Demand for music videos grew in the 1970s because of the harmonisation of single release dates in Europe to combat audio-cassette piracy. Record labels had to use an alternative method to promote new singles on music TV shows because it was difficult to co-ordinate live appearances for the same release window. British record labels began to commission more of the '60s filmed clips so that these could be sent to European music TV shows in lieu of a live appearance. Budgets grew, then hit a crisis in the late 1980s when finance was restructured, and then bounced back in 1991 as the industry saw the new compact disc (CD) take off as a new sales format. The huge revenues accruing from the sale of back catalogues on CD funded the 'Golden Era' of music video in the 1990s (Caston 2015). By 1998, the UK record industry spent £36.5 million on approximately 850 music videos (Caston et al. 2000), a very substantial increase on the estate of £10 million spent in 1984 (Fisher 1984). The 1998 figure is based on data collected by myself and the then video commissioners of East West Records (Nisha Parti), Chrysalis (Carrie Sutton) and Universal (Nijico Walker) in 1999 from a survey that we conducted with UK major, indie and semi-independent record labels in response to ITV's decision to end *The Chart Show*. The figure of £36.5 million reflects the value in sterling of music videos commissioned in Britain but not necessarily produced in Britain because some of the videos would have been contracted to production companies outside the UK.

The apparatus of music video on an industrial scale in the 1980s brought a *potential* conflict between the ambitions of the director-as-auteur and the artist-as-authentic. A new generation of auteur filmmakers, more focused on paying homage to their cinematic heroes than giving voice to musicians, saw opportunities to express themselves through cinema. But routes into the commercial film industry were blocked unless one had parents who worked in the business or could get a trades union card. Film equipment and film stock were prohibitively expensive. The BFI (British Film Institute) Experimental Film Fund, which later became the BFI Production Fund, offered small grants, but from the late 1970s onwards it focused more on features than shorts. Music video offered a way for that generation to access 35mm and 16mm kit, stock and laboratories.

Music video is a product of a collaboration between two industries with two distinctive cultures of production and culturally accepted codes of authenticity: the screen industries in which the film-director-as-auteur has played an important role, and the popular music industry, in which the artist-as-auteur has dominated. Throughout this book, I refer to musicians as *artists* (derived from 'artistes') because this is how they are referred to within the music industry itself. By *production culture* I mean a set of beliefs and institutionalised practices for the production of creative products (whether funded by charity or government on a not-for-profit basis, or by industry for profit). On more than one occasion, this potential conflict has manifested as a serious dispute between the production company and record company about what kind of video should be made. Most music videos arise from a great deal of heated debate about who owns what and who has the right to decide what – arising from the fact that fundamentally, neither side can agree on whether a video is legitimately 'a film' or 'part of the music' – and who, therefore, is entitled to final creative control and a cut of the profits of the revenue arising from the work.

When I refer to the music video for a track rather than the track itself, I put the title in both quotation marks *and italics* to denote that it is an integrated audiovisual work produced by artists within this screen culture (e.g. Radiohead '*Street Spirit*'); by contrast when I refer to the song in isolation, I will adhere to the academic convention of putting it only in quotation marks (Radiohead '*Street Spirit*'). This procedure overcomes the problem that the track used by the filmmakers for the video will have been edited either by them or by the artists' team to fit the picture edit, and is a different audio artistic entity to the version that the label will have released for the single charts. I will include the release date of the video in brackets after the title, but not the country of release.

Barker and Taylor have argued that in the last fifty years, the quest for authenticity amongst artists has been central to the organisation and development of the music industry and music appreciation (2007). This quest for authenticity has manifested in a very particular way in the music video industry. A music video in itself isn't authentic because it is original or truthful. A music video is authentic because it is deemed authentic by a significant community of fans. As Moore says, authenticity is *ascribed*, not inscribed (2002: 210). Music videos are *authenticated* within and by specific communities of artists and fans. If we think about authenticity as consistency between a person's actions and core beliefs – being ourselves, rather than an imitation of what we think we should be or have been told we should be – then it will be this community that deems whether or not the music video content and performance are authentic to the values of the artist and community and, more importantly, to the values the community has attributed to the artist (and these will frequently not be the same, especially when the artist is having a career change). But, as Attias (2016: 131) has said, much of the discourse about authenticity suffers from the assumption that artifice and authenticity are incompatible. If we see authenticity as an ascribed quality, it's perfectly possible to appreciate that the highly mediatised and theatrical music videos of certain artists in the 1970s and 1980s were authenticated by their fans. There is nothing inherently inauthentic about artifice. Bowie's mediatised videos were authenticated by his fans.

The emergence of this *narrative of authenticity* was probably escalated by the popularisation of existentialist ideas through the works of Jean-Paul Sartre (1905–80) in the decades following the 1968 uprisings across Europe – a narrative that affected almost everyone travelling through art school in Britain thereafter. It was escalated by the advent of music television. Andrew Goodwin has argued (1992) that music television caused a crisis of authenticity because mass capitalist media and expanding label marketing departments ushered in a crisis of mediatisation. As well as rooting themselves in authentic cultural and musical traditions, artists strove to convince their fans that they were *real*, rather than phoney, celebrities, or that if they were phoney celebrities, this was a result of their own intentional authentic manipulation of media. The dangers of 'inauthenticity' arising from music video were addressed by MTV's decision to run the *MTV Unplugged* (1989–99) series to recover its own reputation as a platform for authentic artists after over a decade of criticism.

Although this book carries the concept of 'British' in the title, it is not about filmmakers who carry British passports. It's a book about people who have worked on music videos in British creative clusters which often emerged from music scenes (clubs, indie record labels and retailers). The filmmakers within these communities would, I suspect, be troubled by association with a problematic term such as 'British'. In particular, this is a story about Soho, where the independent production sector for music video production emerged in the 1970s. Soho's role in the UK screen industries is generally dated to the 1920s, when a number of business and administration companies involved in the funding and production of film set up in and around Wardour Street W1. From the mid-1960s, the first promo directors used the infrastructure of production companies and other facilities that had developed there to produce their films. In the 1970s they set up their production companies, alongside the post-production companies, TV commercial companies and other independent film and television production companies.

Videos were produced within this cluster for the full fifty-year period on which this book focuses. In the year during which this study of British music videos ended (2016), Soho still dominated the UK's screen industries: a report by the consultancy group BOP found that the entire value chain of film was still available within the square mile of Soho (BOP Consulting 2014). At the same time, Soho has been a centre for the popular music industry. The music video industry emerged within this square mile during the

1960s, when wannabe directors and producers roamed the streets looking for work as runners. They weren't just film fans, they were avid music fans too, and idled their time in the 'Golden Mile' of vinyl, where, in the 1990s, more than twenty independent stores once lined Berwick Street alongside the fruit market and sex shops (whilst the musicians were buying instruments on Denmark Street). As a result, Soho has been the cultural and geographical location in which these two industries intersected and negotiated, from the mid-1960s to the present day, over what is 'authentic' and who is 'the author' in music / film collaborations. Typical of a creative cluster, most of the core creative work of Soho has been done through serendipitous interactions 'on the street, in pubs, coffee shops, record stores, and clubs' (Pratt and Gornostaeva 2009: 120).

I use the term British to pinpoint a set of characteristics of style and practice which have emerged from the production culture of London and other regional centres in Britain from the mid-1960s to 2016. In 2011, Creative Skillset found that 80 per cent of the film production workforce and 98 per cent of the visual effects (VFX) workforce was in London. In 2015, just under half (49.5 per cent) of the UK total gross value added (GVA) for film, TV, video and radio could be found in London and 61.2 per cent for music, performing and visual arts (Rocks 2017: 7). Clusters of record labels and production companies have congregated in Camden, Hackney and Kensal Rise. Significant centres of music video commissions have also existed in Manchester (Factory Records), Sheffield (Warp Records) and Brighton (Skint Records).

The range of passports held by everyone involved in making these videos is huge. Larger still is the variety in cultures of everyone who has taken part. That is not to say that music video has been exempt from the institutionally discriminatory structures determining screen production across the UK in 1966–2016. But a significant number of the creatives who have worked in London's production companies for British record labels are not British, and whilst they often rented apartments in London, maintained homes and representation in at least one other country: Ireland, France, Scandinavia, the USA or Germany, to name but a few. Michel Gondry and Stéphane Sednaoui (France), Jonas Åkerlund (Sweden), Michael Lindsay-Hogg and Spike Jonze (USA), Russell Mulcahy (Australia), Scott Millaney and Tony Kearns (Ireland) have all been leading figures in the industry. A 2017 report commissioned by the BFI estimated that 6 per cent of all audiovisual (AV) industry employment is constituted by European Union members excluding the UK. That figure increased to 25–30 per cent in animation, VFX and video games (British Film Institute Oxera 2017: 10). As this book will demonstrate, British music video's success story is in no small way related to the growth of VFX and post-production in Soho.

It is not automatically obvious, however, that *music video* is the best term for the entire fifty-year period this book covers. The concept of 'promotional clips' or 'promotional films' was used to describe films shot in Britain from the early 1960s to the mid-1970s. In those years, many promo clips were filmed in house at the BBC studios, and promo clips were still relatively rare on terrestrial television. When the clips were filmed outside the BBC by filmmakers such as Peter Whitehead, they were shot and cut on 16mm or 35mm film. But television could not broadcast film prints; the prints had to be transferred to tape via a process developed in house at the BBC called 'telecine' in order for them to be broadcast. When, in the late 1970s, the industry increased its production of promo clips and permission was given by the ACTT trade union for two independently owned post-production companies to operate in Soho outside the BBC, a crucial change took place: the process of telecine became part of the workflow of the music video director and producers, not merely a subsequent technical operation executed by BBC technicians. Telecine became a creative stage in which the director, producer, director of photography (DoP) and telecine operator (later in the 1990s renamed 'colourist') would spend hours, if not days, experimenting with footage and software packages to regrade the footage and add effects, using such materials as women's nylon tights, Vaseline and chocolate. Creative telecine was essentially an invention of the music video industry in partnership with post houses MPC (Moving Picture Company), Molinare, Rushes, VTR (Video Tape Recording) and Framestore, in the hands of innovators such as Jean-Clément Soret, Tom Russell, Aiden Farrell and Tareq Kubaisi from the late 1970s through the 1980s into the 1990s, when it was finally adopted into the workflow for television drama production and feature films.

When, around 1980/1, the concept of 'music video' took hold in labels, initially at MTV and then at the BBC, many outside the industry began to assume, wrongly, that these clips were shot on videotape rather than on film. Barron explains that this happened not because the clips were shot on video, but because the masters were delivered to record labels and broadcasters on videotapes, so record companies would say, 'Give us another one of those videos' (Barron 2014: 9), and passed this language on to the broadcasters. This was compounded when, on 17 January 1981, *Music Week* relaunched as *Music & Video Week* (in 1983 its title was changed back to *Music Week* and an imprint, *Video Week*, was launched). It is factually correct that some clips were originated on videotape for a short period in the late 1970s and early 1980s by directors such as Richard Heslop and David Mallet. But most directors from 1979 onwards preferred not to shoot on tape, and did so reluctantly only if the record label refused to award a large enough budget to shoot on film. Most directors preferred to shoot 16mm or 35mm. Only very reluctantly did the music video move across to shoot on digital film in the 2000s, and in the last year of this study, 2016, some videos were still being shot on 35mm.

In his autobiography, Steve Barron writes that filmmakers continued to use the concept of promotional films after the record labels adopted the terminology of 'music videos' (2014). When *Music Week* launched its dedicated trade paper for the music video industry in 1992 it chose to stick with the earlier concept for its title, *Promo News*. When, in 2007, it ceased circulation as a print title and was taken over by the then editor David Knight it was relaunched as a website, Promo News TV. Knight retained the concept of the 'promo' despite the fact that promos had functioned as *sui generis* television programming since the mid 1980s. Filmmakers today use both the term 'promos' and 'music videos', despite the fact that music videos are neither shot on video nor delivered or screened on video. In the interests of fashioning a vocabulary of music appreciation which is useful to the industry itself, I will use 'promo clips' to refer to musical shorts made from the early 1960s to the late 1970s, and the concept of 'music video' for all works produced after that.

A point here is needed about the mistaken idea that music videos are advertising. Since their academic baptism within cultural studies in the 1980s, music videos have fallen victim to what Winston Fletcher deems 'the traditional British intellectual distaste for salesmanship' (2008: 1). From the beginning (Aufderheide 1986: 57) to the present day (Keazor and Wübbena 2010: 9, Dodds 2009a: 249), scholars have categorised it as a kind of advertising. The distaste was mirrored within the industry; writing of those years in the seminal 1986 collection of essays on British advertising published by the History of Advertising Trust, James Garrett observed an 'antagonism', 'hatred' and 'distrust' towards commercials which prevailed in the 'establishment' 'legitimate' film industry (Garrett 1986: 388). As both 'entertainment' and 'advertising', music video was for a long time left to the domain of cultural studies, where it could be studied as both epiphenomenon of and consolation of capitalism.

To understand why music videos are not advertisements, it's necessary to recognise the advertising model. In the traditional model of television advertising from this period in history, the client would pay the broadcaster to air a television commercial within certain agreed times by booking airtime well in advance. This gave the client control over when and where the advert was seen – which the client wanted in order to reach her target market (e.g. in the commercial break of a prime-time soap). That never happened with music videos. Labels didn't pay broadcasters to screen videos at certain times. They employed pluggers to lobby TV shows in the same way that they lobbied radio DJs. Videos were only ever screened because they were selected by programme editors, station controllers or VJs. In the 1960s promotional clips were often only filmed if an artist had received a concrete invitation from a TV producer to perform on a show but couldn't or wouldn't make it. In the 1970s, the practice expanded so that managers and labels in the UK were starting to commission promo clips even without any guaranteed broadcast. In the UK, the early producers such as MGMM report having to pay the record labels a fee directly in order to license the rights, a licence that they then assigned to the broadcaster.

On the contrary, from the mid-1980s onwards, record labels *charged* TV broadcasters to transmit the videos. After long and protracted negotiations between the BPI (British Phonographic Industry), the MU and the broadcasters in the early 1980s, the BPI negotiated a system whereby record labels would earn money whenever the videos were broadcast on TV through up-front licensing deals. They supplied the videos to TV stations as independently produced content for which there would be a rights copyright. In 1986 record labels introduced the additional caveat that 50 per cent of the video budget would be recouped from the artists' royalties. From then onwards the BBC and MTV paid the labels, and the recording industry exploited music video as it would any other intellectual product in its back catalogue, constantly on the lookout for opportunities to recycle and generate secondary and tertiary income streams. Promos and music videos were content just like feature films and short films paid for by cinemas, broadcasters and VHS distributors, through licences or sales with production funding supplied by the labels.

The dearth of work until recently on music video within British film and television studies can be attributed to two factors. In addition to being inaccurately categorised as advertising, music videos have, for most of the period since the 1980s, been deemed by scholars part of the entertainment industries rather than part of the film industry or art world. Entertainment has not traditionally been highly valued in British film studies. If we turn to Richard Dyer, the problem lies in a (false) historic distinction between art and entertainment located in the mid-seventeenth century, when Molière defended his plays against Church criticism with a populist mandate. At that point: 'Entertainment became identified with what was not art, not serious, not refined. For Dyer, this distinction remains with us today: art is what is edifying, refined, and difficult, whilst entertainment is "hedonistic, democratic, vulgar, easy"' ([1992] 2002: 6). Entertainment is 'not emotionally deep' and has 'nothing interesting to say about the world' ([1992] 2002: 1).

The second reason is that scholars have had very limited access to the industry that produces music videos. Access is a perennial problem in ethnographic work (Ortner 2009). There is little knowledge and understanding of the industrial structure or process of producing music videos, as a result of which misconceptions persist, such as the idea that music videos are produced by advertising agencies (Frith 2019). Music video is one of a number of hidden screen industries, alongside fashion film, advertising, audio production, post-production and VFX, on which there exists very little publicly available data. Yet since the 1950s these have been vibrant, crucial sectors of the British screen industries, and part of a rich and complex ecology of cross-cutting funding streams, research and development (R&D) and talent development (Caston 2019b). This book was conceived to plug that gap. It has also been inspired by my own career in the British music video industry as a producer and executive producer between 1991 and 2003.

It was Derek Jarman in 1991 who, having worked with Marianne Faithfull and the Smiths, suggested I get a job in music videos. My first job was working in the Picture Music International (PMI) division of EMI records in Manchester Square for Storm Thorgerson and Peter Christopherson on films for the 1993 Pink Floyd World Tour. I went on to work as a producer at Christopherson & Co. with Peter Christopherson, Propaganda Films Europe (part of Polygram Filmed Entertainment) and Satellite Films in Los Angeles, and as executive producer at Ridley Scott's Black Dog Films in London.

This career has given me unique insight into an industry which, as I have said, has proven extremely challenging for academics to *access*. What was particularly useful was the fact that I worked both in the UK and the USA, at both Propaganda and Ridley Scott Associates (RSA) / Black Dog; by working on both sides of the Atlantic, signing contracts under both US law and the laws of England and Wales, I was able to study, first-hand, the different ways in which films were produced in Britain and the USA. Whilst I worked mainly in music video, I also produced a number of TV commercials and short films, and produced / managed several TV dramas, feature films and documentaries – which meant I was able to compare the different production cultures of each of these screen media. I could see that music video was more difficult than other sectors of the screen industries for scholars to research because it did not consist of large multinationals such as the BBC independent production companies catalogued by the BFI annual production handbook, or record labels represented by the Association of Independent Music (AIM) or the BPI. The industry is almost entirely freelance and comprised mainly of micro businesses of fewer than three permanent staff, without a professional trade association (it shares the Advertising Producers' Association, the APA). It gave me insights that might have been gained from the kind of ethnographic work undertaken by Powdermaker (1950) or Bechky (2006) and, more recently, scholars within the production studies field (Mayer et al. 2009).

I left the industry in 2003 as the 'Golden Era' ebbed away, to become course director of the BA programme in Music and Media Management at London Metropolitan University, and then course director of Film and Television Production at the London College of Communication. In both cases my ability to teach music video was frustrated by a lack of resources. So, in 2015 I applied for a research grant from the Arts and Humanities Research Council to create research resources for teaching music video.

This book is based largely on research conducted for the grant: seventy semi-structured interviews conducted with filmmakers and record label employees between 2016 and 2018 in London and Los Angeles, and three focus group discussions on the themes of editing, dance and authorship with leading practitioners in the field. Additional data were found using archive analysis of personal collections of production callsheets held by interviewees and those in our broader research group, assembled through a Facebook page, and in ad hoc email correspondence which proved essential when clarifying historical points of accuracy such as dates and names. The trade publication *Promo News* was a core resource. It ran as a business imprint of *Music Week* from 1992 to 2007, when it was taken over by the editor David Knight. The BFI holds the best-quality collection of *Promo* volumes, dating from 1 September 1994 to 1 May 2007 (although there are some gaps). As well as production credits, it published interviews and news items.

This book is also based on knowledge acquired during my previous career. Some scholars may regard this as a conflict of interest that undermines the objectivity of the research findings. I should be clear that I can gain no financial benefit from either the book or the associated DVD. I no longer work in the industry or have any financial ties to it. The filmmakers of music videos do not earn royalties on the videos. 'Going native' is a term from anthropology which highlights the risk of participant observation – a core ethnographic technique. It means becoming so involved with, and sympathetic to, the people being studied, that objectivity is lost. It was a term with which I was familiar because I had studied anthropology as part of my undergraduate degree at Cambridge. In perhaps the most influential text of anthropological theory of the second half of the twentieth century, the anthropologist Clifford Geertz (1973) argued that scholars should move from seeing anthropological research as working with 'scientifically tested and approved' hypotheses (1973: 23) to viewing 'the culture of a people as an ensemble of texts, themselves ensembles, which the anthropologist strains to read over the shoulders of those to whom they properly belong' (1973: 452). In order to identify and understand people, anthropologists need to immerse themselves fully in their culture for a period of time.

The allegation could be made that I'd 'gone native' during my 1991–2003 career, and gone so native that no amount of rigorous intellectual reflection could retrieve my objectivity. But my prior career did not give me any greater insight than excellent anthropologists and media researchers could have gained given adequate funding and time. It did mean, however, that I had already completed what the anthropologists refer to as the initial scoping period of field research in which the scholar familiarises herself with what Bourdieu terms the 'habitus' of the culture (1977: 72, 1980: 53, 1990: 116, 1998: 8) or Geertz called 'local knowledge'. In this period, the researcher establishes the trust that facilitates 'openness' (cf. Born 2004: 14–19), and comes to understand the theoretical framework used within the culture under investigation. What is crucial about this pilot period of time is that it enables the researcher to build up *trust*. It is also important to recognise that universities are not free environments devoid of a similar risk of 'going native'. In his *Homo Academicus* (1988), Pierre Bourdieu demonstrates that the academy is not just a realm of dialogue and debate, but also a sphere of power in which reputations and careers are made, defended and destroyed.

This book is also designed to accompany a boxset collection of music videos curated for the research project: a six-disc limited edition DVD boxset named *Power to the People* (Thunderbird, 2018). This name was chosen to reflect the fact that for the whole of this fifty-year period, music video in Britain has been a medium through which young people could communicate radical ideas about their gender, their sexuality and their personal politics, which were being repressed and ignored by a mainstream media. The collection was not put together to represent a 'canon', because a canon would almost invariably privilege some social groups over others. As Shuker observes, the problem with canons is that history has shown us that they almost inevitably privilege the work of certain powerful social groups (Shuker 2016). Creating a single canon of music videos would be like trying to create a single canon of British pop music. That would be impossible, because musical characteristics that are of value to one musical tradition are not always of value in other traditions; the creation of a single canon and would skirmish over the differences between Sheffield, Manchester and London, between those artists who embraced artifice (David Bowie) and those who did not (the Clash), between those artists for whom video was entertainment (One Direction) and those for whom it was art (Benga) or political protest (M.I.A.). A video only works if it is authentic in the eyes of the fan who legitimises the artist in the identity the artist wishes to hold, and the skill of the music video commissioner, executive, producer and director is to ensure that what is made will be received as an authentic work that completes the music within the moral, cultural, political and aesthetic traditions within which she sits.

I assembled a panel of filmmakers from the industry who had worked in capacities ranging from choreographer to cinematographer to commissioner. I asked them to help identify 200 landmark videos that had innovated in style, technique, genre, issues of gender representation, intellectual property arrangements, exhibition or distribution. I sought to lay markers for a provisional fifty-year history of the industry and aesthetics of British music video; the panel suggested that the collection should not be organised chronologically, but according to themes or topics. In the interviews and consultations conducted for the book and DVD collection, I stressed the importance of representing a diverse body of music genres and music videos and not falling into the trap of claiming to have a single value-free, universal, neutral definition of a great music video. On the contrary, I curated the collection in such a way as to make sense of the medium's history in Britain from the point of view of someone with insider knowledge of the industry.

One of my motives was the poor state of the internet as an archive for music videos. Research indicates that YouTube is used as a cultural archive not only by non-corporate users, but by music labels who are uploading old music videos from the vault (Burgess and Green 2009: 87). But some of the versions uploaded are not the versions mastered by the known (or unknown) directors; some are poor quality, or have the wrong aspect ratio. In the era of MTV and *TOTP* it was often necessary to edit a TV-safe version for broadcast, and it is mainly the TV-safe versions that are found on YouTube rather than the directors' cuts. Others were versions cut for the USA, not the UK market, for example.

The video for Pink Floyd's '*Money*' (1973) illustrates this. I contacted Lana Topham, once production executive at PMI, the company that produced the video for EMI, when I saw that the 'official' video on YouTube could not have been the original video for the 1973 release because it contained footage shot in the 1980s. Although he didn't begin directing videos until the 1980s, Wayne Isham was credited in several places on the internet as the video director of the official video for '*Money*'. Topham explained that Pink Floyd back-projected many of the films she produced for them at PMI at their live tours. '*Money*' was a track for which EMI as PMI produced many films over the years for the band's live concerts. She recalled that PMI produced a film for '*Money*' in 1974 which was directed by Barry Chattington and filmed at East Lane market in Walworth, South London. PMI then made another 1975 version which was a re-edited version of Chattington's video by Peter Medak. PMI also produced a new film for the track in 1994 which was never actually released. Topham watched the video I'd identified on YouTube to see if she could identify it, but said that because the original clip was re-edited even after Medak's version, she couldn't say for sure when this particular one was released – or if it was even an 'official video'. She thought the YouTube version might possibly be the version used for the *Delicate Sound of Thunder* tour in the 1980s.

When Carol Vernallis wrote that music video archives were unstable (2013a: 262), she was not mistaken – but not solely because YouTube is a rapidly changing platform. Throughout the history of music video, record labels have re-edited masters. Labels often don't keep clear records of the work undertaken. Core data ought to have been preserved on the clock at the front of the music video master which contained technical and legal information for broadcasters, but on many masters from the 1980s, the data are missing from the clocks. Added to that, record labels were not obliged by law to credit filmmakers, and there was no obvious place to do so given that videos don't, like features or TV content, have credits. All of this means that viewers, users and researchers cannot know what version they are watching. So a subsidiary ambition for the boxset was to ensure that students knew which version of the video they were viewing. Whilst the public perception is that music videos are everywhere, closer inspection shows that the condition of music video archives is perilous. The production companies and directors often held not only the directors' cut but superior non-compressed versions of the label cuts, because since the late 1990s it was standard industry practice for production companies to master all music videos to an in-house directors' showreel held on D1, a superior format to Beta SP, or Digibeta. I then emailed each director personally to check the version we planned to use, and asked each director whether he or should would prefer to have their work screened in the original academy 4:3 television format, or whether they would like me to crop the video. Dom & Nic chose to remaster all of their pre-2000 work at their own expense, in collaboration with post-production house The Mill.

The chapters in this book are designed to make sense of the boxset of landmark music videos in relation to topics in current academic research. The first theme that I explore is genre, so Chapter 1 is essentially a history chapter which sketches out the broad brushstrokes of a typology. The second chapter looks at editing, which is one of the few crafts other than directing to attract research attention, and interrogates existing academic thought on the notion of a 'fast MTV edit' or disjunctive edit using examples drawn from the landmark collection. The next chapter, on dance, accompanies Disc 3 of the boxset and is a follow-up to an earlier piece I published on dance in special issue of the journal *Music, Sound, and the Moving Image* (2017), exploring in greater depth the argument that British music videos have drawn on a wider range of dance genres than videos produced in the USA. Chapter 5 focuses on an agenda set within cultural studies – gender – which has perhaps attracted more attention than others within music video studies. Using the collection of videos on Disc 6 of the boxset, I argue that British music videos have posited radical alternatives to gender identity in videos since the 1960s to an extent that is not recognised in current debates. Chapter 6 deals with an issue raised in both popular music studies and film studies: authorship. Chapter 7 looks at three aspects of the neglected topic of British distribution – British music television, home video and YouTube – all topics which have been under-researched. Chapter 8 returns to the key themes of Americanisation, art and commerce, and in the final chapter I ask how the evidence and arguments presented in the book impact current scholarship on music video. The aim in all the chapters is to ask how these British videos, and the evidence collected about their production and distribution between 1966 and 2016, impact existing findings and research on music video in the universities.

My intention was that this book should be read in consultation with the DVD collection. One of the key parts of the boxset is the production credits printed on the booklet. I have included these production credits in an appendix to the book for those readers who are unable to access a copy of the DVD. Production credits abound on the internet, with sites such as www.mvdbase.com (an independent database run by a French journalist since 1998) and www.imvdb.com, an offshoot of the larger Internet Movie Database. However, in preparing this collection for commercial distribution, I found that many of the credits given on internet sources for these videos were incorrect. It is difficult to find credits at all for videos dating from before the year 2000. But to expand the field of study in music video beyond an auteur approach, it is absolutely essential to identify the filmmakers involved in the creation of these works. One of the problems is that scholars then reproduce these historically incorrect sources. Researching an important animation video produced at Cucumber Studios, I found that even the Museum of Modern Art in New York had reproduced an incorrect internet credit. In producing the credits for the booklet, I aimed to create a basic dataset for future research.

To this end, a very substantial part of my workload on the grant was to contact all the producers and directors and commissioners of each of the 200 selected videos by email or phone to get the credits. Many emailed copies of the original callsheets. Others rang crew members and debated for days trying to remember who had done what and when. Before the credits were prepared for publication, therefore, I sent every credit listing to the individual producer and director of the video to check personally. It is perhaps because we entered the project as partners with those we studied that we experienced a high engagement and response rate. I supported this by putting the filmmakers in groups as much as possible – a panel and a number of focus groups, where I knew they would be more willing to talk and where some of the contradictions that come out in oral history could be addressed.

2 GENRE

In this chapter I try to develop a theoretical framework for talking about genre that makes sense in relation to the way that music videos have been made and discussed within the British industry since 1966. First I use the loose typology of music videos that has been used in the industry to sketch out a history of the form. Then I move on to examine how the form has drawn on pre-existing genres from the fine arts, film and television, and present examples of genre cycles, parody, pastiche and homage. I discuss the challenges this citational style has generated for authenticity. Finally, I examine the question of whether there has been a correlation between specific music genres and styles of video. By 'genre' I mean a type of plot, lighting style, editing style, camera style and iconography (type of location, set design, costume design and make-up), as well as a set of expectations which the video is designed to trigger in the audience by a series of filmic cues, so that the viewer knows what to expect.

The research conducted for this book shows that since the late 1970s British music video has, in the main, been an unashamed and intentional appropriation art. It has been a *genre* art which succeeds or fails on the extent to which it invokes works from pre-established genres to anchor, authenticate and entertain audiences; genre is a positive, self-aware and intentional act. In director Nick Egan's words,

> [y]ou copy. As directors, we copy Fellini and Kubrick and they copy other directors who've copied, who've copied, who've copied. I love paying homage to these directors. I never tried to pretend that the

'Supersonic' video was not Nic Roeg's *Man Who Fell to Earth* and 'Live Forever' was not *Performance* (1970). I've never had a problem with that.[1]

The concept of appropriation art was coined in the 1980s art world to describe the advent of the citational style in painting and other mediums. Hoesterey explains that the concept was created to capture the very intentional basis of the appropriation in those artists' work and avoid the previously negative connotations of the term (Hoesterey 2001: 10). It captures well the process by which music videos are made, and turns the negative connotations of the concept of genre into positive ones. Within film and television studies, genre works have tended to be valued negatively by their lack of authenticity and originality, and by their supposed collapse into the postmodern. Genre is often negatively associated with the Frankfurt School critique of monopoly capitalism in the Hollywood of the late 1930s, about which Adorno and Horkheimer wrote that 'the hit songs, stars, and soap operas [are] cyclically recurrent and rigidly invariable types' in which 'the effect, the obvious touch, and the technical detail dominates over the work itself' ([1944] 1979: 125).

Within existing music video studies in the USA and Germany, music video critical appreciation is a muddle about genre. Both Carol Vernallis and Saul Austerlitz describe music video as a genre in itself (Vernallis 2004: x, Austerlitz 2007: vii). But in the past, some scholars such as Gow (1992) have presented music video as a category of a different kind, composed of its own distinctive genres. I do not regard music video as a genre. I follow Dave Laing (1984) in defining music video as an *industrial product*. Music video is an industrial product defined by a distinctive supply chain of the model identified by Peter Bloore's work on the film industry for the UK Film Council (2009). Applying Bloore's model, which itself is adopted from Michael Porter's highly influential article on competitive advantage (1985), to an industry like music video which comprises largely micro entities (companies of fewer than five employers), this value chain is maintained by tacit knowledge and networks into which new industry entrants are socialised when they join. Promos and music videos are short films commissioned and released by record labels for mass audiences; they comprise a copyrighted synchronised picture and audio track in which a percentage of the royalties accrue to the recording artist or record label and are generally, but not always, produced out of house by independent production companies or sole traders working from home. The beginnings of this value chain were evident in the 1960s, but it was not until the late 1970s that they were institutionalised within the screen industries into value chains alongside TV commercials, feature films and independently produced TV drama. In the 1980s they were formalised into a set of (mainly verbal) agreements between clients (record labels), producers and exhibitors.

A Brief Overview of Music Videos from 1966 to 2016

During the 1970s, a loose and simple terminology of performance, concept and narrative videos developed which commissioners would use to communicate marketing briefs to video directors. In the 1960s, pop promos for bands such as The Who and Pink Floyd were produced in such a haphazard way that there was no established language, no fixed production budget and certainly no formal contract or even a formal commissioning of the video. A director such as Peter Whitehead would shoot the promo using his own 16mm camera equipment, asking the manager to pay for film stock, and then cut the promo on his Steenbeck at home. The language developed later in the early 1980s and, even then, was extremely informal and avoided by some commissioners altogether. In this section, I explain the principles underlying each of these three terms and identify some of the landmark works.

Performance

The origins of the British *performance video* were generated in early 1950s and 1960s recordings of live performances of British bands on TV shows such as *TOTP*. The early history of these shows and the role they played in familiarising audiences with the tropes of staged recorded performances has been looked at by Evans (2016), Smith (2019) and Fryer (1997). The language of the wide shot and the close-ups on instruments and faces were developed in these pioneering pieces. As Mundy has indicated (1999), a crucial shift occurred when Richard Lester filmed the performance inserts for *A Hard Day's Night* (1964). The sequence showing The Beatles performing '*I Should Have Known Better*' on the train is an example. Filmed on location rather than in a studio, the band mime to the track. The footage is cut together to appear as if the band had performed and recorded both sound and image simultaneously. It established the core principles for editing instrumental and vocal performance to camera, delivering synchronous editing so that the viewer sees the realistic source of the sound (hand on guitar, for example) whilst simultaneously hearing that sound (a guitar chord, for example).

Michael Lindsay-Hogg's video for the Rolling Stones' '*It's Only Rock 'n Roll (But I Like It)*' (1974) is a landmark performance video because it relies solely on performance footage. Performance videos for Manfred Mann and Pink Floyd from the mid-1960s, by contrast, included non-diegetic cutaways. The video works without any cutaways because of the strength and execution of the central premise by the band and Hogg. The band perform the song wearing sailor outfits in a large balloon acquired from a circus. The plan had been to make a more sinister video in which the balloon filled up with mud, but several days before they shot they found that the balloon couldn't hold the mud, so they came up with the alternative idea of foam.² The dynamic of the piece arises from the dramatic tension of the band slowly being submerged in bubbles as the balloon fills up. In his performance, Mick Jagger embraces the theatricality of the artifice of the new-style mediatised video. Few artists in the history of music video would have agreed to dress up as a sailor to be submerged by bubbles in a giant balloon and think their credibility as a rock'n'roll artist could survive. Jagger is the first in the tradition of Annie Lennox, David Bowie and Robbie Williams who absolutely embraces these experiments in dressing up as an extension of, rather than a challenge to, authenticity. '*It's Only Rock 'n Roll (But I Like It)*' retains the cinematographic language of representing musical performance as synchronous through establishing wide shots and pick-up shots of performance close-ups.

The Cure's video for '*Close to Me*' (1985) is a landmark performance video because director Tim Pope, like René Clair and Jean Vigo in the transition to sound years 1928–33, eschews the diachronic relation between sound and image of the early videos. Instead of matching the sound of a guitar solo on the track with a close-up of fingers on the guitar, which had become a staple of the performance video by then, Pope shows metaphoric images (a strummed comb, toy keyboard and clapping). The technique of showing non-representational sources of sound was pushed even further in Zbigniew Rybczyński's video for the Art of Noise's '*Close to the Edit*' (1984), analysed in the next chapter. The video for Coldcut's '*Timber*' (1997), created by Coldcut and Hexstatic as a collaborative political statement against the destruction of the rainforest, uses sound and image similarly: video clips sampled from *National Geographic* and TV wildlife documentaries work in combination with audio effects to convey the artists' message; the sound of a saw is combined with that of a close-up of a Morse Code machine being tapped (SOS – a distress call from the forest).

The creative challenge for a music video director issued with a performance brief was to come up with a sufficiently novel premise for a strong performance video which could not only justify the enclosure of the band in a single small space with their instruments, but also yield a dramatic arc to drive the tension and hold the viewer's attention. In '*Close to Me*', dramatic tension is contrived from the premise that the wardrobe is falling over the edge of a cliff, which simultaneously justifies the enclosure of the band in a small space. Video directors would offer a variety of novel innovations over the years: Dougal Wilson's video for Coldplay's '*Life in Technicolor II*' (2008) construes the band's performance within a Punch and Judy show in an ostensibly quaint English village, whilst Reef's '*Place Your Hands*' (1997) exposes the device of the confined space as a built stage in a film studio. WIZ's video for the Arctic Monkeys' '*The View from the Afternoon*' (2006) builds the dramatic tension from the drummer's performance, a rare occurrence in performance videos; stop-motion in Vampire Weekend's '*A-Punk*' (Garth Jennings, 2008) and photosonics slow motion in Moloko's *'The Time Is Now'* (Dom Leung, 2000) draw the viewer in. The Wild Beasts' *'Brave Bulging Buoyant Clairvoyants'* (OneinThree, 2008) is based on an M. C. Escher lithograph in which the same image continues down to infinity. Toy's *'Lose My Way'* (Joe Morris, 2012) was selected as the most recent performance video for its striking and pure, confident simplicity – a purity which represents the minimalist aesthetic of the YouTube platform.

Concept

The concept video came into its own in the 1980s. In a sense, all music videos are concept videos because they are generated from a concept, but video commissioner / executive producer Liz Kessler explains the principle of a concept video within the industry:

> A concept video is a catch-all term but there was an understanding inside the industry of what it meant. It isn't a performance, although there might be some performance in it. It isn't a narrative, although there might be a bit of story in it. It was a negative definition. When you used it as a commissioner talking to a director, it meant: don't do a straight lift from the song. What you are listening to, and what you see, these have to be one step away from each other. You might hear a love song, but might see a video in which someone is trapped in a time loop, or watch a strange animation from out of space – even though the song is clearly about the girl next door. We did a video for The Feeling called *'Sewn'* (2006) in which we showed the band being sewn up. There was a link but there was a gap: you were going up a level. If the song was about boy meets girl, the one thing you wouldn't be seeing in a concept video was a boy meeting a girl.[3]

In the 1960s, the concept elements of a video were intercut with performance. Intercutting was a technique used by Peter Whitehead in the 1960s to include conceptual footage with performance footage. The intercutting technique was adopted throughout the 1980s and 1990s to cut together the two distinct genres of performance and concept. But the technique was developed in the 1960s pop promos, by directors such as Peter Whitehead. Whilst working on a video for The Animals' *'When I Was Young'* (1967), Whitehead is said to have found the footage in a skip outside the cutting room. He had been searching for footage after becoming concerned that he lacked sufficient performance footage to synchronise to the full duration of the track (Chilcott 2007). As a result, Whitehead's video cuts footage of the band performing the track live with archive reconnaissance footage of fighter planes (Spitfires) during the Battle of Britain from World War II. It is one of the earliest examples of this technique.

John Crome's video for Manfred Mann's *'The Mighty Quinn'* (1968), shot on 16mm, also used the intercutting technique to cut together staged location performance with point of view (POV) shots situated within the diegetic world of Osterley Park in West London. These include shots of the band walking through the park, POV shots on a fisheye lens from a car, and the flashing lights of a bicycle. Gels and Vaseline on the lens are used for effects, as well as double exposure. In music originating from the industrial music scene, the intercutting technique was used by later directors to draw attention to the medium itself in videos such as Cabaret Voltaire's *'Sensoria'* (Peter Care, 1984), a video that had very considerable influence on the editing style at the time. Budgets and set designs for concept and performance videos grew in size in the 1980s. The video for Eurythmics' *'Sweet Dreams'* (Stewart / Ashbrook / Roseman, 1983), for example, includes increasingly extravagant and seemingly disconnected iconography (a cow in a boardroom) within an underlying feminist narrative about male power in record-label boardrooms. Duran Duran's *'The Wild Boys'* (Russell Mulcahy, 1984) was considered at the time by the BPI to represent the culmination of a period of excess in record label expenditure on concept videos, although Russell Mulcahy points out that the budget of $1 million was to shoot an entire video album (*Arena*, 1984) rather than a single video.[4]

The use of pioneering techniques in animation, stop-motion, computer-generated imagery (CGI) and animatronics was not uncommon. A genre of pure concept video omitting all performance developed: Pink Floyd's *'Another Brick in the Wall'* (Gerald Scarfe, 1979), Elvis Costello's *'Accidents will Happen'* (Annabel Jankel and Rocky Morton, 1979), made at the pioneering Cucumber Studios, and A-ha's *'Take on Me'* (Steve Barron, 1985) were examples. Peter Gabriel's *'Sledgehammer'* (Stephen R. Johnson, 1986) used stop-frame animation by the Brothers Quay and Aardman Animation to create the trick film delight of the novelty of 'how did they do that'? Howie B's *'Music for Babies'* (Run Wrake, 1996) was selected for film festivals and had a much longer life than a standard music promo. Concept videos in the 1990s include a number of animatronics videos, such as Walter Stern's video for Massive Attack's *'Teardrop'* (1998), constructed around a minimally animated, lip-syncing foetus within a womb-like setting, inspired by Stern's interpretation of the track drumbeats as heartbeats. The increasing number of pure concept videos was in part a result of the increase in electronic artists. Shynola were still at art college when they made the video for UNKLE's *'Guns Blazin''* (1999). They persuaded the animation department to buy its first computer, and made the video in their bedrooms on consumer technology:

> Suddenly we had tools at our disposal to create anything we wanted. The idea that you could shoot and edit and do effects on consumer

technology doesn't seem that remarkable now, but the effect it has had on music videos is huge.[5]

Throughout the 1990s, video directors used new computer-generated techniques in concept videos to foreground elements of the music. Creation Records boss Alan McGee said it was only when he saw Angus Cameron's video for My Bloody Valentine's *'To Here Knows When'* (1991) that he understood the track.[6] PJ Harvey's video *'Down By the Water'* (1995), directed by Maria Mochnacz, deploys the same technique highlighted by Kessler: showing Harvey performing underwater, it contains a link to the lyrics, but there is a gap between Harvey seen seductively dancing in red, and the lyric narrative about a mother who drowns her daughter. Jonathan Glazer's videos for Massive Attack's *'Karmacoma'* (1995) and Radiohead's *'Street Spirit (Fade Out)'* (1996) again utilise non-normative film techniques: in *'Karmacoma'*, the suspension of linear plot editing and in *'Street Spirit (Fade Out)'* the use of time-splicing, to evoke the sentiment and philosophy of the track in a way which is not necessitated by the music or lyrics, but authenticates the band's musical heritage and foregrounds the mood of the track.

But in the digital era this foregrounding of in-camera and post-production techniques has declined. There are examples of novelty effects – many of the videos for OK Go come to mind, as does Delta Heavy's video *'Get By'* (Ian Robertson, 2012) and Bonobo's video *'Cirrus'* (Cyriak Harris, 2013). But as a general trend, the 'how did they do that?' value of the technique dominates over the 'technique that visualises the emotion, mood, or sentiment or idea underlying the music' that drives the really effective use of these post-production effects in early experimental videos. This, without a doubt, is a partial result of the viewing platform of YouTube, which creates a contrasting viewing experience to music television in which 'less is more'; but it also results in 'innovation fatigue' of an industry. The commissioners we interviewed reported seeing amongst the pitches for new videos many old ideas made in the 1980s and 1990s, of which directors seemed unaware. For concept videos released in the digital era, what stood out were those videos that used technological effects not to test the boundaries of the medium, but to simplify the medium in a manner which evidenced absolute mastery of the technique combined with interpretation of the music, combined with an appreciation of the genre expectations of the viewing audience. The videos for Hiatus's *'We Can Be Ghosts Now'* (Tom Jobbins, 2013) and Benga's *'I Will Never Change'* (Us, 2013) stood out.

Narrative

The narrative video has been a staple of British music videos from the start, much more so than in the USA. One of the first important narrative videos is The Kinks' *'Dead End Street'* (Ray Davies, 1966), but the form came into its own in the period 1979–84. The video for The Boomtown Rats' *'I Don't Like Mondays'* (1979) was directed by David Mallet, director of programmes such as *The Kenny Everett Show* (Thames Television 1978–81). It denotes a narrative, but still includes performance. It was in 1981 that the music video as a mini feature film was really launched, with Ultravox's *'Vienna'* (Russell Mulcahy, 1981). This was one of the first videos that set out to look like a feature film, because although it was not shot on film, the director Mulcahy did not like to shoot on videotape in the 4:3 television frame (required because TV broadcast in the academy frame). So, for *'Vienna'*, he brought DoP Nic Knowland on board and cropped his videos top and bottom with gaffer tape to give a 1:84 cinematic effect. It was a technique he would use frequently in the 1980s, although initially the broadcasters tried to correct it. 'The first time I did it MTV called me up from New York and said, "We've just got your new video, but there's a little technical problem . . . But don't worry, we've blown it up and scanned it."' Mulcahy explained that the black bars at the top and bottom of the screen were put there intentionally: 'No, no, no, they're meant to be there.'[7]

The Human League's *'Don't You Want Me'* (Steve Barron, 1981), released shortly afterwards, took the short film format even further: presented as a behind-the-scenes 'making of' documentary about a murder mystery, the video depicted the breakdown of an affair between 'actress' (Susan Sulley) and 'film director' (Phil Oakey). It was a film about a film, within a film. Barron shot on 35mm instead of videotape and the clapperboard seen in the video bears the inscription 'Le League Humaine', allegedly as a tribute to French film director François Truffaut. Mike Mansfield has described his video for Adam and the Ants' *'Stand and Deliver'* (1981) as a Hollywood musical in three minutes, and the same could be said of *'Prince Charming'* (Mike Mansfield, 1981), which featured Diana Dors.

For the directors of these early narratives, music videos functioned partially as a stepping stone into what was thought of as the 'holy grail' of feature film directing. Both Mulcahy and Barron said that their promos served as show-reels to secure their first films – and in Mulcahy's case, the funder was the same (EMI funded his first feature film after seeing him successfully deliver a run of well-received, effective videos for Duran Duran). After directing the Human League's *'Don't You Want Me'* (1981), Michael Jackson's *'Billie Jean'* (1982) and A-ha's *'Take On Me'* (1985), Steve Barron went on to direct the feature films *Electric Dreams* (1984) and *Teenage Mutant Ninja Turtles* (1990). Mulcahy directed *Highlander* (1986), *Ricochet* (1991), *Shadow* (1994) and *Resident Evil* (2004). Julien Temple had already begun his feature film career with *The Great Rock'n'Roll Swindle*, released in 1979, and Sade's *'Smooth Operator'* (1985), an eight-and-a-half-minute short film intended for cinema release with a TV cutdown for music video shows, and would continue with films including *The Secret Policeman's Other Ball* (1982), *Absolute Beginners* (1986), *The Filth and The Fury* (2000), *Joe Strummer: The Future is Unwritten* (2007) and *London: The Modern Babylon* (2012).

Once established in this period, the narrative music video became an acceptable format for music videos throughout the 1990s, with other landmark works including WIZ's video for Flowered Up's '*Weekender*' (1992), which was shot on S16mm, and presented with full titles and end credits in the style of an eighteen-minute feature film (cut down for TV); Pedro Romhanyi's video for Blur's '*Parklife*' (1994), which referenced *Quadrophenia*, with Phil Daniels in the lead role; Jamie Thraves' seminal narrative video for Radiohead's '*Just*' (1995); Hammer & Tongs' video for Blur's '*Coffee and TV*' (1999), presenting a narrative around a milk carton; and Travis's '*Turn*' (Ringan Ledwidge, 1999), about a push-up challenge. The narrative video was given further stimulus in the 1990s by the emergence of DJ-led electronic music (which had no need to include any performance on musical instruments or from a band), but it was also used for guitar bands. Many of the 1990s narrative directors, including Jonathan Glazer, Garth Jennings, David Slade, Jamie Thraves and Andy Morahan, went on to direct successful feature films.

In the digital era, British and Irish artists have continued with the narrative form. Aoife McCardle's video for Jon Hopkins' '*Open Eye Signal*' (2013) is a minimalist YouTube story, and her video for U2's '*Every Breaking Wave*' (2015 is a thirteen-minute short film dramatising the Troubles in Northern Ireland. Daniel Wolfe's landmark trilogy of videos with artist Ben Drew (aka Plan B) around the fictional character of Strickland Banks (played by Drew) – '*Stay Too Long*' (2009), '*She Said*' (2010) and '*Prayin*'' (2010) – was followed by artist Ben Drew co-financing and releasing his own feature, *Ill Manors* (2012). Both Wolfe and McCardle have directed features.

Genre and Music Videos

So how does this selection of 200 videos, and interviews with their filmmakers, suggest that we think about genre and music video? The performance, concept and narrative typology are not genres; they are formats. One way is to recognise that music videos draw on genres from fields of the visual arts other than film. A great many first-generation music video directors began their careers as photographers. Corinne Day (1962–2010), who co-directed the Oasis video for '*Cigarettes & Alcohol*' (1994), was a photographer. One of David Bowie's early collaborators, Mick Rock (director of '*John, I'm Only Dancing*' (1972), '*Jean Genie*' (1972), '*Space Oddity*' (1969) and '*Life on Mars*' (1973)), was a photographer of Queen, T-Rex, Syd Barrett and the Sex Pistols, to name a few. Directors Nick Egan and Stéphane Sednaoui continued their careers as photographers alongside their directing work. When I interviewed Nick about his video for Duran Duran's '*White Lines (Don't Do It)*' (Nick Egan, 1995), he explained that his video work came from doing album covers and he always thought there was a natural progression in this. 'I always say the artist comes to the camera, not the camera comes to the artist. I'd go to the studio two weeks before and listen to the music.' This determined his entire approach to making music videos: 'I never really considered myself a director, I was an artist. I never respected film. I wasn't like David Fincher. I liked all the imperfections.'[8]

Artistic portraiture, a staple of the music performance video, illustrates this. In his 1952 *Theory of Film*, Béla Balázs argued that the close-up was privileged in silent cinema, and for the same reason it seems to have been privileged in music videos. From the 1980s onwards, the close-up on the face is used to deliver (or construct) an emotional impulse and a sense of personal authenticity in performance. One of the earliest uses of the close-up to foreground lyrics is in the video for Queen's '*Bohemian Rhapsody*' (Bruce Gowers, 1975). According to producer Jon Roseman, the band wanted a video made because they felt the operatic qualities of the song would make it impossible to mime the song on *TOTP* without losing all musical credibility. With so little time, Gowers recorded the video in an outside broadcast (OB) unit, mixing it live onto a tape that he sent straight to the BBC. Godley and Creme's '*Cry*' (1981/5) also exploited the expressive qualities of the human face: the directors used analogue cross-fading technology to show monochrome faces – beautiful, plain, male, female, young and old – all morphing from one to another in sync to the lyrics. The same effect was used for the last twenty seconds of Michael Jackson's video for '*Black or White*' (John Landis, 1991) to morph the faces of Black, Asian and White actors into each other.

John Maybury's video for Sinéad O'Connor's '*Nothing Compares 2 U*' (1990), like '*Cry*', uses a close-up on the face to drench the viewer in emotion and recycles the device of the pop promos for the French 1960s Yé Yé girl bands, such as Françoise Hardy ('*Mon Amie La Rose*' (1965) and '*Voila*' (1967), for example). In Radiohead's video for '*No Surprises*', directed by Grant Gee (1997), the camera is fixed solidly for the duration on the face of singer Thom Yorke, who is gradually revealed by the reflection of a slowly lighted room to be inside a helmet filling with water, on which are reflected the lyrics. These close-ups took the viewer out of time and space into what Balázs called *physiognomy*, a universal dimension of human existence, enabling the viewer to experience the emotions as if they were her own.

Less common is for videos to draw on British television dramas, but a director who has specialised in this is Dougal Wilson. Wilson is unusual amongst British video directors because he cites and appropriates not only television genres more than feature film genres, but distinctively British characters within those genres. In the Temper Trap's video for '*Love Lost*' (2011), Wilson depicts an English school cross-country run in which a motley bunch of grubby and exhausted schoolchildren mime the lyrics whilst triggering mini-explosions on the side of the path. Dizzee Rascal's *'Dream'* (Dougal Wilson, 2004) is a parody of Muffin the Mule. Will Young's *'Who Am I?'* (Dougal Wilson, 2006) interpolates Young with archive footage from the BBC children's programme *Blue Peter* (BBC 1958–). The video's two-day shoot required the erection of a full-scale replica *Blue Peter* studio set and exacting imitation of original camera angles and positioning of studio lighting. A combination of white and green screen was used in order to ensure Young was invisibly integrated into the shots. Newly shot action footage was composited in later, and then match-graded with the stock footage to enhance the 1970s look. Other examples are Wilson's videos for The Streets' *'Fit But You Know It'* (2004) and Jarvis Cocker's *'Don't Let Him Waste Your Time'* (2007).

Many filmmakers draw on established feature film genres such as horror, slapstick, murder mystery and romance. Disc 4 in the boxset contains a collection of landmark love story videos, of which Ultravox's *'Vienna'* (1981) is just one example. If a viewer is not familiar with the genre, this will backfire; a notable example is Queen's video for *'I Want to Break Free'* (David Mallet, 1984). According to an interview with Brian May in *Q* magazine in March 2011, the video was inspired by the long-running British soap opera *Coronation Street* (ITV 1960–). Freddie Mercury played a housewife, loosely based on the character of Bet Lynch, who wants to break free from her life. May's character was based on the (then very well known in Britain) character of Hilda Ogden. The video proved unpopular in countries outside the UK, notably the USA. According to the BBC, it was banned by MTV (*'Queen: Days of Our Lives'*, 2011). May has said that, whereas the parody of *Coronation Street* was understood and much enjoyed in the UK, it was lost on non-British audiences. He sensed that US audiences, failing to see the soap-opera connection, may have interpreted the video as an open declaration of transvestism and Mercury's bisexuality (Sky 1994: ch. 8, and May 2010). According to Whiteley ([2007] 2013a), it also upset their minority audience in the USA, the New York gay scene, where the video was received as a 'misjudged excursion into fantasy video'. The 'seeming flippancy of including straight members of the band in its cross-dressed scenario almost severed [Mercury] from the New York scene. It suggested camp posturing rather than a serious engagement with personal freedom' (Whiteley [2007] 2013a: 26).

For a director to mimic or pay homage to film and television genre, the artist must be willing and able to act, and not all artists are. It is the video commissioner's job to understand what the artist is willing and able to undertake for their video. Carrie Sutton, Robbie Williams's long-term commissioner, explained that Robbie was 'just so good at doing things' and always wanting a challenge so that, when commissioning videos, they were always looking for an interesting role for Robbie to play which involved him learning a new skill or reviving a skill, like horse-riding, from his childhood.[9] In the video for *'She's the One'* (1999), Dom & Nic had Robbie perform the role of a male figure skater with the help of leading dance choreographer Karen Quinn. In Vaughan Arnell's video for *'Millennium'* (1998), Williams parodied James Bond, complete with dinner jacket and references to Bond films like *Thunderball* (1965) and *From Russia with Love* (1963). In Arnell's *'Supreme'* (2000), a tribute to British Formula One driver Jackie Stewart, Williams plays fictitious racing-car driver Bob Williams, and for *'Rock DJ'* (2000), Williams had to learn to dance on a roller disco (with choreography by Arlene Phillips). Robbie's enthusiastic abilities are the exception rather than the norm.

Cycles and Intertextual Referencing

At the beginning of this chapter I wrote that music video was an appropriation art. What is meant by that, and how does this affect current debates about music video, remediation and intertextual citation? Music videos cite other music videos through cycles, pastiche and homage.

The term 'cycle' was used by Griffith (1976) to describe the pattern according to which a genre emerges, crystallises, alters and declines in Hollywood. Like film, music video production occurs in cycles; studying these cycles helps in appreciating the way directors formulate ideas, in line with Horkheimer and Adorno's thesis that in Hollywood, a film made for the mass market and entertainment industry will make an innovation within a tried and tested formula ([1944] 1979). It illustrates the concept of genre as a set of cues and expectations shared by filmmakers and their audience(s).

The sports narrative is an example. Spike Jonze's video for The Chemical Brothers' *'Elektrobank'* (1997) was the first: depicting a gymnast (Sofia Coppola) at an international competition performing her floor routine, Jonze and his DoP, Lance Accord, deliberately created a desaturated 1970s video quality to evoke the genre of genuine sports news footage (it was actually shot on S16mm). The second video was Whale's *'Crying at Airports feat. Bus'* (Ringan Ledwidge, 1998), narrating a world synchronised swimming competition in the style of a 1970s sports newsreel, with visual deterioration added in post to enhance the 1970s look. As with Spike's video, voiceover of the sports commentator runs over the music to strengthen the genre reference. Like *'Elektrobank'*, it was shot on film (35mm) by director Ringan Ledwidge and DoP John Mathieson. The third was Robbie Williams' video for *'She's the One'* (Dom & Nic, 1999), which told the love story of a figure-skating competition revolving around Robbie Williams (the ice coach) and was lit by Dan Landin. The first two videos were commissioned by Carol Burton-Fairbrother in the London office of Virgin Records, and the third by Carrie Sutton. All three were lit by DoPs who went on to successful careers in features, illustrating the extent to which music video functioned often as an R&D wing of the screen industries in which cinematographers had the time, budget and freedom to experiment with different styles of cinematography, lenses, camera and lighting equipment.

Another example is the reverse narrative cycle. In 2002, Jamie Thraves conceived and directed a video for Coldplay's '*The Scientist*' which told the story of a fatal car crash *backwards*. In order to mime the lyrics, Chris Martin had to learn to mime his vocals in reverse. It was a complex shoot and drew on Thraves' expertise as a narrative feature film director. He'd wanted to make a story with a happy ending, a happy beginning but a tragic middle for some time prior to the video. Thraves had begun his career working with the BFI's New Directors Fund following an MA at the Royal College of Art, and he'd already written and directed a feature film (*The Lowdown*, 2000); his video for Radiohead's '*Just*' (1995) had been received as a breakthrough work by the industry. In deciding to present the story in reverse, Thraves was conscious that his audience would be familiar with Spike Jonze's 1996 music video for Pharcyde's '*Drop*'. That video showed the group performing the song backwards. He explains,

> I was very aware making the video that Spike Jonze had already done the Pharcyde video that was backwards. I was playing off that, because I knew that as they saw this video people would think I was ripping him off. But I knew that halfway through, our video would turn into a story, and [the audience] wouldn't be expecting that; people would just be expecting a backwards visual to entertain them. I wanted to do something different that would surprise people.[10]

British audiences were also familiar with another reverse narrative video, Bentley Rhythm Ace's '*Bentley's Gonna Sort You Out*' (Garth Jennings, 1997), which was commissioned by John Hassay at Skint Records. The story illustrates how Thraves set out to delight his audience by giving them something pleasurable and entertaining with which they were familiar (celluloid running in reverse), and then shocking them into encountering a tragic car crash; it's an experiment in a hybrid genre which works well to convey the unexpected horror of the crash for the main character played by Chris Martin.

For Kessler, who has commissioned around 250 videos and produced or executive produced almost 300, cycles and fashions 'bubble up all over the place. In the mid-2000s in Britain there was a phase when every clubbing video seemed to depict old-age pensioners out raving. Around 2013 there was an eruption of alternative choreography arising from the USA.'[11]

Pastiche and Homage

The period 1966–2016 also contains significant examples of pastiche videos. With her video for Blur's *'Song 2'* (1997), director Sophie Muller pushes the parameters of the performance video even further. She reproduces the idea that the band are trapped in a small space, but does so with a deliberate intention to ridicule and parody the genre expectations of rock videos. She explained that she worked with the DoP of The Prodigy's *'Firestarter'* video, John Lynch, to create a similar darkness. The special effects used to pull one of the band against the wall and one away from the wall while Damon Albarn jumped around were created as a pastiche of a rock video. 'Why do bands in rock videos stand in a set whilst lights move, wind comes on and there's smoke? Why are they in the room with smoke?' The video was intended as 'a joke', and Muller was very surprised when it was received as a serious video and nominated as Best Group Video and Best Alternative Video at the 1997 MTV awards.[12]

Muller's *'Goodbye Cruel World'* for Shakespears Sister (1991) spoofed famous melodramas such as *Sunset Boulevard* (1950) and *What Ever Happened to Baby Jane?* (1962). Drawing on genres other than the obvious candidate for the genre of popular music of the artist in order to parody and expose the ludicrousness of media representations in general seems to be a recurring and significant strand in British videos. In his video for Gomez's *'Bring It On'* (1999), Ringan Ledwidge parodied government information films about health and safety at work, road safety and foot and mouth disease from the 1970s. These videos were made by the Central Office of Information (COI) and broadcast in between programmes on primetime TV.

The 1966–2016 collection also contains landmark homage videos. A classic example of the homage is Dawn Shadforth's *'The Importance of Being Idle'* video for Oasis (2005), which pays homage to The Kinks' narrative video *'Dead End Street'* (1966). Shot on Little Greene Street in Kentish Town, London, in black-and-white 16mm using an ITV crew directed by Ray Davies himself,[13] the 1966 promo showed the band members dressed as undertakers and various other characters. Oasis's homage was presented in the genre of a vintage black-and-white movie, with opening credits announcing the title of the film, and starred actor Rhys Ifans. Whilst the rationale for the homage came from the style of the music, it was Shadforth's idea to do the homage to *'Dead End Street'*.[14] The second half of the video contains a 'song and dance routine' which, with Rhys and the band in top hats, conjures up images of Hollywood musicals from the 1930s, and was intended as a parody of the dance sequences found in so many music videos of that time. The Gallaghers play Shadrack and Duxbury, the owners of the funeral parlour where Billy works.

Authenticity and Mediatisation

All of these videos grapple with authenticity. Performance music videos have been produced within a culture that, as Auslander argues, often constructs the live event as real and 'mediatised events' as 'secondary and somehow artificial reproductions of the real' (Auslander [1999] 2008: 3). He borrows the concept of a mediated event from Baudrillard, and defines it as 'a performance that is circulated on television, as audio or video recordings, and in other forms based in technologies of reproduction' (2008: 4). A mediated performance is inherently untruthful to the authentic tradition of real live performance. The mediatised performance video creates a core problem for what Barker and Taylor term 'representational authenticity'. Since 'faking it', in the words of Barker and Taylor, is one of the worst things that an authentic rock musician can do, the 'mediatised performance' at the heart of the promo clip from the 1960s onwards was potentially a major problem. One of the ways in which artists could retain a sense of 'real' and 'authentic' in their mediatised performances was by including footage that appeared to have been shot without their knowledge when they slipped out of character. In '*It's Only Rock 'n Roll (But I Like It)*' (1974), the viewer sees footage of the band reacting to the bubbles as they submerge the band in a manner which seems genuinely authentic rather than staged. But gradually that device receded and, in the videos of Annie Lennox, Freddie Mercury, David Bowie and Robbie Williams, the great theatrical performers of British music videos, such footage is rarely included.

It was in the era of punk and post-punk that faking it became a serious problem in Britain, with the collision between director–auteurs and director–musicians. In the 1970s, as this language for the commissioning of videos evolved, a divide opened up between artists regarding the new mediatised music videos. Don Letts grappled with precisely this issue when he set out to make a video for The Clash's '*London's Burning*' (1977): 'I was looking back further in time, to the old James Brown footage where the film was centred on stage with a couple of cameras locked on to capturing the performance and that really appealed to me' (Letts and Nobakht 2007: 152). Letts didn't want a mediatised video. 'In those early days, videos or promos or whatever you want to call them, were all built around effects – or worse, just nothing but effects' (2007: 152–3). He sought pure representational authenticity, so he put the band and cameras in a boat on the Cadogan Festival Pier. As weather conditions worsened and night fell, the band played on, bringing an intensity and anger to the performance that might otherwise have been missing. This video that was shot is *authentic* because as the night wore on it started to rain, and the anger and intensity of the band's resulting performance gave it an authenticity that Letts was in search of: representational validity, a recording of a true and emotionally real experience for the band.

Imperfections are also crucial to the video for Joy Division's *'Love Will Tear Us Apart'* (1980), which was shot by the band themselves on 28 April 1980. According to Peter Hook, the band had planned the filming in advance because they wanted to release a video for this track as a single. They decided to shoot it at T. J. Davidson's studio, where they used to rehearse. It was the only promotional video the band ever produced, as Ian Curtis died several weeks later. As the group were preparing for their first US tour, Curtis committed suicide on the morning of 18 May. Of the video process, Hook writes:

> We hated the whole idea of a video where you mimed or acted to the track. In fact we were never into it, all through New Order. God, you feel like such an idiot miming. So what we decided to do was hire a PA and a mixing desk, play 'Love Will Tear Us Apart' and record while we filmed, so the video would be a live performance of the song . . . We set up for the filming with a long runway, so the cameras could come in and out on a track, like a mini-railway. Then we went and did a few run-throughs, trying to get the sound right. But we couldn't, because there wasn't a separate room in which to mix the sound . . . It didn't really work, and the tape we ended up with, the soundtrack to the video, sounded pretty rushed and bad . . . Even so, we were very happy with it as it happened. It was raw, dirty and arty. We liked that: it was us all over, of course . . . Our ultimate aim was just to be ourselves, to do things the way we wanted them doing, and we'd insist out of sheer bloody-mindedness . . . You might call them mistakes but at least they were mistakes made on our own terms. Mistakes that became legends. (Hook 2013: 263–5)

As a result of this, the video ended up with an out-of-sync audio track because the label subsequently remastered the video with new audio.

The aspiration to achieve a truly authentic performance in the sense of cultural, musical, representational and personal authenticity within a *mediatised* performance has been pursued. In the early 1990s, Nine Inch Nails (NIN) and director Peter Christopherson collaborated on a video designed to capture the band's pure representational authenticity within a video setting of a simple white cyc. NIN's *'March of the Pigs'* (1994) is a landmark in performance videos because, whilst The Clash and New Order videos attempt to eschew mediatisation, Christopherson's video embraces it. The video is shot in a studio with infinity curves painted white in order to deliver the illusion of nowhere and nothing: no spectacle, no set, no costume, no special effects, no editing. But the handheld camerawork of Simon Archer (a DoP with whom Christopherson often collaborated) is highly foregrounded, drawing the viewer's constant attention to the media construction of the event. What is absent, however, is any editing, and that fact enables Christopherson to deliver mediatisation without the deceit that comes from cutting two or three different performances together to look like a single performance (enabled by non-linear Avid editing a decade later) and by the absence of mime. Christopherson recorded the track live whilst he was filming: he did not have the band mime to vocals. Reportedly, around a dozen takes were done, and the best was selected by Christopherson for the finished video: an authentic media recording.

Correlation with Popular Music Genres?

An obvious question is whether the forms and cycles discussed above correlate with particular popular music genres (defined as 'systems of orientations, expectations, and conventions that bind together an industry, performers, critics, and fans in making what they identify as a distinctive sort of music rather than patterns of musical texts': Lena and Peterson 2008: 698). Keith Negus (1999) has shown that these music genres form the basis for the organisation of corporate music cultures: electronic dance music (EDM), country, heavy metal, folk and so forth. Adopting the 'content analysis' method, Tapper et al.'s investigation of this question yielded inconclusive results (1994). But Fenster's investigation of the distinctive visual styles in US country and western videos of the 1980s provides a fascinating demonstration of the way that genres work intertextually and within cycles (Fenster 1993). As suggested above, research on the fifty-year period from 1966 to 2016 suggested loose patterns and correlations: as well as live rock and stadium bands such as U2, certain Manchester bands such as Oasis, The Stone Roses and Happy Mondays resisted the mediatised artifice of the simulated concept video. Many punk bands and grime artists had issues with mediatisation as well, which I've indicated above.

There was a perception from the late 1980s onwards that heavy metal artists were more willing than many artists to produce high-production-value narrative videos drawing very explicitly on feature film genres such as comedy, slash and horror. Iron Maiden's 'Can I Play with Madness' (1988), directed by Julian Doyle and starring Graham Chapman of Monty Python fame, is a case in point and was one of the first videos to be screened on MTV in 1981. Julian Doyle had edited Monty Python's *Life of Brian* (1979), shot the special effects for *Time Bandits* (1981) and *Brazil* (1985) and directed 'Cloudbusting' (1985) for Kate Bush. 'November Rain' (1992) for Guns N' Roses, directed by British filmmaker Andy Morahan, is also a narrative (intercut with performance), and was alleged to be the most expensive music video made to date (at $1 million). Julien Temple's video for Judas Priest's 'Breaking the Law' (1980) is another case in point, and is analysed in more detail in a later chapter.

There was also a perception that DJ-led electronic music enabled more conceptual and narrative videos because there were no performers to be featured.

This meant that in videos such as The Chemical Brothers' *'Believe'* (Dom & Nic, 2005), Fatboy Slim's *'Right Here, Right Now'* (Hammer & Tongs, 1999), Leftfield feat. Afrika Bambaata's *'Africa Shox'* (Chris Cunningham, 1999) or UNKLE's *'Rabbit in Your Headlights'* (Jonathan Glazer, 1998), the director could focus purely on narrative and story. In our animation focus group, the idea was advanced that animation and effects (FX), CGI and motion capture were particularly popular at that point in DJ-led electronic music of the 1980s, because the artists *as DJs* were opposed to being in their own videos. Animator Maria Manton said that Howie B felt that way, and that the animation videos she worked on with him were created for that reason. The video for Stakker / Humanoid's *'Stakker Humanoid'* (1988) serves as an example. The exploratory, collaborative and 'mixing' methods of creating the animation video mirrored the collaborative, computer-based method for creating the music. Video artists Mark McClean and Colin Scott (aka 'Stakker') sent a demo videotape to Morgan Khan, who invited Brian Dougans to record two demos. The track was originally called 'Humanoid', to be put out by Stakker through Morgan Khan's label Westside Records. In the end, Morgan released it as *'Stakker Humanoid'* by Humanoid to avoid copyright issues, because a dispute had arisen between Brian Dougans and Stakker. It was first released on the dance floor of the iconic London acid house nightclub Shoom.

It was not uncommon in the late 1980s for the visuals to precede the track. The video for Paul Hardcastle's *'19'* (1985) was cut together from footage shot for the documentary *Vietnam Requiem* (ABC News 1982/4), which Hardcastle had watched on TV and which had inspired him to create the track in the first instance. Hardcastle and manager Simon Fuller engaged Ken Grunbaum, the in-house TV promotions person at Chrysalis (Hardcastle's label, where Fuller was head of Artists and Repertoire (A&R)), to cut the video together; with the proceeds, manager Simon Fuller launched his company, 19. EMI's post-punk artists Sigue Sigue Sputnik were very focused on their artwork and visual imagery. The video for *'Love-Missile F1-11'* (1986), created by Hugh Scott Symonds, was conceived by founder and bassist Tony James and depicts a futuristic city reminiscent of *Star Wars* (1977) and *Blade Runner* (1981). The band members are depicted as soldiers, armed with weapons and spaceships. The initial idea was to make a sixty-second trailer to inform the world of the arrival of the band, followed by a promo in which 'the music will take second place'. Tony James explained that

> [W]e want to see two minutes of high-tech sex, gratuitous violence, and generally things exploding in slow motion: rockets, sex, televisions, home computers, BMX bikes, hiring video nasties, it's about films like *Bladerunner* and *Clockwork Orange*. (*South of Watford*, LWT: 1986)

Before they were even signed by a record label, they had created a demo promotional video which they took to show different record labels.

In the animation focus group, Tim Hope said there was an added reason: that the artists were opposed to the idea of celebrity and pop stars. 'The whole rave scene was driven by that because they wanted abstract. They didn't want people, it was all anti-performance. It was all anti: you know, pop stars were dead back then, they were laughable, they were dinosaurs.'[15] This antipathy to the pop star has been a consistent element in British pop alongside the art-school celebration of the pop star, with lead singers such as Damon Albarn catapulting between the two extremes. Concept videos that included no performance were more common to the UK because of a greater antipathy here to the idea of the celebrity pop star, the apparatus of marketing and the duplicity of mediatised performance. All of this underlay the creation of Gorillaz by Damon Albarn and comic creator Jamie Hewlett – a creative group motivated by the idea of a 'virtual band', so that no mediatised performance or marketing would be possible at all.

British artists and filmmakers have been more likely than their US counterparts to experiment with a clash of genre expectations: to invoke a music video genre that is not normally used for a music genre. Amongst artists, Blur stands out as a band ready to parody video genres associated in the USA with other music genres; examples include their video for *'Song 2'*, discussed above, *'Music is My Radar'* (Don Cameron, 2000) and *'Crazy Beat* Version 2' (John Hardwick, 2003); both of the latter are organised around choreographed dance routines. Jake Nava's video for the Arctic Monkeys' *'Arabella'* (2013), like Blur's *'Song 2'*, defies genre expectations of a rock video and bears the signature hallmark of Nava's fashion photographic female empowerment mise-en-scène.

Amongst the British directors invoking video genres not typically associated with music genres is Mat Kirkby. Kirkby began his career in music videos working at the MTV offices in Camden (London) and won an Academy Award in 2015 for his short film *The Phone Call* (2013), starring Sally Hawkins and Jim Broadbent. Kirkby's comedy music video for *'Witness (1 Hope)'* (2001), which constructs Roots Manuva as an anti-hero, runs against the grain of all typical rap and hip-hop videos produced at that time. The video shows Roots Manuva in a comic revenge fantasy, returning to his former London primary school to compete in sports day. The video for English dance act Basement Jaxx's *'U Don't Know Me'* (2005) shows Queen Elizabeth II on a night off in London, drinking, eating a kebab, fighting with bouncers, fighting with a woman in an alley and fleeing police. It plays on the idea of whether the public can ever really know celebrities in the media. Domestically available computer technology has facilitated more affordable CGI videos such as Jesse Kanda's video for FKA twigs' *'How's That'* (2013), which depicts a computer-animated body falling in thin air.

The concept captures the economically effective use of citation by music video directors to locate bands in specific traditions of visual representation. To do this well, directors must be experts not only in film and television history, but in music culture and traditions. When a director deployed a specific genre reference to a film or director, she would have to follow a clear rationale. Jamie-James Medina's video for King Krule's '*A Lizard State*' (2014) paid homage to Alfred Hitchcock with a bookended Hitchcock presentation playing with 90-degree camera angles. When asked if he was worried that King Krule's fans might not recognise the Hitchcock references, Medina explained that both he and Archy (King Krule) were 'Hitchcock fans and that's all we thought about'. But he added: 'There were two Hitchcock biopics in 2012' – a sufficiently recent release date at the time for Medina to hope audiences would recollect – 'and he's still a huge part of entertainment and culture.' Further, he added that 'musically, King Krule's references reach way back sometimes, so I just have to assume that people get it' (Tierney 2014). It was a gamble based on the director and artist's assumptions about the culture capital of their existing and target fanbase.

Without that research, such citation and intertextual referencing could backfire. Aside from the example of Oasis videos, evident from Noel Gallagher's infamous voiceover to the band's DVD release of music videos released between 1994 and 2009 (*Time Flies*, 2010), other more problematic examples have occurred. Dougal Wilson's video for Dizzee Rascal's '*Dream*' (2004) was perceived by some in the industry as a sell-out because it wasn't anchored in Rascal's street culture. Like much of Wilson's work, '*Dream*' parodied British television shows, in this case referencing Annette Mills and Muffin the Mule. The video opens on children's building blocks, and a music-box tune plays as the camera zooms in on a woman at a piano, who says: 'Hello, boys and girls. Shall we see what Dizzee Rascal's up to today? He's such a rascal.' Finding the right balance between speaking only to the subculture from which the artist originated and, on the other hand, expanding your market is a continual challenge for directors. Citation and appropriation work only if the director gets it right, and getting it right means understanding the values, iconographic references, film and music traditions in which the artists have placed themselves.

Notes

1. N. Egan, personal communication, 28 October 2016.
2. M. Lindsay-Hogg, personal communication, 30 June 2015.
3. L. Kessler, personal communication, 1 March 2019.
4. R. Mulcahy, personal communication, 29 October 2016.
5. Shynola, personal communication, 12 May 2015.
6. A. Cameron, personal communication, 17 March 2016.

7. R. Mulcahy, personal communication, 29 October 2016.
8. N. Egan, personal communication, 28 October 2016.
9. C. Sutton, personal communication, 16 November 2016.
10. J. Thraves, personal communication, 10 November 2014.
11. L. Kessler, personal communication, 1 March 2019.
12. S. Muller, personal communication, 19 April 2018.
13. R. Davies, personal communication, 12 April 2015.
14. D. Shadforth, personal communication, 17 November 2016.
15. T. Hope, personal communication, animation focus group, 19 June 2015.

3 EDITING

Music video is an editors' medium. In this chapter, I give a brief history of the changing processes editors and directors have used to cut their films during the period 1966–2016, and examine some differing editing styles and post-production effects that have had a major impact on British music video aesthetics since the mid-1960s. Other than directing, editing is perhaps the only element of making videos that has received systematic attention in scholarship (e.g. Goodwin 1992, Vernallis 2001 and Korsgaard 2017). Many of these arguments were advanced on the basis of a small handful of often American videos. Vernallis argues that, unlike mainstream Hollywood film, music video is not a slave to continuity editing and does not need to preserve time and space in the service of a narrative (2001); the primary aim of a music video is to sell a star and a song, not a story. For Vernallis, editing in music videos responds to rhythmic, timbral, melodic and formal musical features and has more in common with the disjunctive edits of the Russian formalists – Kuleshov, Pudovkin and Eisenstein – than the editing styles of mainstream Hollywood fiction directors. Vernallis points out that it also has similarities to the editing styles of the Nouvelle Vague, often using the 'graphic match' (which joins two frames of similar compositional colour and structure) and the 'jump cut' (brusque edits that make a dramatic change in terms of content, colour or scale) to join shots. Calavita talks of an 'MTV aesthetic trope' arising from 'manic editing that often features flash-cuts, jump-cuts, and the stirring together of varied film stocks, colors, and speeds' (Calavita 2007: 16). Dancyger (2014), for example, sees the legacy of this style of editing in *Natural Born Killers* (1994) and *Crouching Tiger, Hidden Dragon* (2007).

What is often missing from these discussions of editing styles in music video is an account of the creative and social role of the editor in music videos, as distinct from other screen industries. Like the director, an editor is often one of the first people to hear a planned new release. He or she gets to experience the track in its pure emotional form – before the critics, DJs, VJs and fans have interpreted it, before it's been licensed for commercials and films. Her interpretation is a primary and raw one. Every editor will bring something different to the table: as Walter Murch has written, 'You could sit in one room with a pile of dailies and another editor could sit in the next room with exactly the same footage and both of you would make different films out of the same material' (Murch 2001: 12–13). In the USA, editors tend to work without the director present, but not so in the UK. In London, a distinctive craft of music video emerged in the back streets of Soho from the first generation of editors of the late 1970s and 1980s such as David Yardley, who edited A-ha's *Take On Me* (1985) and Dire Straits' *Money for Nothing* (1985) to Tony Kearns. One of the most prolific and acclaimed offline editors of the 1990s and early 2000s, Kearns explained that,

> [w]hat I love about cutting videos was the freedom that it didn't have to make sense as long as it felt great. If it felt good, you could juxtapose things, and that juxtaposition could evoke something that hadn't even been intended.[1]

In this chapter, I will examine the ways authenticity and emotion are evoked through editing techniques and post-production effects. In Britain, post-production has almost always been a process that begins prior to production and not after filming has taken place as the term suggests; this endorses the theory that British videos, more than US videos, are heir to the European tradition of the trick film, in which the novelty of the spectacle and the 'how did they do that?' factor take prominence. The chapter will also highlight styles of editing other than those focused on in existing scholarship. Whilst Goodwin (1993) had rightly argued that directors aim to illustrate elements of the music such as rhythm or time, recent scholars such as Fetveit (2011) have focused on techniques used to exaggerate the latent feeling-state of the track. The interviews conducted for this book showed that a musical disposition was felt to be a crucial prerequisite for editing music videos. For editor Tony Kearns, 'a good edit is a rhythmic edit'.[2] A music video editor is first and foremost a passionate music fan. As editor Tom Lindsay explains, '[t]he music is your script, it's what you cut to, it's your map: the feeling you get, the changes in the music in the verses and the choruses.'[3] Perhaps partly because of this need for a musical sensibility, a great many directors have also been in bands. In discussing what makes a video 'work', producer Scott Millaney ventured the view that it worked if it *moved* the viewer.[4] Creating a powerful and meaningful emotional impact on viewers, it was felt, could rarely be achieved without skilful and musical editing.

Overview: The Editing Process

In our editing focus group, many of the participants agreed that the template for a performance music video lay in films such as Richard Lester's *A Hard Day's Night* (1964), but they were highly critical of the view that fast, disjunctive editing originated on MTV.

> I remember myself and Pedro were quite depressed when we saw this video for the Spencer Davis Group, 'I'm a Man'. It was made in 1967 but it looks like it was made in 1997. It's got all the mad jump cuts; people doing mad dancing in the street; a lightbulb swinging back and forth, really fast, double exposed. Fast cutting and shot on an H-16 Bolex? It was made in 1967.[5]

Art Jones also drew the group's attention to the musicality of the editing of *The Loneliness of the Long Distance Runner* (1962) and *The Knack and How to Get It* (1965).[6]

In the 1960s, promos were shot and edited on film, and this was either done at a director's house or in a commercial edit suite. Director Peter Whitehead owned his own 16mm Steenbeck and cut his promos at home without an editor.[7] For Manfred Mann's '*Mighty Quinn*' (1968), director John Crome rang successive post houses in Soho until he found one that would let him cut the video as a favour without charging a rental fee, because the label had provided no post-production budget. Crome recalls ending up cutting it at MRM, the company of then TV-commercials director Adrian Lyne, who went on to direct *Flashdance* (1983) and *Fatal Attraction* (1987).[8]

By the early 1980s, although most videos were shot on film, many were cut on videotape. The film rushes were transferred with timecode and colour grading to U-matic and Beta SP (introduced by Sony in 1982). The offline editor usually cut on a two-machine U-matic (dry hired at home or in a dedicated offline editing company) and handed the edit decision list (EDL) to an online editor at a dedicated online and FX company to generate a master Beta SP for the label. Copies would be made for or by a video plugging company to send to producers of *The Chart Show*, *TOTP* and MTV amongst others. Beta SP was broadcast quality. The fact that the editors were cutting on tape led to them having a lower status in the editing houses of Soho: Tony Kearns recalls David Yardley being hurt when dismissed as merely 'an engineer' by a feature film editor on the grounds that he was working on videotape rather than film (editing focus group).

Not everyone switched to the new two-machine U-Matic editing, however. Some continued with the feature film and commercials workflow. Tim Pope continued to edit some of his videos on film well into the 1980s with editor Peter Goddard.

> '*Boys Don't Cry*', '*Close To Me*' and '*Inbetween Days*' were cut and finished on film entirely and TK'd from a cinema quality print. Often we'd have two gos at printing to find the best colours. Also, interestingly, all optical effects were done on film, too, which gave them their grungy feel.[9]

Pope would take the neg cut to Ken Robinson at the Video Bureau in Soho or Mike Udin to have it graded and transferred to videotape for broadcast.

By the early 1990s, whilst most videos were still shot on film, the industry was moving to Avid, a non-linear digital editing system that would eventually be widely adopted by the music video industry and subsequently for feature films. The film rushes would be colour graded to Beta SP and Digibeta with timecode. The Digibetas would be retained by the telecine and online company such as VTR, Rushes and MPC, whilst the Beta SP tapes would be couriered to the offline for loading into Avid. In the late 1990s, some directors (for example, Ringan Ledwidge) introduced the television commercials procedure, according to which the final online video would be given an additional mastergrade. From the mid-2000s to 2016, some directors and DoPs began shooting on digital cameras, and the role of the digital imaging technician (DIT) evolved: a person attending the shoot on behalf of post-production to ensure all the digital rushes were prepared correctly for post. But a significant number of directors continued to shoot on film.

Concept Videos

As discussed in earlier chapters, the early 1980s saw the emergence of non-performance concept videos. Stylistic parallels between this genre of music video and early musical shorts such as Len Lye's *Rainbow Dance* (1936), *Kaleidoscope* (1935), *A Colour Box* (1935) and *Colour Flight* (1937) can be drawn. In these videos it is often the editing of the images that creates meaning, rather than the images in isolation. It was in these kinds of videos that the disjunctive editing identified by Vernallis blossomed.

In the post-punk period, abstract footage was cut together for some videos, as documented by Fowler (2017). The video for '*Psychic Rally in Heaven*' (1981) for Throbbing Gristle, directed by Derek Jarman, is an example.

Richard Heslop's video for 23 Skidoo's '*7 Songs*' (1982) is another example and was shot on Super 8mm, VHS and U-matic, before being cut together at the London College of Printing (LCP) and Central St Martins. The colourisation was created using an early colour synth that was installed into the edit suite at the LCP at the time. Having met 23 Skidoo's Johnny and Alex skateboarding, Heslop was asked to make '*7 Songs*' after he'd created live projections for their gigs. He describes '*7 Songs*' as

> a cut and paste piece of work. I was learning to edit as I went along and [it] was a very intuitive process. We were influenced by William S. Burroughs and his cut-up editing technique at the time, and I used chance and random association a lot in this video.[10]

Heslop went on to direct videos for The Shamen, The Smiths, New Order and Happy Mondays.

The live-action version of the Art of Noise's video for '*Close (to the Edit)*' (1984) marks the coming together of avant-garde traditions in popular music composition and experimental filmmaking, and exemplifies Goodwin's idea that sound illustrates image. It was the first of three versions made for the track, and was commissioned by Chris Blackwell at Island Records in New York, which distributed for ZTT Records at the time. ZTT's Paul Morley and Trevor Horne did not like Rybczyński's version and commissioned a second animation version from director Matt Forrest; at some point a third was also made. Rybczyński's live-action video shows three unknown masked performers and a heavily made-up small girl destroying symbols of classical music underneath a railway bridge, edited in perfect syncopation to the beat. It reflects the futurist leanings of both the London-based pop collective Art of Noise and the Polish-born director Zbigniew Rybczyński – a pioneer of 'instant video' editing techniques and a champion of high-definition television (HDTV) technologies. Employing the visual overdubs which would become his signature style, the video won MTV's awards for Most Experimental Video and Best Editing in 1985. The Art of Noise are one amongst several bands for whom a performance video would *not have been authentic*, because it would have directed fans and viewers towards the celebrity-star system which the band rejected, and would have signposted the video as a device for selling music through MTV.

Godley and Creme's video for Herbie Hancock's '*Rockit*' (1984) also foregrounded editing and special effects (SFX). It featured robot-like movable sculptures by Jim Whiting dancing, spinning and walking in time to the music in a virtual (animated) house. Like Rybczyński's '*Close (to the Edit)*' it was recognised at the MTV Music Video Awards with five awards, including Best Concept Video and Best Special Effects. But where the lack of performance or other representational footage of the artists themselves was the desired and explicit choice of the Art of Noise, it appears to have been a marketing decision for '*Rockit*'. In 1984 it was still difficult for Black artists to secure airtime on MTV. Godley and Creme were hired to come up with an idea that relegated Hancock's 'blackness' to the background and gave MTV the visual spectacle and novelty with which London had become associated.

LFO's '*LFO*' (1991) was selected by the editing panel as another landmark work because of the musicality of the editing. The video was directed by Jarvis Cocker, who also directed an early Aphex Twin video for Warp (although John Foxx, Penny Downes, Paul Plowman and Gary Smith are also credited on the *Warp Vision* DVD, 2004). LFO were one of the first artists to sign to Warp Records in Sheffield. LFO's self-titled track 'LFO' also marked Warp's first Top 20 hit. Two other significant videos are Howie B's '*Music for Babies*' (1996) and Future Sound of London's '*We Have Explosive*' (1996). Both were directed by John 'Run' Wrake (1965–2012), a graduate of the Royal College of Art.

Performance Videos

As a result of falling production budgets and rising demand from labels for MTV Europe content, the prominence of editing rose after 1986 because producers were given insufficient funds to build expensive sets or film at costly locations. Directors had to look for cheaper craft techniques to animate the music and to grab the attention of viewers. Into the mix came a generation of DoPs and directors such as Sophie Muller, Jamie Thraves, Dan Landin, Vaughan Arnell, Chris Palmer, Steve Chivers and Andy Morahan. Mainly graduates from Britain's art schools, versed in DIY film culture, post-punk, class politics, feminism and Marxism, these directors neither especially wanted nor were given big production budgets. Having served an apprenticeship at Cucumber Studios with Annabel Jankel and Rocky Morton (makers of Elvis Costello's landmark '*Accidents Will Happen*' video, 1979), director Andy Morahan recalls that, '[o]ur generation didn't have the money. We were relying more on elements of editing in a much more musical way.'[11]

An otherwise very simple video, Morahan's video for George Michael's '*Faith*' release (1987) is significant. Editing and colour grading are the dominant techniques used to animate what is essentially a performance video of Michael playing a guitar near a classic-design Wurlitzer jukebox. Michael is wearing a black leather jacket, Aviator sunglasses, blue jeans and cowboy boots. Talking about the editing for '*Faith*', Morahan explained that whilst initially in his career he would have attended every day of the edit, he had an epiphanic moment where he realised that editors 'were a creative force in themselves'. But he explained that an editor had to be musical: 'I've always liked musical edits, but some people think musical editing is just on the beat.

Well, it's not. It's about anticipating, it's about half beats, it's about the feeling as much as anything.'[12]

Directors such as Richard Heslop chose to edit their videos themselves rather than employ an editor. Heslop's video for The Shamen's '*Ebeneezer Goode*' (1992) was filmed on 16mm black-and-white stock. He cut the film himself on a two-machine U-matic offline player after it was transferred from 16mm. He explained that he enjoyed editing, and used to have a two-desk U-matic edit player sent to his house.

> A lot of those 'bang, bang' edits where the video cuts backwards and forwards, is just literally me cutting: I could just see the tape running in and out on the beat; you can't do that now with digital editing.[13]

He explained that when he pressed the edit button the machine often slipped a frame or two, and that led to the lip sync sometimes appearing a little out. Heslop stopped directing when the industry moved to Avid. His video for '*Ebeneezer Goode*' illustrates the so-called fast MTV aesthetic, as did his later video for Leila K's cover of '*Ça plane pour moi*' (1993), featuring Leila in a car in fast-edited footage graded sepia, which pushes the frantic energy of the track. Because of flashing images in the video, some music channels include epilepsy warnings before airing it; other channels, such as VH1, edited the video to reduce the frame rate of these scenes.

The video for The Prodigy's '*Firestarter*' (Walter Stern, 1996) shows the energy that it was possible to conjure through editing. The premise of the video is simple and in itself not visually gripping (a man in a tunnel mimes to a song), but it works because Stern understood that Liam's extraordinary performance, John Lynch's deep and textured lighting, Tony Kearns' dramatic editing, and the peaks and troughs and energy of the song itself could, if integrated cleverly, create a mesmerising video. Kearns explained that in the edit suite, he had none of the usual arsenal of editors' weapons to cut to create tension and pace, save some close-ups of cockroaches and a 'fantastic track' with 'many peaks and troughs'.

> The limitations made me explore the cutting. The video has one point of view, looking down the tunnel. Its limitations, the location, and the performance are what makes it. There were no rules to follow. John Lynch did the lighting and there's so much going on in each frame.[14]

Director Dawn Shadforth edited her own videos initially too, and explained that her ideas always came 'from the inside of the music'. 'I try not to impose my sort of film, the film that I want to make, onto a track. I have to be led by the music, by the way that music *feels*. That leads me into the idea.'[15] She cut the All Seeing I's '*The Beat Goes On*' (1998) herself on an Avid, which enabled her to achieve more frame-accurate editing; she likened the process to animating live-action footage.

> That video is almost kind of knitted. It's like a piece of tapestry . . . I could never have done that with an editor. It was like a craft project in which I was working with the footage in a very intricate way.

Several years later, Dawn stopped cutting her own material. 'I let them [the editors] do the nitty gritty so I could step back and see the bigger picture.' She felt that 'the actual process of editing so hard – of looking through the rushes and actually managing the machine myself' was underestimated, and enjoyed the process of having an editor to discuss ideas with.[16]

Director Sophie Muller continues to edit her own music videos. Muller described editing as the most creative element of making a video because so much of the meaning in a shot is derived from its position in relation to adjoining shots. This, alongside the editor's role in selecting takes from the performance rushes, can give the editor great creative control. As a result, Muller found it difficult to delegate this part of the creative process. 'I'd be sitting next to an editor saying: "No, try that. Put that frame there. And then, no, no, three frames back, like that. . . ."' This was partly because Muller didn't shoot from storyboards:

> When I direct, I don't do storyboards. I like to leave it as open as possible for things to happen that I hadn't planned, because the most magical things I've ever filmed have been accidents. I like to create a world where these accidents can happen on my shoots. That means I just have to edit the videos myself.[17]

The editors in our focus group shared a high opinion of Muller's editing. Adam Dunlop described Muller as 'the best editor in the world, in music video'. Tony Kearns recalled first seeing Muller's video for '*Song 2*' (1997), which she'd edited herself, and concluding, '*I've got a lot to learn*, haven't I?'[18]

Single-Shot Videos

Single-shot videos are often overlooked in music video because, as Kearns explained, 'the "fast" or "MTV" edit . . . has blighted critical appreciation of music videos'.[19] Several were selected for the landmark collection, such as Sinéad O'Connor's '*Nothing Compares 2 U*' (John Maybury, 1990), Björk's '*Big Time Sensuality*' (Stephane Sednaoui, 1993), Radiohead's '*No Surprises*' (Grant Gee, 1997), Toy's '*Lose My Way*' (Joe Morris, 2012), Coldplay's

'*Yellow*' (James and Alex, 2000), Elton John's '*I Want Love*' (Sam Taylor-Wood, 2001), The Streets' '*Fit But You Know It*' (Dougal Wilson, 2004), Bat for Lashes' '*What's a Girl to Do*' (Dougal Wilson, 2007), Dan Le Sac vs Scroobius Pip's '*Thou Shalt Always Kill*' (Nick Frew, 2007) and FKA twigs' '*Water Me*' (FKA twigs and Jesse Kanda, 2013).

A single-shot video is a video either filmed in one continuous take, or composed of multiple takes cut together to give the impression that the video was recorded in a single continuous take. Most of these examples foreground the artist's vocal performance and lyrics. Single-shot videos have been overlooked in the scholarship. In the film era (1979–2005), the possibility of making videos without edits depended on the length of the track and the aesthetic sought. A 400ft roll of 16mm film running at normal UK speed of 24 frames/s would deliver around eleven minutes of footage. A normal-length single release would be just under four minutes. Thus, it was possible to fit two run-throughs of an artist's performance onto a 400ft roll. If the director and DoP wanted to shoot on 35mm, the margin was much tighter. Problems were further compounded if the team wanted to shoot at high speed in order to create a slow-motion effect.

Massive Attack's video for '*Unfinished Sympathy*' (Baillie Walsh, 1991) illustrates this technical challenge. The unreal atmosphere captured in '*Unfinished Sympathy*', which became known in the industry at the time as 'heavy air', was said to cleverly intensify the psychological internal narrative of the track. In '*Unfinished Sympathy*' the viewer sees Shara Nelson bravely dicing with death as she walks along the sidewalk, narrowly avoiding a couple of street gangs with their dogs, an amputee and a group of drunks. It was photographed in one continuous shot on a Steadicam from 1311 South New Hampshire Avenue to 2632 West Pico Boulevard in Los Angeles. Not only, however, were the vocals mimed, but they were also recorded at the wrong speed. Director of photography John Mathieson explained that Walsh wanted to shoot the video in a single take, but the track was longer than a 400ft roll of stock. So Mathieson and producer Mark Whittock 'had to work out a speed that would creep so the whole track could fit in'. The solution they settled on was to speed up the audio track. This meant Nelson mimed her vocals faster, and the 400ft roll of film stock lasted the full length of the track. This gave rise to the so-called heavy air effect. As Mathieson recalls,

> The way she moved became iconic . . . But it was because of the interlacing between the frames . . . instead of a *chut chut chut* it was a *zchoom zchoom* . . . it made this weird, soft dissolve between the frames; it made the way Shara moved look as if she was in her own distant world.[20]

Narrative Videos

Narrative videos have posed very specific challenges for music video editors because the editor has to cut according to the dramatic points of a plot- and character-driven story as well as the dramatic structure of a track. Jamie Thraves' video for Radiohead's *'Just'* (1995) illustrates this. The editor, Tony Kearns, initially cut two versions. The first version he cut was a story. 'Because I didn't want the music to dictate the edit of the narrative I cut a separate film with a narrative.'[21] He cut it without listening to the music and without syncing the pictures to the track. After this, he cut an entirely separate performance video, utilising the 'many musical moments' in the track 'when you just go, something has to happen here'. He finally cut both the performance video and the narrative film together. 'The buzz I got when I put the narrative down to the track and [found] it just kept hitting 80 per cent of the marks. It was fantastic.'[22]

In her video for Doves' *'Black and White Town'* (2005), by contrast, Lynne Ramsay and her editor chose to cut only to the drama of the story. The editing bears little relationship to the rhythmic, timbral and melodic features of the track. The editing is governed by the principles of feature film continuity editing rather than the musical editing described of Heslop, Morahan, Shadforth, Muller and Jones. Feature film director Lynne Ramsay had stronger roots in film editing than music video editing. In the essay 'The Evolution of the Language of Cinema' (1950), André Bazin describes the invisible editing identified with the tradition of D. W. Griffith (and the classic American cinema) over the aesthetics of 'montage' associated with Vernallis's Russian filmmakers. Shot on a council estate in Glasgow, the *'Black and White Town'* music video creates a 'window into the world', not a window onto the world as experienced and structured by the music. It hides the music, and hides its own filmmaking apparatus. The version of the video that Ramsay delivered to the label was re-edited in order to strengthen the relationship with the music.

As a result, the 'official version' on YouTube and Vevo is credited to 'Alan Smithee' on the Music Video Database. Alan Smithee is the pseudonym used by a director when she wants to disown a film. I have not been able to find out what happened to the version that Ramsay originally delivered to the label, but Ramsay's director's cut of the video, featuring different footage, can be found on the DVD in the boxset version of the *Some Cities* (2005) album; this is the version that Ramsay has authenticated. The politics of Alan Smithee have been subject to some considerable discussion in the industry. The concept was used by British commercials director Tony Kaye, in the case he filed against the Directors' Guild of America in 1998 regarding his work on *American History X* (1998) for New Line. The use of the term by directors highlights very deep-felt issues regarding creative control on films, of the kind that surface at their worst when production cultures collide – in Ramsay's case, the culture of independent British film production clashed with British music video culture. In Kaye's case, the production culture of British television commercials clashed with Hollywood film. 'As soon as we appreciate Smithee figuratively as a way to perform the conflicts and issues surrounding creative control and collective authorship, the signature functions as performance' (Saper 2001: 42).

'*Black and White Town*' illustrates how, in order for it to work successfully, a music video story constitution must be effective *through* the dramatic music, not despite the music. The first and primary interpretation of the world lies in the song – whether instrumentally or in the lyrics. This is not to say the editing must be visible. There are examples of invisible editing which is also rhythmic editing, such as Oasis's '*Falling Down*' (WIZ, 2008) and Madonna's '*Drowned World / Substitute for Love*' (Walter Stern, 1998). Editors sometimes edited the track itself so it could service the rhythm of the story more fully in narrative videos such as these. It was common practice throughout the 1990s to remix a track to suit the video. Chris Cunningham's video for Aphex Twin's '*Come to Daddy*' (1997) was remixed to accommodate dialogue in the middle. Liz Kessler explains that this continued in the 2000s.

> Approx 25 per cent of the videos I commissioned at Island between 2001 and 2007 had original versions, some included spliced tracks, it was common practice. It fell out of favour for the reason that the BPI charts restricted the number of formats that could contribute to the chart position so doing a specific vid mix became counter-productive, it actually reduced chartable sales. This has now of course all gone away again some time ago as streaming is key and formatting doesn't play the same role as it did in achieving high chart entry.[23]

'*Time to Dance*' (2009) was the second video Daniel Wolfe had made for French electro-pop duo The Shoes, and a trusting working relationship had already been established. Like Kearns, editor Tom Lindsay initially cut the story mute, without any music, in order to get the crucial dramatic elements of the narrative in place. Lindsay used the stems to score to picture, which The Shoes sent to him as individual components (bass, drums, keyboard, etc.). He explained that they asked the band if they could use another track ('*America*', 2008) at the front of the video, because he and Dan thought it worked as an intro. He himself mixed '*America*' into '*Time to Dance*' for the video, whilst remixing the '*Time to Dance*' audio as well. Together, he and Wolfe created a new audio track for the video – 6:51 in duration, as opposed to 3:16 (the original audio duration of '*Time to Dance*'). Having created this new track, they then 'tweaked the picture to fit the score perfectly'.[24] So although this video was commissioned for the single release of the track '*Time to Dance*', it cannot be described as an *accompanying video*. Like the Island videos commissioned by Liz Kessler, the *'Time to Dance'* video is a separate self-sufficient audiovisual work.

Psychological Realism and Authenticity

For twenty-five years, from the mid-1970s through to the late 1990s, the music video industry functioned as a crucial R&D sector in telecine and VFX for the screen industries in Britain as a whole by pushing the creative and artistic boundaries of both the hardware and software. Artists, directors, editors and post houses were at the fore, experimenting with new machines and software packages to see how they could push the film rushes to emote the audio to extreme degrees. Some of the technologies were developed for beauty purposes, such as K-Scope at VTR, and with much controversy. But others were developed by experimental and competitive directors in Soho in order to represent the internal states of the music and song. In his essay on mutable temporality, Fetveit (2011) has identified some later examples of this work, but the tendency started as early as 1975 with Queen's *'Bohemian Rhapsody'*.

Mike Lipscombe's video for Tricky's cover of Public Enemy's *'Black Steel'* (1995) is a conceptual work that pushed new Flame software to represent the mood of the track. Throughout most of the video, Martina Topley Bird can be seen vocalising the lyrics whilst other people and animals appear in the background (a darkly graded ominous beach). Intercut are shots of a drummer and guitarist playing their instruments. Just for the 'switch on, switch off' part, Tricky is visible, holding his hands towards the camera. *'Black Steel'* used two-point tracking with efold animation to create infinite tracking; this allowed multi-layered compositing. The 1990s saw a rapid transformation in music video as a result of silicon graphics, Flame and Inferno, as shown in Radiohead's *'Street Spirit'* (Jonathan Glazer, 1996), McFly's *'Room on the 3rd Floor'* (Si and Ad, 2004), Radiohead's *'House of Cards'* (James Frost and Mary Faggot, 2008), Coldplay's *'Strawberry Swing'* (Shynola, 2008), The Ting Tings' *'Shut Up and Let Me Go'* (Alex and Liane, 2008) and Klaxons' *'Twin Flames'* (Saam Farahmand, 2010).

Angus Cameron's video for My Bloody Valentine's *'To Here Knows When'* (1991) illustrates not only this conceptual performance approach, but also the extent to which a video can bring a track more life, more power and more meaning than when it is experienced merely as audio. The video was shot on 16mm and Super 8 using a small crane as well as 'a van full of lights and every strobe we could lay our hands on'.[25] Cameron and Montague shot 'an impressionistic performance of the band with the camera on the crane describing lazy circles around each band member'.[26] In order to capture what Cameron describes as the 'mesmeric, almost orchestral looping theme' that pervades the song, he decided to depict something that would resemble a 'moving Rorschach ink blot'. Cameron also asked the band's other vocalist and guitarist, Bilinda Butcher, to pirouette slowly round and round on the spot while crossing and uncrossing her arms. The video was put together entirely in a Beta SP online suite at Component Editing, by Nigel Simpkiss. Other techniques employed to achieve the 'psychedelic' effect included using solarised negatives of the Super 8 that had been telecined at VTR. 'We recoloured some of the blue smudges and then set to work layering and re-layering the footage of Bilinda's dancing to get the hypnotic "ink blot" effect,' recalls Cameron. The number of layers employed at any given time was as many as twenty-eight – unprecedented for the time, given that the video predates digital technology. The erratic rhythm and flash frames were also used to give the video what Cameron describes as an overall feel that captures the 'classic Valentine's paradox'.[27]

Much of the emotional work of music videos is achieved through colour grading, which was created for music videos in the 1980s long before it was used in TV or feature films. Although academic attention to colour has increased recently, with a number of publications (Dalle Vacche and Price 2006, Coates 2010, Cowan 2015), as well as Sarah Street's comprehensive histories of colour from 1900 to 1955 (Street 2012, Brown et al. 2013), a history of telecine colour grading has yet to be written. In 1987, when director Andy Morahan made his video for George Michael's *'Faith'*, telecine had also been added into this mix. One of the key contributions of music video in this transition to videotape was to turn the craft of telecine into an art. When broadcasters at the BBC decided they wanted to screen content that had not been shot on videotape but had been originated on film, they encountered a problem. The difference in frame rates between film (generally 24 frames/s) and television (30 or 25 frames/s, interlaced) meant that simply playing a film into a television camera would result in flickering. A variety of technologies were developed and experimented with to overcome this problem and generate flicker-free content.

'Faith' illustrates the early development of telecine as part of the creative process in music video production, because it was only possible as a result of the recent appropriation by Soho's post-production houses specialising in music video of software that could isolate and adjust a single colour within the screen palette. Morahan explains, in relation to the Pet Shop Boys' *'West End Girls'* (1984) video that he directed, that,

> [w]hen I look at *'West End Girls'* I think it looks like a documentary. The grading of it was so unsophisticated. Then you look at *'Faith'* a couple of years later; well by then Da Vinci had come in, and you could be much more aggressive with the way you graded film. Because we video directors had been working closely with the post-production companies, we were the first in on all these new techniques. We were ahead of the commercials people who were using telecine as a way of

mastering for broadcast. In those days it was a Pandora's box: 'Oh, we can do this! Oh, we can do that!'[28]

The video for '*Diane*' (1995) illustrates the hugely important role that colour grading was starting to play in music videos. The song concerns the murder of St Paul, Minnesota, waitress Diane Edwards by Joseph Ture in 1980. Northern Irish metal band Therapy? covered the American original version. The video was commissioned by Robin Dean at A&M Records and directed by WIZ. Colourist Tareq Kubaisi recalls,

> I was trying to grade something using one of the control balls but I'd mixed it up. I realised I was adding colour into the blacks, which, if you go into the BBC manual, you'd see is wrong. But it looked amazing. It was the colour of the blood in her womb. It was this green rich black with amber tones flooding through. I remember the hairs on the back of my closely cropped head going up, which was my barometer for whether things were going right. It was an accident. I've always just worked on instinct. I don't build things up correctly. Sometimes I think, 'What on earth did I do there?' But that's how to get to whatever subliminally colours say.[29]

Radiohead's '*Street Spirit*' (1996) is another important video for technological innovation. It was directed by Jonathan Glazer and shot during two nights in a desert outside Los Angeles. One of the features Avid subsequently offered was an effect whereby editors could speed up and slow down human motion change ('ramping'). Previously this had to be achieved by over- or undercranking the camera. The panel in our editing focus group believed '*Street Spirit*' was one of the earliest landmark uses of the effect, and it was seen by the industry as radical at the time. The editor was John McManus. He and his assistant Neil 'would do their own tables about how, you know on graph paper, on how to ramp the footage. And it hadn't been done before.'[30] Glazer has subsequently described this video as 'a turning point' in his own work in which he'd found his own voice as an artist. 'I felt like I got close to whatever mine was, and I felt confident that I could do things that emoted, that had some kind of poetic as well as prosaic value. That for me was a key moment' (Kaufman 2001). In recent years, however, there has been a backlash against reliance on post-production. For London Grammar's video for '*Wasting My Young Years*' (2013), all the effects were created in camera: a huge pinhole camera was built to create the images.[31]

A full analysis of the changing roles of editors and post-production houses would be useful, but the examples examined in this chapter undermine any attempt to furnish a single universal model of music video editing and suggest that Vernallis's account of disjunctive editing – endorsed by Korsgaard – applies only to a minority of videos produced in Britain between 1966 and 2016. It is generally the concept videos of the 1980s that adhere most obviously to that model. But many of the single-shot and narrative videos that are amongst the most acclaimed videos produced in Britain do not adhere to that model at all. Moreover, the comments of the editing panel and analysis of editing styles in the pop promo films and early British promos suggest that the fast editing style was rooted in the editing rooms of Soho 1965–7, rather than a response of producers to MTV. The interviewees for this chapter felt that music video editing required a musicality and a set of craft skills that, in the past, would have been learned in often unofficial apprenticeships as runners and in the post and offline houses of Soho, after which a runner might be promoted to assistant editor and then given an opportunity to cut a low-budget video for an up-and-coming director – supervised by more experienced editors in the company. But with falling budgets in the digital era and the availability of affordable domestic editing packages such as Adobe Premiere Pro, increasing numbers of editors have begun to work from home using domestic equipment. This was perceived by our editing workshop to account for a general decline in the craft of video editing from the mid-2000s onwards.

Notes

1. T. Kearns, personal communication, editing focus group, 26 November 2015.
2. T. Kearns, personal communication, editing focus group, 26 November 2015.
3. T. Lindsay, personal communication, editing focus group, 26 November 2015.
4. S. Millaney, personal communication, 12 April 2018.
5. T. Kearns, personal communication, editing focus group, 26 November 2015.
6. T. Kearns, personal communication, editing focus group, 26 November 2015.
7. P. Whitehead, personal communication 1 October 2015.
8. J. Crome, personal communication, 8 February 2016.
9. T. Pope, personal communication, 24 September 2018.
10. R. Heslop, personal communication, 15 September 2015.
11. A. Morahan, personal communication, 10 May 2016.
12. A. Morahan, personal communication, 10 May 2016.
13. R. Heslop, personal communication, 15 September 2015.
14. T. Kearns, personal communication, editing focus group, 26 November 2015.
15. D. Shadforth, personal communication, 17 November 2016.
16. D. Shadforth, personal communication, 17 November 2016.
17. S. Muller, personal communication, 19 March 2018.
18. T. Kearns, personal communication, editing focus group, 26 November 2015.
19. T. Kearns, personal communication, editing focus group, 26 November 2015.
20. J. Mathieson, personal communication, 8 January 2018.
21. T. Kearns, personal communication, 26 November 2015.
22. T. Kearns, personal communication, editing focus group, 26 November 2015.

23. L. Kessler, personal communication, 22 February 2019.
24. T. Lindsay, personal communication, 23 May 2017.
25. A. Cameron, personal communication, 17 March 2016.
26. A. Cameron, personal communication, 17 March 2016.
27. A. Cameron, personal communication, 17 March 2016.
28. A. Morahan, personal communication, 10 May 2016.
29. T. Kubaisi, personal communication, 18 January 2018.
30. A. Jones, personal communication, editing focus group, 26 November 2015.
31. L. Kessler, personal communication, 22 February 2019.

4 MOVEMENT AND DANCE

When many people think about music video, it is as the heir to the musical. Most of the scholarship on dance in music videos has, not surprisingly, focused on that. In his book on British musicals, John Mundy dedicates a section to music video, arguing rightly that the music video only makes sense when viewed within the larger history of twentieth-century music on screen (1999). Sherril Dodds argues that music video is heir to the 'innovative and dazzling film techniques' of Fred Astaire and Busby Berkeley's 'eye-catching and opulent screen-dance images' (2009a: 252). Beth Genné (2018a, 2018b) argues that music videos adopted the street dance traditions of René Clair, Ernst Lubitsch, Rouben Mamoulian, Fred Astaire, Gene Kelly, Stanley Donen and Vincente Minnelli. McRobbie and Buckland both argue that, as in later dance films such as *Dirty Dancing* (1987), *Fame* (1980) and *Flashdance* (1983), dance in music video can serve as a metaphor for social identity, romantic fulfilment and other 'fantasies of achievement' (McRobbie 1984, Buckland 1993).

But British dance videos are not simply an heir to the US street dance musical. Our study showed that dance has emerged as one of the most dynamic cycles of production in British music video in recent years, with choreographers such as Aaron Sillis and Holly Blakey emerging from distinctively British dance traditions. In Britain, dance videos have tended to represent the social experience of the fans and the dance culture of the clubs in ways that authenticate the artist and their music within their cultural and economic roots. In this chapter, I ask how British dance music videos function as an appropriation art governed first and foremost by authentication. I will sketch out what,

I hope, is not too superficial a history of the videos. In a previous publication, I argued that British choreography tended to be more messy and realistic than US music videos (2017a). Here I argue that British music videos have tended to show more attention to the representation of *internal emotional states* than US videos. The chapter is offered as a contribution to the expanding literature in dance-on-screen studies which was partly constituted to remedy a 'continuing neglect of music in dance analysis' (Evans and Fogarty 2016: 1). Sherril Dodds, regarded as the founder of this subdiscipline of dance studies, defines it as dance choreographed for television in which 'it is not only the body that creates the "dance", but also the camera and the cut' (Dodds 2001: xv, xiv). In the proceedings of the 2006 American Dance Festival, for example, Pearlman proposes *editing* as a form of choreography (2006) by way of proposing a new discipline of study in which the apparatus of filmmaking is conceived of as part of the formal integrity of the choreography.

As in previous chapters, I will draw out some of the ways in which British music videos have intentionally appropriated and cited cultural and artistic dance forms between 1966 and 2016. In his interview for this book, British music video choreographer Paul Roberts argues that there is no such thing as originality in the field today. He began his career as a dancer for East 17 and Take That, and cites the video for Hurts' '*Wonderful Life*' (2010), which he choreographed for Dawn Shadforth using the inverted angles of celebrated US choreographer Bob Fosse. 'As choreographers, we always hark back to the days gone by. And we take those times and influences and then go, "well, how can we make it our own?".'[1]

Movement Direction

The first step is to appreciate that all choreography takes place within paradigmatic practices of performance of the kind analysed by Carlson (1996) and Auslander ([1999] 2008). The figure of Lindsay Kemp is crucial in appreciating the extent to which British artists in the 1970s began to use carefully controlled exterior performance in order to represent both interior mental states and philosophical statements. Kemp was a mentor to a nineteen-year-old David Bowie, casting him in a production of *Pierrot in Turquoise* in 1966. He is credited with helping Bowie shape the Ziggy Stardust persona, and appeared both on stage in the singer's 1972 *Ziggy Stardust* tour and in the video for '*John, I'm Only Dancing*' (Mick Rock, 1972). Kate Bush enrolled in Kemp's interpretive dance courses with an advance from her original EMI record contract; and she later recruited the choreographer to appear in her 1993 short film *The Line, The Cross and the Curse*. The notion of performance as performance-of-the-body was peaking in the late 1960s and early 1970s, to be replaced, in the 1980s and beyond, with an orientation that emphasised spectacle and disembodied experience. This was to be replaced yet again in the 1990s by a turn towards language and the performative (Carlson 1996: 108, 111, cited in Waldrep 2016). The disembodied spectacle phase was typified in the USA by the videos of avant-garde band Devo and the choreography of Toni Basil, who created David Byrne's dance for the Talking Heads' *'Once in a Lifetime'* video (Byrne / Basil, 1980).

Movement direction is an industry term for a paradigm of *directed performance*. At the close of the period examined in our study, 2016, there were three types of movement direction. The first is visible movement direction. This is signposted as having been authored by the choreographer. Significant examples are Garth Jennings' videos for Radiohead's *'Lotus Flower'* (2011) and Atoms for Peace's 'Ingenue' (2013), both created by the innovative Wayne McGregor CBE, resident choreographer of the Royal Ballet and associate artist of Sadler's Wells. Aletta Collins' choreography for Will Young's *'Losing You'* (Henry Schofield, 2012) also falls into this category, as does Supple Nam's choreography for Peace's *'Money'* (Ninian Doff, 2014). Nam's pioneering collaborations with post-production FX teams have shown how choreographers can utilise the latest technologies (The xx's *'Islands'* (Saam Farahmand, 2009). His choreography for The Chemical Brothers' *'Midnight Madness'* (Dom & Nic, 2008) includes not only post-production FX but creative stunt direction. It was Nam's collaboration with post-production house MPC and directors NE-O at Stink to remediate the Gene Kelly choreography from *Singin' in the Rain* (1952) for the VW commercial *'Singin' in the Rain'* (NE-O, 2005) that first brought him to major industry attention and earned him a prestigious Design & Art Direction (D&AD) award.

The second type of movement direction is invisible. It is intended not to be noticed, but to be experienced as authentic flow from the artist. The primary underlying intention is to make it appear that the movement has manifested naturally and organically from the artist's own personal relationship to the music. Choreographer Natricia Bernard explained, in relation to Florence and the Machine's *'Drumming Song'* (Dawn Shadforth, 2009): 'She's not a pop star where you can go "Five, six . . ."' because she is 'a free spirit'. Choreographing fixed dance moves would have been wholly inauthentic to Florence's personality: '[T]he hair needs to be part of the movement as well as the clothing, everything . . . all of it is meant to be a reflection of Florence.'[2]

The third type of movement is visible, but intended to be perceived as flow from the performers' personalities. It's evolved from what was called 'loose choreography'. In earlier years, pop acts were generally more comfortable with semi-choreographed routines of the kind created for Bananarama by Bruno Tonioli for *'Venus'* (Peter Care, 1986) and the moves created by Paul Roberts for Steps' *'Tragedy'* (Dave Amphlett, 1999), which were simple enough for primary-school children (a primary target audience) to imitate. These simple dance moves could be extraordinarily effective in marketing bands to new audiences if they caught on. According to John Stewart, Bananarama's video for '*Venus*' was so well liked by the VJs and producers of MTV that it was selected for heavy rotation and, in his view, played a major role in the single reaching number one in the US charts. But Roberts says this kind of choreography has been rare in recent years, because '[a]s the years have progressed, it's become all about the looseness and looking like you're natural. Gone are the days of the formulated dance moves.' Instead, says Roberts, 'bands, especially the One D boys, want to be very honest and very true to themselves'. For Roberts, this is rooted in deeper changes in the industry, because 'a lot of artists have more say today in what they want to be and how they want to be perceived and the label and management allow them to do that now'. By contrast, twenty years ago 'it was decided in a boardroom meeting; the label and management would tell them what they wanted.'[3]

THE HOLLYWOOD MUSICAL

The influence of Hollywood musicals on British music videos can be seen in a number of ways. The first is the chorus line, which formed a vital element of Hollywood musicals. A chorus line is a large group of dancers who together perform synchronised routines. Busby Berkeley began to enhance the traditional dance number with ideas drawn from the drill precision he had experienced as a soldier during World War I. In films such as *42nd Street* (1933), *Footlight Parade* (1933) and *Gold Diggers* (1933), Berkeley choreographed a number of films in this unique style. His numbers typically begin on a stage but gradually transcend the limitations of theatrical space: his meticulously choreographed routines, involving human bodies forming patterns like a kaleidoscope, could never fit onto a real stage and the intended perspective is viewing from straight above. The chorus line is a primary element in Arlene Phillips' choreography for Elton John's '*I'm Still Standing*' (Russell Mulcahy, 1983) and a lesser feature of Queen's '*I was Born to Love You*' (David Mallet, 1984/5).

It was also a core concept of Michel Gondry's video for Daft Punk's '*Around the World*' (Michel Gondry, 1997), commissioned by Paul McKee at One Little Indian in London. The video, choreographed by Biana Li, seems to appropriate the preferred top shots and geometrical lines of Berkeley's films: five groups of dancers' movements are synchronised with the different sounds of the track as they move around a giant platform representing a vinyl record. The B-boys move in time with the bass line, the bathing beauties dance to the synthesiser and the space explorers circle with the vocal track. Similarly, for his video for the Chemical Brothers' '*Let Forever Be*' (1999), Gondry, working with choreographer Keith Young, used ground-breaking video and film effects to depict a young woman's nightmares with a *virtual* chorus line. Gondry has said he wanted to create dance videos in which the camera and edit were put at the service of the dance, and were not edited into fragments.

A second way in which the influence of Hollywood musicals can be seen is through individually choreographed routines. In the late 1990s, US choreographer Michael Rooney (son of Hollywood actor Mickey Rooney) brought the Hollywood musical style to the UK in videos for Björk, Fatboy Slim and Kylie Minogue. He worked on three landmark videos commissioned by British record labels. In Björk's *'It's Oh So Quiet'* (Spike Jonze, 1995), the choreographed camera of Jonze's video is reminiscent of Berkeley's film style and peppered with homages to Hollywood film musicals. The video made a huge impact on the music video industry in London by reinventing the wheel: bringing the Hollywood musical to life for a generation of British audiences and music fans who had previously never heard of Astaire or Kelly. Jonze hired Rooney again to choreograph his second video for Fatboy Slim, *'Weapon of Choice'* (2001), which featured Christopher Walken dancing and flying around the empty lobby of the Marriott Hotel (now the LA Hotel). In his third major British work, Rooney collaborated with Dawn Shadforth to choreograph Kylie Minogue's *'Can't Get You Out of My Head'* (2001) after working with Minogue on her 2005 *Showgirls* tour.

The Hollywood musical is also very evident in two videos directed by Sophie Muller: Sophie Ellis Bextor's *'Murder on the Dancefloor'* (2003), choreographed by Litza Bixler, and Duffy's *'Rain on Your Parade'* (2008), choreographed by Natricia Bernard, the latter recalling Judy Garland's performance of the *'Get Happy'* number in *Summer Stock* (1950). Despite an intense grounding in postmodern and feminist theory attained in her MA at the Royal College of Art (RCA), Muller graduated with a continued passion for Hollywood musicals, with which she had fallen in love as a child visiting the Everyman Cinema in Hampstead with her father. Muller says *The Sound of Music* (1965) remains her all-time favourite film.[4] The Hollywood influence is also evident in Phil Griffin's comedy video for Basement Jaxx's 'Hush Baby' (2006), which was inspired by the musical *Hello, Dolly!* (1969).

But the influence of Hollywood musicals is also felt indirectly through the slick high production values of US dance videos, which themselves were made in the tradition of the Hollywood musical. Michael Jackson's *'Thriller'* (John Landis, 1982) was cited by British choreographers Aaron Sillis, Natricia Bernard and Paul Roberts as the inspiration for their careers. Choreographed in the USA by Michael Peters, it was screened as a late-night premiere on Channel 4 and BBC's *TOTP*. Janet Jackson's *'Rhythm Nation'* (Dominic Sena, 1989) was also hugely influential in the UK: directed by Dominic Sena and choreographed by Anthony Thomas, the sheer scale and polish of the choreography, costume, photography and editing of the synchronised dance of the video set a standard that has rarely been achieved since. Together, these two videos established a style that was opulent, dramatic and very slick, and that would be inherited and consolidated in the 1990s R&B and rap videos of Hype Williams, characterised by fisheye lens work and glitzy wardrobes. Dawn Shadforth explained that she was influenced by Hype Williams, who had directed TLC's *'No Scrubs'* (1999). When she made Minogue's *'Can't Get You Out of My Head'* (2001) Shadforth 'was obsessed with Hype Williams doing Missy Elliott and Busta Rhymes – it was the frame cutting, the movement, the bombastic-ness of the ideas. I really love those videos a lot.'[5]

Dawn Shadforth's video for Hurts' *'Lights'* (2015) sits within the Astaire tradition genre of dance drama. In dance drama, the exposition of plot, narrative and character is communicated through dance, rather than dialogue scenes interrupting musical scenes involving synchronised vocals. The lead singer – Theo – undertook dance training over a period of eight months in order to play the main role. At seven minutes long, the video exceeds the song, and audio was remixed to support the dramatic structure of the video. Shadforth describes it as a genuinely collaborative work that tells the story of two eccentric outcast souls who find love with each other on the dancefloor. The camera was choreographed into a 360-degree set by Shadforth and DoP Robbie Ryan. Whilst the video is shot through with gritty British realism (especially in the characterisation of the girl), the video transforms into distinctive Hollywood escapism in the final exterior scenes as the pair dance on top of the car. That final shot evokes the lyrics of the celebrated Fred and Ginger number from RKO's *Follow the Fleet* (1936): 'There may be trouble ahead / But while there's music and moonlight and love and romance / Let's face the music and dance.'

But *'Lights'* bears British traits too. It offers what Dyer ([1977] 1981) has termed the utopian solution to real social needs and contradictions of the classic musical. With its observations about social cliques and outsiders, the video harks back to the early British ballets of Ninette de Valois and Frederick Ashton, which sought to secure an identity distinct from Russian ballet; in those ballets, as in *The Red Shoes* (1948) and Lee Hall's *Billy Elliot* for the stage (2005) and cinema (2000), choreographers and directors sought to capture the experience of ordinary British people. Another example of utopian redemption is the video for Canadian band Arcade Fire's single *'We Exist'* (David Wilson, 2014). The video begins with US actor Andrew Garfield – in the role of a transgender woman – shaving her head and getting dressed. At a small-town local bar, she's harassed and assaulted by some bar patrons. She collapses and, in a dream-like sequence, escapes to dance with a group of male dancers in matching plaid half shirts and jean shorts. In the final moments of the video, she walks through a portal to Arcade Fire's Coachella concert. In a similar vein, the video for the Avalanches' *'Since I Left You'* (2001), directed by Rob Leggatt and Leigh Marling, tells the story of two miners in a black-and-white world who find a passage into a dance studio situated in a colour world. The majority of the video consists of the miners dancing with two ballerinas. All these figures transform the disparate and out-of-place into something new and joyful and redeeming.

The Star Dancer

As scholars of the Hollywood musical and dance on screen have observed, the musicals were often arranged around set dance routines for stars such as Gene Kelly. In researching dance for the landmark collection, it was difficult to avoid the conclusion that a number of videos could best be described as star dancer performances, because their very premise was an exhibition of the unique choreographic and dance performances of the lead vocalists. In all cases, the choreography is authored by the artist herself. The first example was Kate Bush's video for *'Running Up That Hill'* (1985), which was choreographed by Bush in collaboration with the Detroit-born African American dancer Dyane Gray-Cullert, who had a background in Martha Graham technique and with whom Bush had been studying ballet (Thomson 2012: 201). In the video, Bush and Michael Hervieu perform a fusion of ballet and contemporary dance with frontal photography. According to Thomson, the video's 'ballet moves, low-key colouring and lack of lip-synching' were 'too esoteric for US audiences' and a clip of Bush's performance on *Wogan* (BBC 1982–92) was used in its place (Thomson 2012: 224).

Another landmark example is Jamiroquai's video *'Virtual Insanity'* (Jonathan Glazer, 1996), which was choreographed by Jay Kay himself. Not only does the video pay homage to the Astaire tradition of the star dancer, but it also pays homage to the theatrical stage as the authentic home of pure dance as Jay Kay dances across the apparently moving floor of a highly contrived production set. Director Jonathan Glazer had studied theatre design at Wimbledon, and had spent much time in preparation planning the motion of the set walls so that it would appear to be the floor that was moving, rather than the walls. The video created the 'how did they do that?' novelty effect of early British trick films such as William Paul's *'Upside Down / Human Flies'* (1899). From the œuvre of FKA twigs, there are many examples of these set pieces. Twigs trained as a dancer, and earned a living as a paid background dancer in music videos for other artists such as Ed Sheeran and Jessie J. Twigs sometimes choreographs alone, and sometimes with long-term collaborator Aaron Sillis. In *'tw-Ache'* (2014), directed by Tom Beard, FKA twigs dances with Sillis and Denzel Daniels in slow motion in a beautiful examination of the human form, and in *'Cellophane'* (2019) she invents an intricate pole dance.

APPROPRIATION: AFRICAN AMERICAN DANCE

Dance scholar Sherril Dodds argues that whilst music video 'has served as a wealth of choreographic innovation during its twenty-five-year existence' (2009a: 259), it only does so by appropriating and reconceiving popular dance traditions for its own purposes (2009a: 248). In such appropriations, 'the dance may be distorted, simplified, glamorized, or loaded with meanings that may bear little relevance to its earlier form' (2009a: 248). There are many examples of such appropriation in US music videos, and in the section above we saw examples of the appropriation of traits from Hollywood musicals. In this section, I look at Beyoncé's video for *'Single Ladies'* (2008), which was directed by British filmmaker Jake Nava and raises some of these issues about the appropriation of African American street dance in the larger context of existing research about appropriation. It can be seen as an example of what Beth Genné (2018b) terms the 'street dance' tradition, invented when Astaire and Kelly not only adopted dance moves from the street, but took their choreographed dance sequences off the studio floor and out into exterior street locations for filming. Amin defines African American dance as 'the embodied performance traditions that both emanate from and have been reshaped by persons of African descent living in the United States, via the growth and development of the early colonies and the trans-Atlantic slave trade' (Amin 2018: 45). She reverses the tendency of other authors to assume a pre-existing 'White, cultural scaffold upon which African American aesthetics came to rest'. Instead she sets out to examine the ways that 'African American dance itself is . . . the scaffold upon which other aesthetic predilections are grafted' (Amin 2018: 45). Beyoncé's *'Single Ladies'* (2008) illustrates Amin's argument, but some information about the British context is needed.

In the early 1980s, Malcolm McLaren introduced US breakdancing to the UK with his video for *'Buffalo Gals'* (1982). The video, which used footage shot in New York of the New York breakdance collective Rock Steady Crew, was one of the first opportunities British audiences had been given to see graffiti, breakdancing, DJing, MCing and b-boying. Although the Sugar Hill Gang had introduced Britain to rapping with their track *'Rapper's Delight'* (1979), they hadn't introduced the dance or street culture. *'Buffalo Gals'* was released in Britain around the same time as *'Thriller'* in 1982. The use of non-choreographed street dancers established a new style of dance video: by the summer of '83, breakdancing had been adopted on the streets of the UK. *'Buffalo Gals'* was later referenced in Neneh Cherry's *'Buffalo Stance'* video (1988), directed by John Maybury. It was also a reference point for many subsequent British hip-hop and R&B videos such as Jake Nava's 1998 video for Beverley Knight's *'Made It Back'*, showing British street dancers performing their individual pieces, and was a platform for Max and Dania's breakthrough video for So Solid Crew's single

'*21 Seconds*' (2001). So Solid Crew were the UK hip-hop collective that first brought grime and underground garage to mainstream attention; '*21 Seconds*' was a hit, and secured the group a number one and a Brit Award.

'*Single Ladies*' was directed by Jake Nava, who had spent the late 1990s and early 2000s making videos for Mark Morrison, Mis-Teeq, Shola Ama, Glamma Kid, Ms Dynamite and Beverley Knight in the UK. His mission had been partly political. He felt that Black artists were sidelined by the British music industry. 'I wanted to make high-end videos for less money for Black British acts,' explains Nava. 'It was a semi-political agenda for me, I wanted the people who look like the people I was at school with, my age. I wanted them represented. I wanted them not to be ghettoised. I wanted them to step up'. But Nava didn't want to make a cheaper imitation of US R&B. He wanted to make distinctly English videos. 'When I was making Mark Morrison's video,' he explains, 'I definitely was trying to make the English side of the story and have a video on MTV which could be next to a Hype Williams video without being laughed off the table for looking a little bit cheaper.'[6] Fusion had long interested Nava. His father was an avant-garde performance artist turned painter 'who originated from the barrios of Mexico'. Nava grew up 'trying to make sense' of his father's 'alienation as a dark brown man in England' . . . 'wanting to create a landscape where the black faces around me did fit in'.

'*Single Ladies*' was one of a long line of videos Nava would make with Beyoncé. In total, Nava has made nine: '*Baby Boy*' (2003), '*Crazy in Love*' (2003), '*Beautiful Liar*' (2007), '*Single Ladies (Put a Ring On It)*' (2008), '*If I Were a Boy*' (2008), '*Flawless*' (2013), '*Grown Woman*' (2013), '*Partition*' (2013) and '*Naughty Girl*' (2014). When Beyoncé left Destiny's Child, she had her research team find a director to help her furnish a different kind of video for the launch of her solo career, something distinct from the Hype Williams / Paul Hunter look that dominated the USA at that time. She liked the look of Nava's work, particularly a narrative piece of filmmaking that he'd created for English electronic act Lo-Fidelity All Stars.

When she asked him to direct the video for '*Single Ladies*', Beyoncé suggested he look at a version of a Bob Fosse routine on the internet, '*Mexican Breakfast*', which someone had laid down to a hip-hop track she liked. Nava says that 'essentially we remade that film' – but they did so in the biblical sense of reinterpretation, because it was not at all intended as a literal remake, rather as an adaptation for modern times.[7] The choreography was interpreted and reinvented by Beyoncé's long-term choreographer Frank Gatson. It had roots in African jazz, so the core performance of the video was already a reinterpretation. As Nava explains, 'Beyoncé's choreographer [Frank Gatson] was very influenced by Bob Fosse. Bob Fosse was into an almost over-enunciated female femininity. Frank also exaggerated femaleness.' So Gatson's choreography brought a contemporary aesthetic to the work.[8]

To this complex mix, Nava brought a 'European fashion vibe'. Most other video directors were using built production sets, but Nava decided to have none.

> Like *i-D* magazine, I understood that if you've got the right background you can stick someone in front of the white wall and it would look amazing – if the person was wearing the right outfit and the lighting was right.

Nava brought styling and make-up references from a British *Vogue* shoot and he flew a London make-up artist in for the other two girls: 'it was quite a specific thing with wet-look eyes, dark eyes underneath the wet', a look which ended up influencing Beyoncé's own make-up. He also sought to fuse the USA's hip-hop aesthetic and US fashion photography, so hired Steady G, 'a Steadicam guy who had done a lot of Hype Williams' videos' and cameraman Jim Fealy, 'who had worked with Bruce Weber' (American fashion photographer and occasional film director). Amongst the other creative contributors, it was Nava's producer, Ben Cooper, who suggested that the limbo go all the way round the studio. He felt the contribution of his editor, Jarrett Fijal, was huge, because '[i]t's very clearly not a single shot, [but] people think it was, and [that] is to Jared's credit, because we used a couple of takes and Jared made it look like it was one shot.' Nava felt that the post FX operator, Lewis at 20/20, also made a major contribution.[9] For Nava, however, the main creator of the video was Beyoncé herself. Not only did Beyoncé bring the core idea of *'Mexican Breakfast'* to the table, she also brought the execution and the ownership. 'Whatever I brought to her, [Beyoncé] would always execute it in a way that was always better than I could have dreamed of. She's the de Niro of performance.'[10]

On social media, when the video was released, Beyoncé was accused by some of stealing the choreography from a White man (Bob Fosse) and a White genre (the Hollywood musical) (Thomas 2014). Thomas points out that Beyoncé was in fact reclaiming a dance that Fosse had appropriated from African American dance traditions. Jazz dance (the genre of *'Mexican Breakfast'*) is 'a dance form in which historically whites have emulated the stylistics of African American social dance without giving due credit or renouncing their "white privilege"' (Thomas 2014: 293). In the America of the 1950s creatives such as Fosse were neither obliged nor expected to credit Black artists; 'racial segregation and prejudice', argues Thomas, 'allowed for cultural ignorance or amnesia in support of a fantasy of white innovation and genius' (Thomas 2014: 293–4).

Appropriation: Ballet and the Dance Film

British music videos have drawn on ballet and modern dance traditions since the 1980s. An acclaimed work from that decade is New Order's *'True Faith'*

(Decouflé, 1987), said to have been inspired by Bauhaus artist Oskar Schlemmer's *Triadische Ballet*. The video shows two male performers dressed in surreal costumes leaping about and slapping each other. It was both directed and choreographed by choreographer, dancer, mime artist and theatre director Philippe Decouflé. As Jordan and Allen point out, 'the dance appears less as an interpretative expression of the song text, than as a tangential element of design . . . There is no reference here to the world of popular dance, either on the stage, or in the disco.' Instead, the 'movement reflects the interest of many contemporary British and continental choreographers in gestural vocabulary' (Jordan and Allen 1993: 72).

One of the criticisms of dancers coming to work in music video was that the cinematography and editing of music videos interrupted and destroyed integral choreography – and this, indeed, was a criticism Bush and Gondry had made of the way in which music videos used dance. In an interview with the Canadian television programme *Good Rockin' Tonite* (CBC 1983–93) in November 1985, Kate Bush discussed how she wanted 'to do a serious piece of dance' for '*Running Up That Hill*':

> I'd seen quite a few videos on television that other people had been doing and I felt that dance [. . .] was being used quite trivially, it was being exploited: haphazard images, busy, lots of dances, without really the serious expression, and wonderful expression, that dance can give.

This motivated Bush 'to make a very simple routine between two people, almost classic, and very simply filmed' (Childed 2018). In a sense, it reflected a clash of the production culture of choreography in classical dance forms with the production culture of music video, which constantly veered towards the exhibition of spectacle and effect in the form of editing and post-production.

In 2016, The Chemical Brothers released Dom & Nic's video for their track '*Wide Open*'. The video deliberately maintained minimal interruptive cinematography and, instead, used the apparatus of post-production special effects to foreground the pure choreographic performance. In so doing it was designed to achieve the simplicity aimed at by the pioneers of dance music video such as Kate Bush. It did not result from the typical commission process, largely because it arose from the kind of long-term collaboration between artists and directors described elsewhere in this book, which has tended to maximise the chance of synergies because the directors have prior experience in authenticating the artists' music. Dom & Nic had already directed seven videos for the band when they first heard the track on their eighth studio album, *Born in the Echoes* (2015), after it was released. In the music, they felt they saw a dance film, so they approached Ed and Dom (The Chemical Brothers) to ask if the band would be interested in commissioning a video. Ed and Dom said 'yes', and the video was released in 2016.

They wanted to produce the video as a *dance film*, which presented the entire dance in one single take, rather than as a music video. They also wanted to portray a private, important moment in the life of a dancer and continue the theme of loneliness that had characterised all their videos for The Chemical Brothers. So, to convey this internal narrative, they devised the idea that Sonoya (the dancer cast to perform the piece) becomes a 3-D printed version of herself through the dance. They brought on board Academy Award-winning post-production house The Mill and acclaimed British choreographer Wayne McGregor, who had previously choreographed two music videos with Radiohead and Atoms for Peace, so was familiar with the shorter rehearsal periods of music video. But Dom & Nic nevertheless asked The Chemical Brothers for five weeks instead of the standard two weeks' pre-production time in order to rehearse both the dance and camera movement. When recording the performing, they tried to achieve the 'liveness' of a non-mediatised dance performance that one might see on the stage at Sadler's Wells: 'We didn't want it to be a performance that felt rehearsed and could be repeated. We wanted it to feel like a one-off moment in time.' Dom explained that,

> Because we wanted it to have the authenticity of pure dance the video had to be one take. We wanted the camera to be part of the choreography, like a character. This is why she looks at the camera. This caused a lot of challenges for post. The match moving, the CG model of Sonoya, had to be hand-animated frame by frame. Every joint, every finger had to match the performance. It was really important to us that it was an authentic performance with no cuts. So we chose the best take, whether it had mistakes or not. It's all one take. All of the movement is her [Sonoya's] movement. We thought [the viewer] would be able to tell, even on a subconscious level, if it wasn't Sonoya's movement or if you felt it was a CG animation at any point.[11]

British choreographer Aaron Sillis explains that in the world of ballet and contemporary dance, a choreographer would have perhaps six months to develop a piece. But in a music video the choreographer will rarely have more than half a day's rehearsal. In the past, this, plus the tendency for directors to cut out much of the choreography in post, has deterred many choreographers from wanting to work on music videos. But in the last fifteen years Sillis has seen the situation change, and believes that boundaries between dance film and music video have been broken down. This may be because of the greater simplicity of post-2006 digital video dance cultures.[12] Certainly, in the dance world more generally, choreographers such as Matthew Bourne, Akram Khan and Wayne McGregor have helped to break down barriers between the elite world of dance and the popular world of music. In 2006, Akram Khan collaborated with Kylie Minogue for her *Showgirl* performances, and in 2013, The Feeling released their video *'Boy Cried Wolf'*, a simple video showing Edward Watson (principal dancer at the Royal Ballet) performing in an aircraft hangar in North London, choreographed by Arthur Pita.

The work of British director / choreographer Holly Blakey represents this new aesthetic. Blakey studied dance at Roehampton and, like Sillis and FKA twigs, began her career as a dancer. Her video for Gwilym Gold's *'Triumph'* (2015) is an extraordinarily simple work built around the performance of Nandi Bhebhe. It is shot entirely in black and white. The cinematography and editing of the video are placed at the service of Bhebhe's performance, capturing the raw, urgent dance. Holly Blakey explained her rationale: 'I wanted to show her massive power, beauty, resilience, create something almost lucid and fertile in a way that I wish we saw women represented more often' (*Nowness* 2015). Evans and Fogarty (2016) differentiate dance films from music videos by the fact that, in a dance film, the choreography will originate from the pure dance concept; it would be anathema to build a concept from and for music. The skill of choreographers / dancers such as Blakey and Sillis is to build the choreography from both the dance concept and the music. As well as his work for FKA twigs, Sillis, who had previously assisted Michael Rooney, has choregraphed a number of landmark British music videos including *'Julia'* (2014), one of five dance videos for Jungle directed by Oliver Hadlee Pearch.

Appropriation: Club Dance

In industry language, a 'dance video' is not a video based on choreography, but a video for a dance track, usually EDM (electronic dance music). These videos anchor the music. Rarely is a choreographer employed. They highlight the limitations of existing theories of music video, which focus only on the relationship between sound and image to explain how a music video works. In collaboration, choreography and cinematography can animate the music through appropriated dance genres. But if the dance represented in the video doesn't represent the dance culture from within which an artist originates, then the video doesn't have *cultural authenticity*, a term which overlaps closely with *cultural authorship*. In club dance videos, the video represents the dance culture of the fans. The video is not an isolated text, it is a social experience, on a par functionally with a live gig or a DJ-ed party, and the video needs to interpolate the viewer in a communal experience: to bring a sense of collective unity in listening to and experiencing the music.

Among the landmark examples included in our collection are the video for The Prodigy's *'Out of Space'* (Russell Curtis, 1992), which reflects the underground rave scene of the early 1990s. It shows the band in the countryside:

Keith Flint is dressed up wearing white overalls, a face mask and fluorescent gloves, sniffing Vicks VapoRub, whilst he and various other band members dance and muck about. The video for Faithless's 'We Come One' (Dom & Nic, 2001) not only depicts the ravers, but the police brutality perceived to control and repress youth culture and the alternative lifestyles and moralities of groups who found freedom in dance in those years. Moloko's video for 'Familiar Feeling' (2003), directed by Elaine Constantine, portrays the Northern Soul dance club culture, and was followed up by her feature *Northern Soul* (2014).

Drugs have been central to British club culture, and in seeking to represent the communal music experience, many also represent the internal drug consciousness in the videos. For Shadforth, Avid offered an opportunity to represent the hallucinogenic, communitarian and sensual dimensions of club dance when it was introduced in the late 1990s and is illustrated by her video for the All Seeing I's 'The Beat Goes On' (1998). The premise for the video came from the band's name, and the endoscopic camera was used to visualise the idea of an 'all seeing eye' at a party. She explained that she used the frame cutting technique to visualise an altered head space, 'to visually describe how your head might feel at the end of a night of hard-core partying'. The time slippage, split screens and people moving at different speeds were techniques used to 'represent this idea that everybody is in a slightly different headspace to each other ... in their own very warm and lovely little bubble.'[13]

When electronic dance video directors have set out to exploit the cinematography of FX, however, they have tended to employ choreographers to assist with the kind of precision choreography needed. Examples include Futureshock's 'Late At Night' (NE-O, 2003) which, set in Japan, shows actors body-popping to the music; it was conceived and directed by British directing duo NE-O (who had directed VW Golf GTI's 'Singing in the Rain' 2005 with Supple Nam). Shadforth's video for Basement Jaxx's 'Red Alert' (1999) does just this. It tells a story about a diner that is hit by a meteor, which turns everyone into robot-like people; their robotic movements were partially created using choreography by Litza Bixler, and partly by frame cutting on Avid by Shadforth. Tim Lawrence's essay in Malnig's collection (2009) examines the emergence of the 'solo dancer' in disco and club culture of the 1970s, and is absolutely crucial to understanding such representations of solo dance in club dance videos of the 1990s and 2000s as Breach's 'Everything You Never Had' (The Sacred Egg, 2013). Motion capture was a technique used increasingly in the 2000s. This video, choreographed by Supple Nam and directed by The Sacred Egg, captures the emotional arc of the solo dancer experience of the 1970s discos and clubs described by Tim Lawrence by reproducing multiple dancers.

Appropriation: British Authenticity and Dance Genres

When asked about the differences between UK and US choreographed videos in this fifty-year period, the interviewees consistently pinpointed the greater production budgets and rehearsal periods of US videos. But choreographer Litza Bixler felt that 'a very British thing' was to employ street dancers on British videos, rather than trained dancers. She said that US artists much preferred to work with professional dancers, and that 'time and time again' she was hired in Britain to cast non-dancers. In part, this is embedded in a production culture of 'street casting' in British music videos:

> They love normal people dancing here in Britain. It's their favourite thing. In their view, it makes it more authentic. More real. That authenticity in music, for me, originated here. Most of the time when I am asked to choreograph in Britain, it's usually a non-dancer . . . They can't look like dancers in Britain.[14]

The '*Praise You*' video for British artist Fatboy Slim, released in the UK in January 1999, typifies the trope of the ordinary dancer, although in reality it was highly contrived by Jonze. The video was commissioned by John Hassay at Skint, after Jonze sent Norman Cook (Fatboy Slim) a video of himself and a friend dancing incompetently but passionately beside a boombox playing '*The Rockafeller Skank*' (1998) outside Grauman's Chinese Theatre in Hollywood one night. Cook and Hassay commissioned him to make the video for an alternate track. In the faux-amateur video, 'Richard Koufey' and a fictional crew, the 'Torrance Community Dance Group', execute their awkward routines by the Hollywood Walk of Fame. Masquerading as an author-other-than-myself is something that Jonze has always done, forging his career in film under the pseudonym of Spike Jonze when his real name is Adam Spiegel.

The 'ordinary dancer' trope is also evident in Moby's video for '*Body Rock*' (Fredrik Bond, 1999), which was commissioned by London's John Moule for Mute Records for the UK release of the video, and produced by London production company Harry Nash. Based on the premise of a crazy man dancing on a council estate whilst a car catches fire, Moby and Mute eventually released a compilation of the casting sessions of ordinary British dancers filmed in the casting suite of production company Harry Nash as an alternative video. The popular dance genre was reproduced again by Ricky Gervais in a 2002 episode of '*The Office*' (BBC 2001–3).

A very different presentation of the non-professional dancer is Raine Allen-Miller's video for Salute's '*Storm*' (2016). It depicts a woman dressed from head to toe in a Union Jack print dress dancing across a living room decorated as a nod to first-generation African British families. Allen-Miller described it as 'a celebration of the incomparable mix of cultures and the unique blend of people that makes this country so incredible – what makes Great Britain so great' (Cliff 2016). It was made on the eve of the Brexit referendum, and intended as 'a really celebratory film about what is great about Britain: through immigration people bring culture into this country'. Allen-Miller was shocked when the majority voted to leave the European Union.

Authenticity has dominated and determined what kind of dance tradition is appropriated, which dance film genres are homage, and whose artistry and authorship is invoked as the choreographer – and indeed whether the concept of choreography is invoked at all. As seen in previous chapters, British directors have tended to mix dance and music genres in ways that defy expectation. The Young Fathers' video *'Shame'* (2014), directed by Jeremy Cole and choreographed by Blakey, illustrates this. The video features a White dancer / actor / model, Joshua Hubbard, as the main character, Terry. It illustrates the unexpected clash of genre expectations that British artists and directors have been keen to experiment with, mixing a popular music artist with the 'wrong' genre of video.

Hype Williams was the inspiration behind Natricia Bernard's choreography for the Arctic Monkeys' *'Brianstorm'* (Huse Monfaradi, 2007), which married the rock music genre with a choreographed dance video. In her interview, Natricia explained that the jarring clash of genres was intentional. Monfaradi was, she says, 'very specific' in wanting an 'old-skool, hundred-grand hip-hop or R&B video' with 'the screens, the girls, the pumping and the hair'. 'I said, "What, to *this* track?" And the producers were like, "Yeah!"'[15]

Don Cameron's video for Blur's *'Music Is My Radar'* (2000), choreographed by Blanca Li and commissioned by Food / Parlophone, was another unusual marriage of genres. These examples illustrate that in Britain, dance videos have not just been commissioned for dance acts. It was predictable that dance videos would be commissioned for EDM acts such as Daft Punk, Fatboy Slim and The Prodigy, and urban and R&B artists in Britain such as So Solid Crew – but not that they would be made for non-dance acts like rock bands. Equally, British directors Max and Dania mixed things up a little by creating a British costume drama dance extravaganza for British urban R&B artist Jamelia's *'Money'* (2001). The video was choreographed by Priscilla Samuels, a key figure in British pop choreography who had worked with S Club 7, the Spice Girls, Westlife and many other British pop artists.

The kind of slick, high-production-value American R&B videos directed by Hype Williams and Paul Hunter were parodied in Chris Cunningham's video for Aphex Twin's *'Windowlicker'* (1999). Hoesterey defines parody as a work of art 'that imitates an existent piece which is well known to its readers, viewers, or listeners with satirical, critical or polemical intention' (Hoesterey 2001: 13–14). The dance solo was choreographed by Vincent Paterson, who had worked with Michael Jackson. Cunningham says he asked Paterson to 'come up with some really immature and perverted takes on Buzz [sic] Berkeley's movies' (Adams 2014: 9). Cunningham's '*Windowlicker*' represented a perhaps long overdue summary of the British industry's frustration with the American dance video throughout the 1990s. But as a close-knit and supportive community, that frustration would not be expressed in negative comment, but rather in a comedic and ironic fashion by the director, then in a position of greatest creative freedom.

In her interview for this book, Carole Burton-Fairbrother reflected on the 1990s: 'One thing I do think the Americans did brilliantly is choreography. Their choreography used to be so great on a lot of these videos. I think they definitely beat us at that actually. But we are more creative.'[16] The majority of those I interviewed agreed that the US industry has tended to make more spectacular, high-concept, high-production-value videos with bigger sets, chorus lines, locations and costumes than the UK; and they are typically much tighter, slicker, more meticulously executed and choreographed, as a result of their longer rehearsal times and preference for casting professionally trained dancers rather than real street and club dancers. With their smaller production budgets, UK pop and R&B artists struggled to achieve those standards. In some quarters, there was a sense that the British couldn't *do* dance so well for a while. But by the early 2000s it was obvious that British artists did support choreographed dance – just not the obvious genres of British artist. It was the rock bands, experimental artists and EDM artists who pushed the boundaries of what was possible, technologically and formalistically, within the genres of dance video, dance film and dance performance itself.

Notes

1. P. Roberts, personal communication, 1 Feburary 2016.
2. N. Bernard, personal communication, 1 February 2016.
3. P. Roberts, personal communication, 1 Feburary 2016.
4. S. Muller, personal communication, 19 March 2018.
5. D. Shadforth, personal communication, 17 November 2016.
6. J. Nava, personal communication, 12 December 2016.
7. J. Nava, personal communication, 12 December 2016.
8. J. Nava, personal communication, 12 December 2016.
9. J. Nava, personal communication, 12 December 2016.
10. J. Nava, personal communication, 12 December 2016.
11. D. Hawley, Dom & Nic, personal communication February 9, 2016.
12. A. Sillis, personal communication, 22 September 2015.
13. D. Shadforth, personal communication, 17 November 2016.
14. L. Bixler, personal communication, 3 March 2016.
15. N. Bernard, personal communication, 1 February 2016.
16. C. Burton-Fairbrother, personal communication, 15 January 2016.

5 GENDER

In the Moonlandingz' *'The Strangle of Anna'* (2016), the vocalist gendered as female reveals menstrual blood stains on her white dress and stuffs her mouth with cake whilst singing (Rebecca Taylor). The vocalist gendered as male feigns a variety of satirical dance poses, with fried eggs stuck to his nipples by clingfilm (Johnny Rocket, aka Fat White Family's Lias Saoudi). It was filmed in three hours, using some old cans of film that director Dawn Shadforth had been keeping at home. 'It's a video that's not really a video for a band who are not really a band,' said Shadforth (Knight 2017).

The representation of female sexuality has arguably received more attention than any other subject in music video scholarship since the early 1980s, often drawing on Laura Mulvey's essay on the male gaze (1989). Successive content analyses of gender roles produced by scholars in the MTV period examined negative images of women as sex objects (Baxter et al. 1985, Brown and Campbell 1986, Sherman and Dominick 1986, Vincent et al. 1987). Lieb has written that, '[m]ore than any other cultural force, MTV made beauty and sexuality a primary factor in a musician's career' (2013: xv), whilst Austerlitz has written that '[m]usic videos, for the most part, are intended for men's eyes, providing them with endless opportunities to delectate in the spectacle of beautiful women performing for their pleasure' (Austerlitz 2007: 4). Issues regarding gendered representation remain a key focus in scholarship (e.g. Beebe and Middleton 2007, Railton and Watson 2005).

The objective of this chapter is to counter that focus. *'The Strangle of Anna'* is an example of gender fluidity and the breakdown of the binary divisions between masculine and feminine which we have seen in music video in Britain since the mid-1960s. I believe this is a specifically British *tendency*. Below I present a number of examples from our collection that illustrate the ways in which fixed concepts of gender (and indeed sexuality) have been challenged by British artists, based on the paradigm developed by Judith Butler ([1990] 2002) in which the gendered self is a cultural construction. As Wallis argues, using Irving Goffman's concept of gender display (1976), artists *perform gender* (Wallis 2011: 172). Our study shows that, far more than in the USA, British music video has been a progressive influential site for the articulation of alternative transgressive gender identities and sexualities, identities which fall outside the heteronormative gender dichotomy. It is beyond the scope of this book to produce a comprehensive analysis from 1966 to 2016, so this chapter makes the argument based on a number of case studies from the landmark collection.

In preparing this chapter I have drawn on Sheila Whiteley's writings on Siouxsie Sioux, Annie Lennox, Mick Jagger and Freddie Mercury (1997a, 1997b, 2013a, 2013b) and West and Zimmerman's work on Annie Lennox (1987), and have taken background information from Coates (1998), Leonard (2017) and Davies (2001) on gender issues in the music industry and press. I have also been influenced by Rosamund Gill's critique of the content analysis paradigm (2007); as she points out, the dominance of irony, parody and pastiche makes any attempt to establish an evidence base for sexual objectification in the kinds of content analyses advanced by Baxter et al. (1985), Brown and Campbell (1986), Sherman and Dominick (1986) and Vincent et al. (1987) very tricky to establish.

Whilst in the 1960s, gender performance was still ideologically binary, scholars have argued that the origins of later gender fluidities lie in The Beatles' 'groomed appearance' and 'resistance to formal representations of masculinity' (King 2016: 62, Bannister 2017) as well as Jagger's dandyism and flamboyance (Gregory 2002, Whiteley 1997b, Hawkins 2017b). Whilst the boys wore higher heels, the girls took to low shoes, flattened their breasts, avoided curves and wore trousers. Edie Sedgwick, Mia Farrow, Jean Seberg and Audrey Hepburn all popularised the short pixie hair cut. But despite these changes to the iconography of femininity, 'female singers of the era primarily interpreted songs written by others, a practice at odds with the ideology of authenticity in rock that developed in the late 1960s' (Coates 2010: n.p.). This, combined with the ample use of close-ups on British music television shows, emphasised women's looks and failed to establish women as authors of their own musical work, performance and image. By contrast, wide shots of male bands emphasised their fully musically authored performance.

Two videos from the punk and post-punk era illustrate dramatic shifts in the representation of women artists. Marianne Faithfull's film '*Broken English*' (Derek Jarman, 1979) is unusual because it contains a mixture of found footage, including excerpts of Jarman's films and Super 8 and 16mm footage of Marianne Faithfull. For an artist whom Coates describes as having 'validated' Jagger's 'cock rock' (Coates 2010), with this film Faithfull repositioned herself as a self-conscious and politically aware independent female artist after a long absence associated with drug addiction and homelessness. Made to promote three tracks, the film was shot in a DIY punk style with contributions from directors Richard Heslop and John Maybury. Jarman's plan was for it to be screened in cinemas. 'Punk', writes Coates, 'opened a real space for women in rock as an expressive menu of their experience in and out of rock culture . . . [it] helped to put aside the notion that "women in rock" were there to be decorative and pretty.' Coates points out that Faithfull's 'ravaged' voice was a perfect expression of punk feminism and 'contrasted dramatically with that of her 1960s recordings'. It could 'be read on its own as a feminist critique of the options available to female performers in that decade' (Coates 2010: n.p.).

Siouxsie and the Banshees' video, '*Happy House*' (Piers Bedford, 1980), presented a visual critique of women's domestic entrapment. Siouxsie mimes to the vocals wearing a harlequin outfit in a fake studio house, with a demeanour and a confrontational attitude rarely before seen in videos, and without a hint of 'the male gaze'. Whiteley argues that Sioux feminised rock through her confrontational style and image (2000: 113), partly influenced by her early involvement with the Bromley gay scene and such London clubs as Chaugeramas, the Masquerade and the exclusive lesbian club, Louise's in Poland Street, and Vivienne Westwood's 'inner circle of punk women performers [who] were encouraged to act out their sexual fantasies appropriately dressed in her designer clothes' (Whiteley 2000: 108–9). Siouxsie has claimed that Derek Jarman pitched to shoot the video, but that his budget was considered too expensive by Polydor.

The next major breakthrough occurs in 1978 with Kate Bush's first single, '*Wuthering Heights*' (1978). The video for this broke with the then dominant codes for constructing the female body. It did not dismember or objectify Bush's body, nor disempower her authorship by editing the footage into sexually alluring close-ups of the kind with which British television audiences had become familiar when viewing female artists. Two videos were released. In one version, Bush performs the song in a dark room filled with white mist, and in the other she dances outside. According to scholar Ian Cawood, Bush took direct control of the visual side of her work following her experience with Gered Mankowitz at the beginning of her career, 'when she was provocatively photographed after a vigorous workout in a thin pink leotard' (Cawood 2016: 55).

From the outset, Annie Lennox subverted gender roles in her videos by presenting, variously, androgynous, masculine and over-enunciated feminine performances. In '*Love is a Stranger*', filmed in 1982 and produced by Jon Roseman, Lennox wore short hair, inviting parallels with artists such as Jean Seberg. Hair would later be identified as a tool used by Sinéad O'Connor to control her subjectivity (Negus 1997). The video went on heavy rotation on MTV, but also caused a panic – prompting MTV to ask for Lennox's passport to confirm she was female (West and Zimmerman 1987). In *'Sweet Dreams'* (Stewart / Ashbrook / Roseman, 1983), Lennox dressed up as a record company executive in a suit for a board meeting. Many of the videos for Eurythmics' *Savage* album (1987) centred on Lennox interpreting the Madonna–whore complex in the form of a neurotic, mousey housewife and an extroverted blonde vamp. Almost all of Lennox's videos from 1987 onwards, including the *Savage* album, were directed by long-term collaborator Sophie Muller.

The *'Little Bird'* video (1993) from Lennox's *Diva* album was directed by Muller. In this video, Lennox-lookalikes dress as the many different personae that Lennox has used in her videos (both solo and as part of Eurythmics). Men as well as women auditioned for these roles of Lennox. Lennox herself also performs in a cabaret-esque setting. She was in the late stages of pregnancy with her second daughter, Tali, during the filming of the video. In the video for *'Why'* (1992), we see Lennox getting dressed in her diva outfit. Lennox gazes at herself in a mirror as she puts on her outrageously glamorous make-up. Within art history, the woman looking at herself in the mirror has been constructed as an act of extraordinary narcissism and defiance. Significant works include Giovanni Bellini's *Naked Young Woman in Front of the Mirror* (c. 1515), the nineteenth-century paintings by Degas and Toulouse-Lautrec of women dancers and prostitutes getting ready for their performances, and Velázquez's seventeenth-century *Toilet of Venus* (c. 1647–51), in which Cupid holds the mirror for Venus as she admires herself, begging the question whether the gaze is male or female.

Muller also directed the video for PJ Harvey's *'This is Love'* (2000), which announced that 'cock rock' was female. Harvey performs the track on her electric guitar, in a white suit with red lipstick, alone in a studio. It's a genre of performance normally associated with the masculine rock culture documented by Norma Coates (1997). At this point, Muller had already directed *'Good Fortune'* (2000) and *'A Place Called Home'* (2001) with Harvey, and had established a productive working relationship. The white suit, Muller points out, was Harvey's choice; at conception stage, the idea for the video was very much intended as a joke.[1] The video subverted the idea that only men can do rock, whilst women can't do rock because they have to dress up to attract the attention of the male gaze – and this automatically renders their performance inauthentic in the context of masculine rock culture. The work of Bayton (1997), Leonard (2017), Reddington (2016) and Clawson (1999) has all highlighted the challenges women face as rock artists and the almost phallic status of the electric guitar (cf. Tracey Thorn, cited in Negus 1997: 15).

Sade's video for *'No Ordinary Love'* (1992) also defies stereotypes, this time racial and ethnic stereotypes used to portray Black women artists. It was directed, again, by Sophie Muller, and tells the story of Sade as a mermaid who surfaces and walks the streets of an American city as a desolate bride. As with her video for Blur's *'Song 2'*, Muller appropriates a video genre not conventionally associated with the genre of popular music (soul and smooth jazz). Julien Temple had already created a narrative video for Sade intended for cinema release, showing that Sade was an artist committed to exploring the full potential of video. Several scholars have found a persistence of gender and racial stereotypes in music video, despite changes in society that have raised the status of women and ethnic minorities (Emerson 2002, Railton and Watson 2005, Ward 2003). Jean-Paul Goode's video for Grace Jones's *'I've Seen That Face Before / Libertango'* (1981) also defies stereotypes. With her cropped hair, pronounced features and often masculine-styled attire, Jones had never articulated a passive or objectified screen presence. Although Jones was American, the video was commissioned in London. It opens with a shot of Jones wearing a tall black hat, her face concealed under a three-piece paper mask; when these are removed and her trademark haircut is displayed, Jones starts to sing straight into the camera while playing the accordion. The camera then zooms out to reveal that the video set is located on the roof of a tower block, inverting Balázs' theory that the close-up drives the viewer towards the universalism of the physiognomy, and taking the viewer back into the concrete hard reality of urban context.

With her video for *'Water Me'* (2013), directed by Jesse Kanda, FKA twigs repossesses the objectified female face of Japanese manga, anime and over one hundred years' worth of cartoon imagery of sexy, cute girls with overstated eyes or eye-popping expressions, such as Betty Boop. In a single-shot, uncut take, twigs' face becomes wider and her eyes larger and more doll-like. A tear falls. Her face is transformed from twigs the authentic artist to the objectified girl of manga. The track *'Video Girl'* (2014), with a video directed by Kahlil Joseph, was written about her experiences when she stopped being a background dancer hired to appear in other artists' videos, and became an artist who was in theory in control of her own voice and image (Battan 2014). By 2015, twigs was directing her own videos. In her self-directed *'Glass & Patron'* (2015) we see twigs caressing a large pregnant belly, giving birth to a colourful fabric, and then bending that same body, sans bump, into impressive shapes with stunning fluidity.

British artists and directors have also created sexist and derogatory representations of femininity in the guise of parodies, with which many of the interviewees felt uncomfortable. Robert Palmer's *'Addicted to Love'* (Terence Donovan, 1985), The Prodigy's *'Smack My Bitch Up'* (Jonas Åkerlund, 1997), Benni Benassi's *'Satisfaction'* (Dougal Wilson, 2000) and Eric Prydz's *'Call on Me'* (Huse Monfaradi, 2004) are notable examples. The latter two videos completed a decade of 'bums and tits' videos instructing women to enjoy good old-fashioned saucy seaside humour, and 'shut up and stop being so sensitive'. The video for *'Satisfaction'* (version 2) featured women – many of them Playboy models – in skimpy 'construction outfits', demonstrating a variety of power tools. The cycle ended with a spat between Miley Cyrus and Sinéad O'Connor, following Cyrus's controversial performance with Robin Thicke at the 2013 MTV Music Video Awards. Lily Allen entered the debate with her video for *'Hard Out Here'* (2013), which was intended as feminist critique and satire, but widely interpreted as insensitive racial and sexist stereotyping.

What of masculinities? In 1998, Coates pointed to a rock discourse that sought to give the impression of an archetypal male rock performer, and Connell has ventured a definition of the hegemonic masculinity which in contemporary Western societies has dominated R&B and urban genres as 'practices and embodiment that justify and institutionalize the central position of patriarchal men and the suppression, discrimination or symbolic exclusion of women or of men who embody and/or express alternative masculinities' (Connell 2005, Connell and Messerschmidt 2005). In his national comparative study of masculinity in indie rock, Bannister looked at *homosociality* as 'a male-defined social hierarchy based around one's susceptibility to accusations of homosexuality [which] engenders a split between male friendship and homosexuality: one is properly masculine, the other effeminate and taboo' (2006: 92). He found the UK was less overtly homosocial, less openly macho and more androgynous in its performance styles than the USA or New Zealand, and that labels like Cherry Red and Rough Trade promoted a generally gentler, more PC approach than in the USA and New Zealand (Bannister 2006, 2017). Hawkins (2017b) has argued that British male pop has been characterised by the dandy figure, giving as examples Adam Ant, David Bowie, Ray Davies, Mick Jagger, Jay Kay, Robert Palmer, Robert Smith and Sid Vicious:

> Voyeuristically offering himself up as an object for spectatorship, the pop dandy is a phenomenon of the recorded form. Tantalizing the fan, and assuming many guises, he can be demure, sensual, sexually naïve, or bold, cock-sure, rough and vulgar; or even passive, regressive, and a psycho-case. And, mocking his own self-loathing, the dandy exhibits an outward expression of superiority, an embodiment of the Wildean idea of the self as a work of art. (Hawkins 2017b: 5)

How were these masculinities impacted by the medium of music video? Bannister argues, as Frith and Horne had done twenty years earlier (1987), that

> [t]he commodification and feminisation of the star was deeply troubling for many male rock performers, as it was for the whole indie ideology of

independence. The idea of the star as commodity is anathema to the traditional masculine split between the artist and his art. (Bannister 2006: 99)

Laura Mulvey had also earlier argued that the male body could not withstand the sexual gaze (Mulvey 1989). In the 1970s, male rock stars came up against the sexualisation of music consumption. They, like women, became the objects of desire (Frith and Horne 1987: 155). In Frith and Horne's view, this caused strife because 'once pop stars began exploring the semiology of glamour, then women could employ their superior experience and expertise' (1987: 155).

In our study, the video for George Michael's '*Faith*' (1987) stood out. It is a landmark work in the representation of fetishised masculinity. When George split from Wham!, he faced some major decisions about how to market himself as a solo male artist. For his seminal '*Faith*' video, he hired Central St Martins graduate Andy Morahan. The video objectifies his sexuality as his persona is broken up into a series of individual body parts by close-up cuts to shots of his chin and behind. The jukebox starts by playing '*I Want Your Sex*' (1987) and is then interrupted by a pipe-organ version of Wham!'s '*Freedom*' (1984) before starting into the song. '*Faith*' was the second single from George Michael's debut solo album of the same name. The first single released from the album was '*I Want Your Sex*', which had been banned by many UK and US radio stations for its sexually suggestive lyrics. As Drukman has argued, George Michael was 'fetishised perhaps like no other male performer, before or since' in the '*Faith*' video (1995: 92).

> Dressed in faded blue jeans and a distressed leather jacket, [Michael] does not strain against male objectification . . . On the contrary, Michael softens his image just enough to actively invite the gaze, gay or otherwise. 'Just enough' – without tipping over into what Kaplan calls 'soft' androgyny or what Aufderheide calls the 'daring statement' (1986: 126) of MTV androgyny. (Drukman 1995: 92)

The videos of Take That in the 1990s similarly fetishised the male body. They rekindle the iconography of the Dave Clark Five's video for '*Nineteen Days*' (1966), which showed the band members' bare torsos as they water-skied in a lake; it is arguably the template for subsequent boy band videos. The video for Take That's '*Back for Good*' (1995), directed by Vaughan and Anthea is a simple, moving portrait of the band. It is shot in black and white and shows the band walking and dancing in the rain as well as performing the song in a shelter. Most of the external footage was shot on a backlot at Pinewood Studios. A 1958 Chevrolet Impala and a 1951 Mercury Custom, both customised in the styles of the 1950s / early 1960s, feature in the video. For McDonald (1997), the emotions evoked are yearning and loss.

Although it was largely apolitical, glam rock was a musical style accompanied by a flamboyant dress code which emerged during the early 1970s and has had a huge influence on the lexicon of masculinities in the UK as analysed by Leonard (2017). With the exception of Suzi Quatro, there were no female glam rock artists. Gregory asks whether masculine glam rock arose as a reaction to the rise of feminism. Was it a crisis of masculinity? Although Marc Bolan is often cited as the first male of the British glam rock scene, it is David Bowie who exploited music video within the glam rock iconography to its full.

Bowie had already been recording and performing for several years before his breakthrough hit *'Space Oddity'* in 1969. He did not become widely known until his creation of *'Ziggy Stardust'* in 1972 with photographer Mick Rock. Although there is much scholarship on Bowie's pioneering role as a visual performing artist (e.g. Chapman 2015b), as Wright points out, very little of this scholarship focuses specifically on the music videos (2017). Not only were videos a vital part of Bowie's own artistic output, but they were also regarded as extremely influential in Britain by everyone I interviewed for this book, and not only because they challenged heterosexual binary constructs of gender. His influence on subsequent artists and directors was inestimable, even though his self-representation through multiple personae has presented challenges for scholastic interpretations of *authenticity* and the authorial voice. Dillane, Devereux and Power have offered an analysis of the 'Pierrot' character in and making of Bowie's *'Ashes to Ashes'* (David Mallet, 1980) video (Dillane et al. 2015). This is the video which has probably received most attention in Bowie's œuvre within music video scholarship.

Bowie called into question the limits of then dominant definitions of gender and sexuality in Britain, creating not transvestitism or camp but the defamiliarisation of the body in a way that can only be compared to the work of feminist performance artists. As Waldrep says, in his performances 'Bowie made the male body new again, removing centuries of encrusted meaning to suggest the possibility of new interpretations of it' (Waldrep 2016: 52). In the 1970s, his explorations in feminised body apparel and performance questioned the limits of the gendered body in ways that were also being questioned in the New York gay and disco scene. Whilst in interviews of the early 1970s Bowie declared that he was bisexual, Cagle argues that Bowie presented a muddled sexuality, rendering a positive model 'of sexual identity outside of the heterosexist models' (Cagle 1995: 13). Although Bowie's achievement may in part have been to bring the radical gender questioning of New York to London, rather than to invent something new, this does not undermine his own role in that cultural movement or the impact it had on successive British generations.

Nineteen eighty-four was a crucial year. It was a year in which there was a very public fight over the dominant heteronormative ideology and status quo regarding masculinities and sexuality. Frankie Goes to Hollywood's *'Relax'* was released in October 1983, the debut single of an act signed to Trevor Horn on ZTT Records. The premise for the video seems to have been developed by Paul Morley. The video was set in an S&M-themed gay nightclub and featured a glamorous drag queen (amongst other colourful characters). According to the director (Bernard Rose), Dave Robinson, who – unbeknownst to Rose when he was commissioned to create the video – had been drafted in by Chris Blackwell to run Island from Stiff, refused to run with Bernard's video when he saw it.

> I was in post-production for the 'Relax' video and I suddenly got a phone call from Dave Robinson out of the blue. And I was like 'What's he calling me for?' And he goes, 'I'd like you to bring over the "Relax" video, bring it over now and show it to me.' And I was like, 'Why do you get to see it, it's nothing to do with you,' and he said, 'Well actually it is, you're delivering to me.' And I was like 'Oh no.' No one had told us that. And so I took it in to show Dave Robinson. And he looked at it. And he said, 'What's the use of that, it's just filthy, I can't show that on children's television. Alright – I'm not paying you for it.' It's basically what he said. And he was just like, completely dismissive.[2]

In the end, it wasn't screened. Godley and Creme's video for '*Two Tribes*' (1984), however, was happily screened by the BBC as a representation of masculinity.

When asked, in 1987, 'Do you think that music is the best medium to get your ideas across to people?', director Peter Christopherson is said to have replied, '[n]o, I think film and television is by far the strongest because it's a way of really affecting all of us' (quoted in Neal 1987: 121). As well as being a founding member of Hipgnosis, Christopherson was an early member of the transgressive performance collective COUM Transmissions, who went on to form influential industrial music band Throbbing Gristle with Chris Carter, Cosey Fanni Tutti and Genesis P-Orridge, and later Coil. In the experimental audiovisual duo Psychic TV, Christopherson and P-Orridge began to distribute experimental music videos with the vision that Psychic TV could become an alternative underground video network to counteract the mainstream music business and MTV. Christopher's video for Coil's '*Tainted Love*' (1984) illustrates this philosophy. It was a powerful narrative about HIV and AIDS, released at a crucial time: in 1983 Britain had seventeen reported cases of AIDS, and by 1984 that number had risen to 108 cases with forty-six deaths. The British government had responded not by supporting and protecting the gay community, but by stigmatising and isolating gay men. With Christopherson and his partner in Coil, John Balance, playing the roles of the affected lovers, Christopherson's video told the story of a tragic romance ended by AIDS. All proceeds were donated to the Terrence Higgins Trust. In 1985, the

Museum of Modern Art in New York held an exhibition titled 'Music Video: The Industry and Its Fringes', which included *'Tainted Love'*. Whilst corporate America responded to British video as a marketing tool, US art institutions were quicker than their European counterparts to recognise the artistic qualities of British video.

British videos played no small part in tackling head-on the homophobia that was rife in Britain in the early 1980s. Bernard Rose's next video, for Bronski Beat's *'Smalltown Boy'* (1984), also dealt with homophobia and was screened on *TOTP* (*'Tainted Love'* was not). It presented a narrative about a small-town boy who, having been victim of a violent homophobic attack, leaves home for the more diverse city streets and larger gay community of London. Rose says he was hired by the label rather than by the band because the band did not like his video for *'Relax'*.[3] He was asked to work with two of their filmmaker friends, Constantine Giannaris and Isaac Julien, to craft a visual narrative. Rose explains: 'Essentially the video was a dramatisation of Jimmy's story. He was from Glasgow. It was life. Not literally but figuratively. Some of the pictures in the montage were his.'[4] So again we see a video in which the director deploys his skills to articulate the voice of the artist, rather than his own.

Freddie Mercury and Queen also profoundly challenged heteronormative visuals of masculinity, particularly in videos such as *'I Want to Break Free'* (1984), discussed in the next chapter. Less widely noted is what Stockdale terms Mercury's critique of Britishness (2016). She argues that the roots of much of his glam rock dandyishness arose from his non-normative ethnicity and upbringing. But, as with his sexuality, Mercury did not discuss religion or ethnicity in his interviews.

> By using the dandy as his foil, Mercury joins a pedigree of British performers who came from the outskirts of cultural authority to send up the essential symbols of culture. As a former imperial subject pushing his way into the realm of British pop music, Mercury used glam and its campiness to send up Englishness in a way that slipped past those he targeted for critique. (Stockdale 2016: n.p.)

Britishness, gendered discourses of pop, dominant masculine discourses in urban and R&B music in the USA and hypersexuality have structured the visual and ideological environment for Black British men. In their analysis of R&B and hip-hop culture, Connell and Messerschmidt argue that contemporary R&B and hip-hop culture articulates a particular form of hegemonic masculinity which is hypermasculine, hypersexual and heteronormative (Connell and Messerschmidt 2005). With director Jake Nava, Glamma Kid and Mark Morrison articulated their masculine authorship primarily through US video genres. The video for Seal's *'Killer'* (1991) is included in our landmark collection because it broke the mould of such heteronormative representations. It nonetheless won nominations for Best Male Solo Artist and Breakthrough Video at the MTV Awards, and won Best Video at the Brits (1992). It was also a technical landmark, produced using computer-generated science-fiction-themed imagery, largely built around a partial recreation of the M. C. Escher print *Another World* (1947). The creation of the science-fiction world by South African director Don Searll, who has made a career directing stereoscopic animation, live-action and post-production as well as hi-tech 3-D SFX, involved shooting blue screen with multiple cameras and mattes (Simpson 2013).

The hypersexualisation and commodification of the male body is taken to extremes in Vaughan Arnell's video for Robbie Williams' *'Rock DJ'* (2000). It features Williams trying to impress a female DJ by stripping naked and eventually resorting to removing his skin and muscles, ending up as a skeleton. Arnell had already directed *'Angels'* (1997), *'Let Me Entertain You'* (1998) and *'Millennium'* (1998) for Robbie. Although the idea for *'Rock DJ'* wasn't Arnell's, it was created within a working relationship that Robbie and Arnell had developed with their commissioner Carrie Sutton, which was more like the 1960s process than the standardised pitching process of the late 1990s. The video in a sense answers the question about masculinity and the male gaze raised at the start of this chapter. In her essay, Mulvey had said that masculinity could not cope with the gaze; the answer of this video is 'no, it can't'. The video can also be interpreted as a biographical narrative about the fame and celebrity that almost killed Robbie. It was a controversial video for a solo male artist because it did not make Robbie look attractive; it did not sell his beautiful body to a sexually admiring target audience.

James Blunt's video for *'You're Beautiful'* (2005) inverses hegemonic masculinity by presenting the gendered male as not only fragile, but subject to the heterosexual female gaze. Directed by Sam Brown, it seems to objectify Blunt's naked body in a manner previously preserved for female solo artists. Blunt removes the upper portion of his clothing in a cold, bare, snowy setting and places all of his personal belongings on the ground. While he is doing this, seagulls circle overhead like buzzards. At the end of the video, he jumps off a cliff and falls into the water while he sings the lyrics: 'But it's time to face the truth / I will never be with you.' It seemingly shows a male as 'incomplete' without a woman, a 'victim' of love, as a woman is often shown to be; and as such, it challenges heteronormative portraits of heterosexual masculinity as in control, independent and aggressive. It was, according to Rich Skinner, who commissioned the video, perceived at the time as a brave and risky video for a male solo artist to release, presenting himself as a victim of powerful, dominant love from a significant other.[5]

On the other end of the spectrum of non-heteronormative portraits of naked men is the video for Fat White Family's *'Touch the Leather'* (2016). Fat White Family, sometimes referred to as a psychedelic Ouija pop group, are an English rock band, formed in 2011 in South London. This video was directed by Roger Sargent, and sees frontman Lias Saoudi singing the song while a naked man on a skateboard rolls past in the background. Mark Craig has referred to it as Guy Ritchie homoeroticism meets *Scorpio Rising* (Craig n.d.).

Behind the Scenes

One of the recurring questions in feminist scholarship is whether films made by women are less likely to objectify female subjects (e.g. Smith 1995). Until the early 1990s, women directors were rare; Lindy Heymann, Maria Mochnacz and Sophie Muller were exceptions. However, many women artists – PJ Harvey, Sade, Annie Lennox, Shakespears Sister – chose to work mainly with female directors. Today there are more women directors amongst them, including Dawn Shadforth, Tabitha Denholm, Aoife McArdle, Franny, Kim Gehrig and Sarah Chatfield. Since 2000 we have also seen the rise of the woman artist–director, notably FKA twigs and M.I.A. (Maya Arulpragasam). M.I.A.'s video for *'Bad Girls'* (2010) was directed by Romain Gavras, a French–Greek director, and was written by Arulpragasam. Gavras had already collaborated with M.I.A. on the video for *'Born Free'* (2010), which was not shown on YouTube in 2010 – owing, it was said by the singer, to the video's graphic depiction of genocidal violence. *'Bad Girls'* is no less powerful an address to attitudes towards female autonomy in Arabic and Muslim countries using Sharia law. It was taken as a critique of Saudi Arabia, where at that time it was illegal for a woman to drive unless accompanied by a male companion.

When director Sophie Muller graduated from Central St Martins and then completed her MA at the RCA, she did not think a career in film was an option because there were no women directors in the 1980s. In 1975, an enquiry into the status of women in film and television conducted for the ACTT showed that women's employment had deteriorated since World War II (cited in Muir 1988). Women constituted only 15 per cent of the workforce (a decline of 3 per cent since the 1950s), and were mainly employed in low-paid, low-grade and low-status administrative support roles (Muir 1988: 143–4). Therefore artists such as Marianne Faithfull and Siouxsie Sioux had little choice but to hire male directors – as did Kate Bush, although Bush took at the very least a co-directing role in her videos. When Muller began directing, she says her only role model was Kate Bush because Bush wrote and produced her own material. Unlike other artists, Bush's creative œuvre was entirely a result of Bush's own vision. The impact on Muller was profound. 'She was the only person that I related to. I thought: I want to do that. I want to be like her.'[6] Bush is an artist who has often taken full control of all aspects of her artistic production, including songwriting, arrangements and the creation of music videos (Moy 2007: 72–88, Morini 2013: 285). When we contacted her for permissions, it was agreed that to reflect the true extent of her work on the videos she would be credited as co-director of both '*Running Up That Hill*' (along with David Garfath) and '*Cloudbusting*' (along with Julian Doyle).

Muller has directed more than twenty videos for Annie Lennox and Eurythmics, and has a long-time collaboration with producer Rob Small. The video for '*Why*' (1992) illustrates the collaborative process between Muller and Lennox. The account of their working process also suggests that the auteur model of practice does not suit women's way of working. There was no script, just an idea that they would shoot some videos for Annie's *Diva* album. Muller went to Lennox's house to film her performing the tracks in order to get some ideas. Lennox 'stood against the wall and sang the song over, and over again' whilst Muller filmed her. Muller reports, 'I'd say try like this and try like that, try it more angry . . . no, try it more humorous . . . but nothing worked, nothing was happening: we couldn't get there, so we decided the video should be about nothing.'[7]

On the shoot day, Lennox tried on some feather boas and other Hollywood paraphernalia, dressing up as a diva, and suddenly Muller understood what the video was going to be about. Muller says it became *about* Lennox herself. It became about Lennox putting on her warpaint and transforming from being a shy person who had been away from the industry for a while having a baby. 'It was like she was saying, "Here I am."' Muller said she had always been so impressed by Lennox's capacity to become someone else in her videos, but also mystified by it. 'I was always trying to find out: Why are you changing? How did you change? What happened? Did you feel it? Did you feel yourself changing into this person?' Muller continued, '[i]t was such a simple thing, but it was so hard to do because I was saying nothing [as a filmmaker]. There was no text: it was all about what Annie felt underneath.' For Muller, the fact that she and Lennox had worked together on so many videos enabled them to make this video about something that neither woman could put into words. 'I don't think anyone else could have done that because it came from our relationship.'[8]

Muller pitches to her artists by *listening* to them rather than *speaking* at them. This subverts the auteur model. Women who have had to fight to be heard will sometimes – but not always – gravitate to a place where they can be heard, and have someone pitching their corner helping them to be heard. 'I've been very, very lucky because I don't have that kind of "*I* have something to say, and this is how *I'm* going to say it."' Instead of approaching a project with her own cinematic vision, Muller approaches her projects in order to listen. She describes this as a kind of 'humility' that is atypical of the 'arrogance' that is sometimes celebrated and even required within an exceptionally competitive film industry.[9] It could be interpreted that this is in fact the reason for Muller's success. Female artists gravitated towards her because they could see in her someone highly expert and talented who would not impose her ideas on them, who would use her skills to realise their ideas – and in the realm of commercial and art film production, that was extremely unusual. Sophie Muller reports that PJ Harvey's *'This is Love'* 'was shot on reversal, because all her videos are shot on reversal because she really loved that look'. I asked Sophie, did Harvey technically know that it was reversal stock she wanted? 'I don't know if she knew, but, I, I interpreted what she wanted.'[10] After *'No Ordinary Love'* (1992), Sade worked only with Sophie Muller. Muller also began a long collaboration with Shakespears Sister, e.g. *'Goodbye Cruel World'* (1991), which features Siobhan Fahey and Marcella Detroit spoofing famous melodramas such as *Sunset Boulevard* (1950) and *What Ever Happened to Baby Jane?* (1962).

For Dawn Shadworth, this aversion has a regional and age dimension: 'I think I'm probably quite bossy but in a quiet way. Bobby from Primal Scream once said, "I know when you mean 'no' Dawn: it's when you don't say anything,"' suggesting that this was a control strategy Shadforth had developed in order to avoid being perceived by her crew and artists as overtly 'bossy'. Silence, rather than confrontation. Shadforth explained that 'I think it's something to do with being a young woman working with a much older male crew.'

> Coming from up North, even the idea 'I am a director' seemed utterly pretentious. It made it hard for me to even own that name 'director' when people might say, 'ooooh you're a director, are you?' So I think I was always a little bit apologetic. My strategy was to be very sweet and charming to get my way; and by never saying 'no'. But now I'm more comfortable with all of that. I'm better at being forthright.[11]

But none of the interviewees felt that positive representations of women could be achieved only by women directors. In the 1990s, a body of progressive videos was produced by a generation of male directors seemingly more alert to female autonomy, power and pleasure. The Chemical Brothers' *'Setting Sun'* (1996), directed by Dom & Nic, depicts the so-called 'ladette' culture of the 1990s, raising issues about women's ownership of their bodies, and posing challenging representations of women far removed from the stereotyped male gaze. In his video for Björk's *'Big Time Sensuality'* (1993), Stéphane Sednaoui invokes the ghost of a British Pathé film of 1927 to represent Björk as a late-twentieth-century flapper: a free urban spirit in charge of her own dance, her own pleasure and her own image. Jake Nava talked of the valuable influence of growing up with a mum (Mica Nava) who was 'a cutting-edge feminist and activist':

> All of us are inevitably influenced by our primary socialisation. [In the 'Single Ladies' video], it's definitely true that part of what I was doing with Beyoncé was showing that women could be really sexy and project their sexuality without being victims. If you are a young male growing up surrounded by a lot of feminist discourse it's going to cause you to question your sense of masculinity. It felt important to me to say, hang on, it's cool for women to dress up and feel hot. Empowerment doesn't mean you should repress your libido.[12]

Vaughan Arnell has been one of the most prolific directors enabling artists to articulate their identity through gendered performance. He directed the 1998 *'Outside'* video for George Michael, which drew on genre styles of soft porn and newsreel to position a satirical two fingers to the judgements against Michael after he was arrested in a public toilet in the USA. In the mid-1990s, Arnell created the iconic video for the Spice Girls' *'Say You'll Be There'* (1996) at a point at which the band had already asserted their claim on 'girl power', a concept they had harnessed from the Riot Grrrl-associated bands of New York in the 1990s (Schilt 2003). Among the British equivalents were Elastica and punk bands such as Siouxsie and the Banshees. The *'Say You'll Be There'* video presented the Spice Girls as a band of female techno-warriors who use martial arts and high-tech-influenced weapons to capture a hapless male. It reasserted the girls' battle-mantra of 'girl power' and visualised, in a satirical comic style inspired by *Faster, Pussycat! Kill! Kill!* (1965), the new world order according to the Spice Girls. The shots of male bondage are unexplained and function as symbols of male disempowerment, just as the rest of the clip serves to assert the power and fighting abilities of the women. The clip is presented as a narrative, with movie credits at the start introducing the Spice Girls as fantastic characters such as 'Trixie Firecracker'. Dibben argues that the video neither privileges nor challenges traditional representations of femininity. She argues that whilst the Spice Girls are posing for the male gaze as desirable, sexualised women, they are simultaneously posing for young women to interpret them as autonomous and powerful. Dibben argues that in common with other popular texts, the Spice Girls offer resistance to patriarchy using the patriarchal constructions of femininity in oppositional meanings (Dibben 2002).

Validating this reading of the video is the interview that I conducted with Carole Burton-Fairbrother, who commissioned the Spice Girls videos in the UK offices of Virgin. Burton-Fairbrother said she saw a pressure on women to be sexy in the industry in general and the USA in particular. But she did not see that pressure on the female artists for whom she commissioned videos in

London. 'Apart from the fact that it was degrading women, I thought it was so boring. In London we didn't have to do that.'[13] The Spice Girls videos were about their individual personalities.

> They were absolutely in control. They were not five little puppet girls: they were five girls who yearned to be in that position, and then once they were in that position they were just off and running on their own. Totally under their own banner.[14]

In summary, in music videos, young people in Britain from the mid-1960s onwards found a media outlet to venture alternative and challenging definitions of gender excluded from mainstream television culture and feature film content. Since the late 1970s, women have fought within the British music industry and have managed to gain significant control over their image by collaborating with non-auteur filmmakers such as Muller. Men and women alike have subverted gender stereotypes and tropes around sexuality in progressive ways that have not yet been captured in music video studies.

Notes

1. S. Muller, personal communication, 19 March 2018.
2. B. Rose, personal communication, 26 October 2016.
3. B. Rose, personal communication, 26 October 2016.
4. B. Rose, personal communication, 26 October 2016.
5. R. Skinner, personal communication, 10 April 2015.
6. S. Muller, personal communication, 19 March 2018.
7. S. Muller, personal communication, 19 March 2018.
8. S. Muller, personal communication, 19 March 2018.
9. S. Muller, personal communication, 19 March 2018.
10. S. Muller, personal communication, 19 March 2018.
11. D. Shadforth, personal communication, 17 November 2016.
12. J. Nava, personal communication, 12 December 2016.
13. C. Burton-Fairbrother, personal communication, 15 January 2016.
14. C. Burton-Fairbrother, personal communication, 15 January 2016.

6 AUTHORSHIP

This chapter looks at the patterns and tropes of collaborative authorship in British music videos since the mid-1960s. One could argue that the so-called Death of the Author has left authorship studies inoperable, but a language for the critical appreciation of music video which incorporates a theory of intentional creative practice is a precondition for the future production of music video appreciation and industry history. Who made what, and when, also has major financial and legal implications for musicians and filmmakers, because in most capitalist economies, it determines who does and does not get paid for copyright. In the discussion below I look at law, auteurism, the textual voice and social authorship – the degree to which the video articulates values, attitudes and iconography perceived as *authentic* to the music community in which the artist claims to have originated.

British music videos are made at the intersection of two production cultures: film and music. Both the film and music industries comprise human beings holding and continually reaffirming certain conceptions about the processes, crew hierarchies, legal and economic rules for production articulated through discourse(s) (Robins 1997: 4). But they often hold very differing conceptions of these, so the scope for something to go awry from the collision of these two cultures is huge. The diagram here identifies and illustrates the production process for a music video. It shows the parties with potential claims to authorship on a legal or empirical basis. The sheer complexity of the diagram shows the considerably different centres of creative, economic and legal power which are involved in music video production. To explain the licensing and rights of the

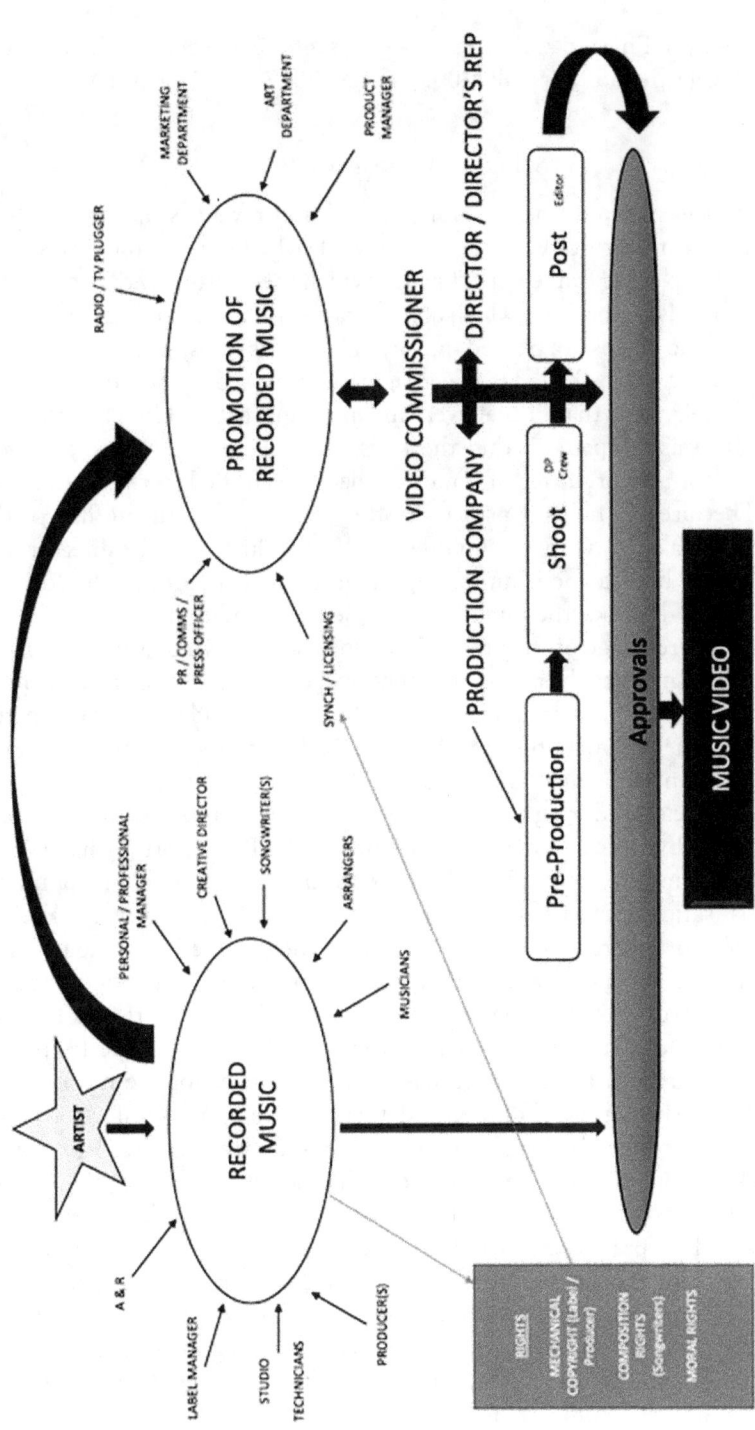

Figure 6.1 Music Video Production (credit Mark Evans).

music industry in England and Wales (the law is different in Scotland), the reader is referred to Frith and Marshall (2009), Grice (2013) and Harrison (2017).

Legal Authorship

In Britain, it has been in the domain of rights and revenues that the clash of music and screen cultures has been felt most clearly. In most capitalist economies authorship is the framework through which the courts identify copyright, which, in turn, is the basis on which corporations trade in media (Doyle 2013). Although music videos are treated in copyright law as films, directors and producers of music videos have far fewer rights in their work and far less power to control their work than if they were independent feature film producers.

How did this happen? Within the laws of England and Wales, the individual director and producer of a music video are entitled to two authorship claims. The director holds a primary authorship claim as the author of the script (known as 'the treatment' in music video production). The director and producer then hold a joint authorship claim as the authors of the 'derivative' audiovisual work, 'the film'. In principle, this would mean that they are entitled to a percentage of the profits from commercial exploitation (e.g. from sales and licensing, or advertising revenues on YouTube). But the record labels stipulate in their contracts that such royalties are included up front in the (labour) fee for the work, thereby ensuring that no further royalty payments need to be given to the director.

It is also because, during the 1980s, the labels en masse instituted a practice, endorsed by the 1984 recommendations of the BPI report (Fisher 1984), of defining themselves as the legal film producer in the production contracts. The labels' rationale was that they, not the production company, bankrolled the production (whereas in feature films it is the production company that puts together the finance deal), and because they, not the production company, own the 'title work' of the song (asserting that the dominant title work is not the director's video treatment, but the artist's track), they are the legitimate producer. The record labels would bankroll the budget for the music video from their marketing expenditure, and then recoup those production costs from revenues from artists' sales (singles, albums, streaming, advertising, etc). The 1984 BPI report further recommended that no additional copyrights were extended to any contributing creative party in the music video. It therefore became standard practice for actors to be contracted on an in-perpetuity, all-media and throughout-the-universe buyout not used in advertising, feature film or television. This has meant that when labels decide to exploit the product in a new media or platform, they do not need to renegotiate control, secure any further consents or make any further royalty payments. One of the core activities of a media company is to find new ways to recycle old products to maintain copyright revenues (for example, when the labels resold their product on CDs in the 1980s). By this method, the record labels ensure that all future royalties are payable only to the publishers and recording artists, including the session musicians. The record industry contracts directors as a service industry to execute the music, much as it would hire a catering company to provide food at events.

Directors in Britain have faced a harder position on moral rights, too. In the USA, moral rights are not recognised in law (Fine 2010, Grantham 1999). Thus it is standard practice for writers and directors to exchange the products of their labour for money. The work of art is not considered part of the artist's personality, as it is in the European *droit de l'auteur* culture. Provided the economic exchange is deemed just and proportionate, an economic purchase suffices. In Europe, by contrast, artistic works are produced within a discourse of the artist's soul and body. In France, moral rights are enforced as inalienable – the author retains rights over the work as an extension of his or her personality. In the UK, moral rights were incorporated in the laws of England and Wales in 1988 in a weak way in the view of some, such as Ginsberg, to protect the interests of large US corporates like record labels, for whom moral rights would interrupt commercial exploitation of intellectual product (Ginsberg 1992). British music video directors have always felt themselves to sit in an uncomfortable place where, like European artists, they experience themselves as artists, and experience the videos – sometimes – as deeply personal works. They were not credited as the authors of the works on *TOTP*, *The Chart Show* or MTV, and they were not consulted on the integrity of the works, and this was a cause of discontent for many directors in the 1980s and 1990s. The directors had no legal power to enforce their credits as directors. By contrast, and ironically, directors in the USA, where there is no moral rights framework, were able to secure credits on MTV. This probably illustrates that having a powerful and effective professional trade body is more important than a law, because laws have no value unless enforced. The US Music Video Producers' Association (MVPA) was much more powerful than its UK counterpart.

Authorship as 'Signature' or 'Hallmark'

Although Goodwin (1993) warned against applying concepts from film theory to music video, scholars such as Vernallis and Ueno (2013) have adopted the concept of an auteur. These scholars have used it to elevate music video in much the same way that film studies appropriated the concept from literary studies in the 1970s to elevate film studies to the stature of literary studies in the Universities (English 2001: 270). Others use the theoretical assumptions surrounding it without invoking the word itself (e.g. Donnelly 2007b, Rogers 2013). The scholars were not alone. *In the absence of any effective professional trade association or legal framework* to claim the economic value of their intellectual property as the authors of their work, music video directors have looked to the concept of an auteur to claim cultural value as compensation. Cultural value compensates for the failure of the existing copyright regime to recognise their economic and moral rights.

In the 1990s a notion of video directors as auteurs developed in the British and American music video industry, with roots in the discourse of 1980s British directors such as Russell Mulcahy and Steve Barron, who saw music video as a stepping stone to a more illustrious career directing feature films in Hollywood. The *New York Times* assessed the situation astutely in a 1995 article, 'Out of Crass Commerce Arises the New Auteur'. I have argued elsewhere that for many decades, music video lay at the base of a cultural hierarchy of screen industries. In 1998, the former founder of British indie label Island Records, Chris Blackwell, established Palm Pictures to distribute film and music content, and in 2003 he launched The Directors' Label to distribute a series of DVDs dedicated to the work of individual music video directors such as Gondry, Romanek, Cunningham and Glazer. Vernallis wrote that the Palm Pictures DVDs 'enhance our sensitivity to music video directors as *auteurs*' (2013a: 263; my italics).

The auteur framework doesn't work in music video production because it obscures what is really significant about music video production. Pauline Kael identified part of the problem when she wrote that,

> [o]ften the works in which we are most aware of the personality of the director are his worst films – when he falls back on the devices he has already done to death. When a famous director makes a good movie, we look at the movie, we don't think about the director's personality; when he makes a stinker we notice his familiar touches because there's not much else to watch. (Kael 1963: 15)

It follows from Kael's logic that when a director makes a music video in which she deploys cinematic devices or themes used for different artists earlier in her career she's done to death, the viewer of the new video may be less likely to reflect on the artist and song and more likely to recall those earlier works in the director's œuvre. In choosing a particular director, and in collaborating with that director on a mutually agreed and developed idea, the artist employs the director to articulate something important about the artist's own identity and beliefs.

Nevertheless, scholars claim to have found in some directors' work evidence of auteurism. I use Sarris's definition of an auteur as a director whose 'technical competence' and 'distinguishable personality' are evident in the work, and who is concerned with 'the ultimate glory of the cinema as art' (2001).

In Britain, Jamie Thraves is an award-winning feature film director who has advanced the genre of the plot-driven narrative music video, whose personality is evident in his work for what Gilbey has termed a Thravesian trademark: 'the eruption of unforeseeable violence' (2011). His work was not distributed by The Directors' Label, so his name is less familiar to the public, but on Sarris's criteria he is a legitimate candidate for 'auteur status'.

The director singled out most often for celebration as an auteur in Britain is Chris Cunningham, whose work was distributed by The Directors' Label. On the basis that Cunningham's work 'exhibits a good degree of consistency', Dean Lockwood describes him as an 'auteur of the abhuman' (2017: 199). He continues: 'Cunningham has been granted the privilege of auteur status, rare in music video' – inviting the questions, by whom? When? But Lockwood answers: 'This was cemented by his being lionized, somewhat transparently, in a 2003 novel, *Pattern Recognition*, by science-fiction writer William Gibson' (2017: 199). Lockwood goes on to cite the passage from the novel, pointing to the existence of The Directors' Label collection, and Carol Vernallis's support for it, as further evidence that Cunningham is an auteur. James Leggott has written of Cunningham's 'anatomical obsessions and attraction towards transgressive imagery' (2016: 2) and especially 'imagery involving mutated, traumatised or robotic bodies' (2016: 3). Cunningham is the exception rather than the rule, and to build an entire theory or approach around the exception is *to fail to understand the medium itself*.

Cunningham is arguably more of an art film maker than a music video director. Like John Maybury before him, Cunningham could find the music video industry frustrating when the involvement of managers, commissioners and sales reps can create conflicting and inhibiting pressures. What is really interesting is how Cunningham has applied and negotiated his skills, themes and cinematic style to articulate the voices of so many different artists – from Björk to Portishead, Madonna, Leftfield – in ways that have enabled those artists to feel their music and their identity has been *expressed* and *authentically represented*. The more interesting approach, rather than looking for similarities between his videos, is to look for the differences in the skilful way that he was able to address the different needs of each track and each artist. In that lies the extraordinary accomplishment of a music video director, rather than a film director.

In an industrialised service industry such as music video, the major creative power of the director lies in the decision whether or not to collaborate with the artist on a track: whether to accept the commission, or seek out the commission. Most directors will tell you they rise and fall on that skill, which is based on an experienced understanding of what kinds of tracks work well with four-minute videos (usually to do with structure, drama, peaks and troughs), what musical tradition an artist wants to be interpreted within, what visual anchors to use within the video to trigger authentication by the fans, and whether the record company and management will support their creative process. A director will also need to have knowledge and understanding of budgets, collaboration skills and management. The crucial skill of the director is to determine: will this idea work for this track with this artist and that management team / record label, in the budget and time frame I've got?

Most of the directors interviewed for this book are *extremely* fussy. They didn't begin their careers saying 'yes' to any commissioned work. They sought out tracks they thought would work well for a video, in the same way that a choreographer such as Akram Khan will seek out pieces of music or musicians whose music would work well for a new dance piece. The next major step will be for the director to ascertain that they and the artist want the same thing, and can work together and will support each other. And at that point, the brilliance of the director will lie in the fact that the viewer or critic cannot see or hear her voice because he or she is giving voice to the artist, particularly in performance videos. Important examples are Sophie Muller and Vaughan Arnell. It is not particularly desirable, therefore, that the director's personality stands out more than the artist's – which is what auteur theory demands it should do.

So the skill of a music video is often for the director to use his or her expertise – technical, social, creative – to articulate the artist's voice. Pedro Romhanyi is an example of this. Pedro directed four of the videos in our landmark collection: Pulp's '*Common People*' (1995), Blur's '*Parklife*' (1994), Paul Weller's '*Changing Man*' (1995) and the Manic Street Preachers' '*Design for Life*' (1996). 'I like to think I didn't have a signature technique or trick that I did . . . I would work from the music,' explains Romhanyi. When he was invited to script for 'Parklife', Romhanyi read Martin Amis's book *Money: A Suicide Note* (1984) because he'd heard that Damon Albarn was influenced by it. When he heard the track, 'it sounded to me like it was about this place called Parklife, which does and doesn't exist; and the characters you find there and their ways of life; like Martin Amis, it was using archetype and caricature; and it was verbose, and it was playful.'[1] According to Romhanyi, Blur were involved in creating the characters and storyline – especially Albarn, who enjoyed the performance and narrative side of videos.

By contrast, when Romhanyi created '*Changing Man*' for him, Paul Weller didn't like having to make and front videos. Romhanyi explains that the lyrics, although in the third person, were about Paul:

> his different layers of personality, and his often antagonistic extremes: there's a line 'to light a bitter fuse'; it's all in there lyrically [. . .] So I didn't really want him hiding behind as the band leader, I wanted it to be just about him as a man.

In order to root this portrait in the authorship of Weller and his band, Romhanyi looked at Paul's visual materials – photographs, album covers and so forth – and settled on the album cover for *Stanley Road*, which had been designed by Peter Blake. Romhanyi used this as a framework for the video: flat blocks of colour, stark in a white space, and multi-coloured picture frames. For Romhanyi, a music video director has to 'explore the baggage that your artist brings with them – good and bad. You can have a great video but if it doesn't really fit the artist [who is fronting it] you can think it's great, but it doesn't hit the chord. . . .'[2]

Pulp, by contrast, were very enthusiastic about, and involved in, the making of '*Common People*' (1995). Romhanyi attributes this to both their art school backgrounds (RCA and Central St Martins College), filmmaking interests and the fact that Jarvis had directed videos for Warp earlier in his career. 'Pulp, like Blur, came from an alternative background, but they wanted to entertain. They were this new breed. They wanted to make entertaining things.' Romhanyi showed them a film by Zbigniew Rybczyński titled *Tango* (1980) as a reference, and from that they came up with the video premise. 'Lyrically,' said Romhanyi, 'the treatment almost wrote itself.' He was initially worried because the visuals adhered closely to the lyrics. Romhanyi explained that, '[if] the visuals are too on the nose it becomes hackneyed, or it makes the lyric worse, or makes it seem banal' and '[t]his normally makes a bad music video.'[3] A video, he explained, should add value and fulfil the formula 1+1=2. If it merely reflects the lyrics, it can end up 1+0 or 1–1. On the shoot, Jarvis 'just took [the kids] aside and he taught them [the dance] there and then. It was brilliant. It was absolutely brilliant. Again, pure artistic self-expression to dramatize the song.'[4]

The Personality of the Artist

There is a considerable literature comprising case study analyses of artists' videos. Whilst many look at individual videos, some look at the corpus of an artist's music video work (Madonna, Kate Bush) or the entire corpus of the artists' visual representations and performances (David Bowie, Annie Lennox). Several of these are contained in Gina Arnold et al.'s new collection: David Bowie (Wright 2017), FKA twigs (Fairclough 2017), Beyoncé, Björk (Brozzoni 2017). Some of this work is interesting, some better researched than others. In Britain, some of the artists considered the most musically expressive and visually arresting were Radiohead, The Chemical Brothers, Massive Attack and Björk.

In general, many of the most significant conceptual videos were commissioned by bands who embraced video-making as a part of their creativity. Massive Attack are one such band, emerging from the Bristol trip-hop scene as a multimedia artwork band with a distinctively British and Bristol version of hip-hop.

3D, aka Robert Del Naja, is a British artist, musician, singer and songwriter. He was a graffiti artist before becoming a vocalist. His work has been featured on all of Massive Attack's record sleeves. The graffiti artist Banksy cites his work as an influence, and he is regarded as a pioneer of the stencil graffiti movement, bringing hip-hop and graffiti culture from the USA to Bristol in the early 1980s.

That Massive Attack have collaborated with some of the leading British video directors of the 1990s and 2000s – Baillie Walsh, Jonathan Glazer, Walter Stern, WIZ, Ringan Ledwidge – is a result of the band's focus on their artwork as a defining feature of their *authenticity*. Glazer's video for Massive Attack's *'Karmacoma'* (1995) features the band in near-narrative fragments of drama set in a hotel, with very distinctive references to the films of David Lynch and Quentin Tarantino from the late 1980s and early 1990s. As testament to the band's commitment to the visual art, they feature within the oddball world created by Glazer, in which someone has been shot. In a Lynchean way the video evades a linear narrative. There is an *Eraserhead* (1977) character at the typewriter, an Uma Thurman *Pulp Fiction* (1994)-type girl, and a Marilyn Monroe / Cindy Sherman-type blonde in a leopardskin coat staggering around, with *Twin Peaks* (ABC 1990–1)-type iconography in the hotel. Discontinuous editing mixes up space and time, although there is a deliberate purporting to narrative (which is not the case in some of the earlier videos, and which makes it more than just a series of dream sequences).

Like Massive Attack, The Chemical Brothers have collaborated with many leading British directors –Walter Stern, Michel Gondry, Spike Jonze – but they have also collaborated regularly with Dom & Nic. Working so frequently with a particular directing team allows a long-term understanding to build, and it means that directors have the time to get to know the artists, their fans, their interests, their political views and the music videos and films that they like. I asked Dom & Nic about their experience of working with them. 'The Chemical Brothers search out people they want to work with and then they very much let you do what you want to do. They don't interfere.'[5]

Dom & Nic were perhaps from the outset extremely keen to articulate the voice of the artists because they began their careers working for Nic's brother's band Supergrass (his brother is Danny Goffey). This added an incentive not to make an auteur film driven by a separate idea. He says it was 'a good way to move forward' and learn how *music video was a different kind of filmmaking*.

> The ideas come from the music. We don't have a book of ideas that we're desperate to pin onto a track when it comes along. We are completely free to think of whatever we want to. With The Chemical Brothers we're more free than what we would be, say if we did something for an artist who needs to be featured. It's a complete blank canvas and you've just got a piece of music, and we can go and make a film. Video can quite easily

destroy songs if you put them together and they don't match. We have so much respect for the artists, we are fans of their music. We don't want to then bolt something onto what they've created, like a car bumper that drags it down. It should be the opposite.[6]

Dom & Nic explained that because they were of the same generation as The Chemical Brothers they often tried to represent what was happening at that moment in time. In *'Setting Sun'* (1996), they represented rave culture. In *'Believe'* (2005), they represented automation. They felt that there was a recurring theme of isolation and solitude in the videos they had done for The Chemical Brothers, as well as a recurring story element around hallucination. Neither of these themes were present in the work they'd done for other artists such as Supergrass – a band whose music and personalities invited very different themes.

The Personality of the Record Label

The idea of the studio as an auteur is examined by Christensen (2008). Before attributing the artistic merits of Chris Cunningham's work solely to his auteur abilities it is worth considering whether they were partly facilitated by the in-house style of Warp Records, which commissioned his video for Aphex Twin's *'Come to Daddy'* (1997), the breakthrough work selected for heavy rotation on MTV which led to multiple commissions from artists such as Madonna for Cunningham. For founders Rob Mitchell and Steve Beckett, music video was far from just a marketing strategy. It was seen as an integral part of the creative work of Warp, demonstrated by two collections released by the label: *Artists: Warp Vision, The Videos 1989–2004* (DVD, 2004) and *Motion* (VHS, 1994). Beckett consistently commissioned avant-garde and experimental directors such as David Slade and Jarvis Cocker to collaborate with their artists and, when the decision was made to pass the process to a dedicated video commissioner in 2004, they hired a commissioner with a track record in video art: Robin Gutch, previously commissioning editor of Channel 4's Experimental Film and Video department. In 2002 they established Warp Films, which produced signature works such as *Four Lions* (Chris Morris, 2010) and *This Is England* (Shane Meadows, 2006).

When we interviewed him for this project, Steve Beckett confirmed that in his view Warp videos had a signature style, citing videos for Battles' songs *'Atlas'* (2007), *'Tonto'* (2007) and *'Ice Cream'* (2011), as well as the Autechre videos and videos directed by David Slade and Chris Cunningham, as illustrating that style. Beckett explained that Warp always sought 'a simple aesthetic that's going to grab you, not a complex mini feature-film that you're going to cram into two minutes.' He wanted to hear the director say, 'I've got to do this video, I love this band, let me get inside it.' For him, it was essential to hear that the director had both 'a connection to the artist and a connection to the individual song, and had developed the video not from a separate film script idea but from listening to the song and understanding the band's personality'. The song had to sell the artist in some way, and, if a new band, probably feature in the video.[7]

Other contenders for the status of auteur record labels could be 4AD, which released its *Lonely Is an Eyesore* compilation in June 1987 with a VHS and Beta of the accompanying music videos. Mute Records, led by Daniel Miller, with its roster of interesting experimental artists, was also more inclined to commission conceptual videos; many were commissioned out of house by freelancer John Moule. ZTT is another example of an important label that was inclined to commission risky videos that might not get airplay on MTV or terrestrial television; director Bernard Rose has spoken of the problems that occurred in this clash of 'house styles', when Island Records took over the distributing side of video. Island censored videos commissioned by Morley and Horn at ZTT that pushed the boundaries of the medium at that time, such as Frankie Goes to Hollywood's *'Relax'* (1983). Skint Records, with commissioner John Hassay, consistently supported experimental and conceptual music videos in their commissions for Fatboy Slim and other artists. In the literature that exists on music videos, it would be good to see in the future some analysis of the enormous commitment to video and film art made by the commissioners and managing directors (MDs) of these record labels. It is a very noticeable gap in the literature.

The Personality of the Video Commissioner

At some of the smaller indie labels, videos would be commissioned by the label MDs; at others, labels would hire a freelance commissioner. Some semi-independents would use the in-house video commissioner at the parent label. Commissioners varied in the extent to which they simply executed their employer's house style or brought their own creative visions to bear on their work. Ollie Weait challenged the corporate house style of Warner's. During the 1990s, many Black British artists felt unsupported by the labels, particularly in music video, where labels were not willing to commit budgets to match the high-production-value US R&B videos. Within the marketing department of Warner's was Weait, who worked with video commissioner Nijico Walker and sometimes commissioned directly.

> He was trying to get R&B, urban and soul music taken seriously in the corporate culture. Along with Mickey D at Warner Brothers, Ollie was trying to work out how to promote street music in the mainstream, because it had bubbled up from the street a bit more. He understood what was happening in club culture. He was someone inside the corporation trying to enhance the possibilities and the budgets we could work with.[8]

The British music video scene was dominated in the 1990s by four powerful and visionary commissioners at the major labels: Carole Burton-Fairbrother at Virgin, Dilly Gent at Parlophone, Carrie Sutton at Chrysalis and Trudy Bellinger at EMI. The experience of most women in the industry in the 1970s was that their route into music video was commissioning, because the director role was dominated by men. In the '70s and still in the early '80s, commissioning was treated as an administrative role for a medium of as yet unknown cultural and economic relevance. The new post of commissioner was not therefore sought out by men, and was readily handed over to highly creative and dynamic young women who were seeking ways in which to express their creativity and independent thinking. Carole Burton-Fairbrother began her career at Virgin as a secretary.

One of the ways these women expressed their ideas and had a huge influence on creativity in Britain was by seeking out new, up-and-coming directors from showreels and film school graduation events. Carole Burton-Fairbrother gave both Michel Gondry and Jonathan Glazer their first commissions. Dilly Gent explains the creative role of a video commissioner:

> Even now, people don't know what that title means. They really don't. I was explaining to someone the other day and they said, 'So you're like a director?' And I said 'No,' and then they said, 'So you're like an executive producer?' No. And so I said, 'Okay, in the '90s when I was video commissioning, the process was incredibly creative. I'd get the track, I'd live with the track for days. If it was Radiohead, I would live with it for months, because I would get the demo from bands. That was obviously an exceptional circumstance. I'd sleep with it. It would be in my car, in my home. I'd start visualising what I think it should be then I'd talk to the band about it. The band might say they don't want to be in it, or they want to be filmed in the desert. Then I would start thinking about it, visualising it. Then I would reach out to the directors who I thought were right, then they'd write treatments.[9]

Gent was always looking for new voices, such as Grant Gee, who directed '*No Surprises*' (1997). She recounts that she found him through a snowboarding documentary on TV. The end credits used 'really cool motion graphics of the snowboarders' and she thought 'I've got to find out who did that.'[10] She met him, liked him, and hired him to start working on the band's documentary, '*Meeting People Is Easy*' (1998). His first idea for 'No Surprises' wasn't right.

> So I just kept going 'The flat line, the flat line. You've got to listen to the song. The flat line.' I couldn't stress it enough. For me, it had had to be like that. And then he wrote the treatment [for the video that was subsequently made] and I thought, 'Dear God, where did that come from?' He's the most talented person I've ever met in my life.[11]

The Personality of the Executive Producer

Less likely to occur in the scholarship are analyses of signature traits of the executive producers (EPs). This is partly because the names of these individuals are largely invisible to the scholars who have written about music video, and partly because the auteur paradigm blocks out the creative significance of other players – despite the fact that Sarris (2001: xii) and subsequently Bernstein (2008) have suggested the role of auteur *producers* is a worthy concept. Executive producers have the power to sign directors. Once signed, the executive and director's representative will lobby labels and artists to secure commissions or act as conduits when commissioners send tracks out. They will also often take an active creative role in the development of the script, using their knowledge of an artist's career and style (many executives began their careers as commissioners).

Liz Kessler, executive producer at production company Academy – home to Jonathan Glazer, Walter Stern and Us (Chris Barrett and Luke Taylor) amongst others – explained that where the producer physically made the product, the executive controlled the project from pitch to delivery. At a boutique company like Academy, the executive producer protects the brand. Academy's in-house style was to make high-end cinematic music videos that didn't look like music videos, and as a result the executive producer would sometimes decline a track because the brief was too conventional or the turnaround time was too short to allow her directors to make something really distinctive and different. But her job was also to protect the directors, and that meant ensuring they had sufficient in-house and client support to develop their ideas before a pitch (both in terms of time and technical research) and then deliver it to the signature high standard. The executive, Kessler explains, was always the 'straight talker'. Everyone else could sell the idea, inspire with the vision, and joke, but the EP's job was to 'talk straight' with the video commissioner. Together, the EP and the video commissioner bridged the gap between popular music culture and practices at the label, and the film culture and practices in Soho's production and post-production houses.

There was a widespread consensus amongst the interviewees that John Stewart at Oil Factory was one of the most highly regarded executive producers in the industry. Oil Factory was home in the 1990s to Sophie Muller, Pedro Romhanyi, WIZ, Dom & Nic, Richard Heslop and Jamie Thraves. Video commissioner Carole Burton-Fairbrother said of working with Stewart at Oil Factory that 'you felt you were on the same team'. That void and clash between production cultures didn't exist. This may be partly because Stewart had begun his career with one foot in either camp – one in the film industry, and the other in the music industry. Oil Factory was founded by Annie Lennox and Dave Stewart in 1984. John Stewart, Dave's brother, then working at the BFI, became involved in several early Oil Factory productions. He then left his post at the BFI and, with business partner Billy Poveda, purchased the company from Lennox and Stewart. They turned it into a production company that would dominate the 1990s music video scene, in terms of its reputation for presenting the directors most willing and able to work inside the music to deliver authentic artistic work. Under John Stewart, Oil Factory only signed directors who worked from the music outwards. Dom & Nic, who were signed to Oil Factory early on, felt it was pivotal in their career; it meant they were taken seriously by commissioners and could learn from other more experienced directors at the company such as Sophie Muller.

Author as 'the Voice'

The voice enunciated within the video is what Goodwin would term 'the implied author' (1992: 75). There is no consistent rule, but in general, filmmakers are commissioned to produce works in which it appears that the implied author is the artist. Chris Sweeney explains the concept in relation to '*Hard Out Here*' (2013), which he made for Lily Allen. 'It's almost like you have ring-side seats, while being invisible. Apart from the odd person on Twitter, no one out there thinks that I made it. As far as they're concerned, Lily made it' (quoted in Knight 2013).

No matter who came up with the idea or who made it, it must appear as if the artist authored the video, and that the video conveys the artist's view of self / the world / the music. The video for '*No Surprises*' (1997) perfectly illustrates this. Commissioner Dilly Gent explains, 'I remember sitting with Thom at some band dinner and going, "Thom, I'm still worried, you know, to make this work properly you've got to do it for real, you've got to hold your breath. It can't be fake."' On the set, he wore

> what looked like an astronaut's helmet. It had these rubber flaps on the bottom. He had his thumbs through it so he could literally release the water very quickly. But it was so tight around his face. I couldn't watch it. I had to go and sit outside the studio. We did speed up the track, so it wasn't the full length of time. But he was underwater singing away, holding his breath, it wasn't fake.[12]

Fans as Authors / Music Communities

Music artists are authenticated by fans and music cultures, as Frith and other scholars have argued, and they act as spokespersons for certain music cultures. The landmark collection includes a number of videos which the panel did not feel were worthy of inclusion on artistic grounds, but which illustrated the importance for some bands of achieving street authorship over and above artistic authorship. The Prodigy's *'Out of Space'* (1992) video is an example of this. By the time it was made, director Russell Curtis had already directed several of The Prodigy's earlier videos (*'Wind it Up'*, *'Charly'*, *'Fire'*, *'Everybody in the Place'*). Of the production, Curtis explained:

> We shot it in one day near where the band lived in Braintree. Most of the day was spent hanging out in their various houses! It was just me, Bluey Durrant, who was the AD [assistant director] and editor, and a producer. It was a tiny budget, shot on 16mm on a Bolex. In one of the old Prodigy video compilations there is some 'making of' footage; me sitting on the ground with the Bolex and 16mm film spilling out everywhere! There wasn't a treatment or anything like that – I just shot them messing around and dancing at various local spots. A big old Cadillac that Keith was car surfing on – I think it was the same car we used in 'On a Ragga Tip' by SL2.[13]

'Out of Space' scores high in authenticity in the sense proposed in the Introduction: as a matter of interpretation which is made and fought for from within a culture. As Moore says, 'it is ascribed, not inscribed' (Moore 2002: 210). The silly, hedonistic humour of the video is authentic to the rave culture in which the band originated; Keith Flint sniffs Vicks VapoRub dressed in a mask and yellow gloves. As well as genuine footage of the band's live shows to authenticate their roots, the video intercuts footage of ostriches.

Another example is Flowered Up's *'Weekender'* (1992), directed by WIZ in documentary style on 16mm, colour with a total run time of 18 mins. The anti-nine-to-five message of *'Weekender'* is backed by samples of Jimmy (Phil Daniels) from The Who's *Quadrophenia* (1979). It was perceived by fans to be an authentic representation of what it's like to be high on drugs. The film was also shown on Channel 4 and championed by Annie Nightingale and Pete Tong, and secured attention outside of the music press and television. British newspaper the *Daily Star* ran a piece claiming that 'Sick rave band Flowered Up has made an outrageous film showing drug abuse kids.'[14]

Jake Nava explained his process for enabling Ms Dynamite to anchor her videos in the authorship and authenticity of the garage scene. It illustrates the skill and sensitivity required for a director to ensure that an artist's existing fanbase feels the artist has remained faithful and authentic to their roots, whilst new fans from a different demographic are attracted to the music by an additional visual hook. Ms Dynamite had come from the garage scene. Her music had evolved with more mainstream potential, and she had ended up becoming a priority act for the label who allocated her a 'good budget'. Nava felt, 'here is a new British female artist who had a really fresh sound that felt eclectic.

She had one foot in America and one foot firmly in England' and wasn't, like some other acts of the era, being derivative of America: she was rapping with an English accent, yet with a strong production sound 'put together by a big American producer . . . It was less street than some of her stuff, but the street didn't dislike it and the mainstream were drawn to it.' Nava describes making *'It Takes More'* (2002):

> The first video that I did for her was conceptualised by her and her crew. They came with the idea that she's on a fake music video set. She looks around her and feels like, 'I'm being manufactured . . .' So she jumps in the hired car to go back to her area where they are having a big street party. Everyone comes out and joins: people from all walks of life, *real* people. A little kid – an abstraction from these regressive gangster rap videos – looks down from one of the flats and sees Ms Dynamite's more positive representation. He is drawn to her. The video says: be true to yourself.[15]

In their interviews for this book, directors Sophie Muller, Andy Morahan and Dawn Shadforth described making music videos as a collaborative practice. Only when 'all the stars are aligned' and the artist and label and management are on the same page does a great video happen. In some videos the legal author, dominant creative author, main power-holder, performer and textual voice resides in one and the same person (in the videos of Kate Bush, for example). But whilst Kylie Minogue is the textual voice of *'Can't Get You Out of My Head'* and holds some element of legal authorship in the track, the origination of the video idea and the power and control exercised to make it were Shadforth's, who felt it a more 'director-authored' piece than the previous work on which they had collaborated. The key collaboration is between the artist and the director, and it's in the power of other corporate figures to find a director who is driven by a vision that empowers the artist, announces her voice and channels her voice to her audience. There remains a very strong case for students of a new 'music video appreciation' to seek out 'signature styles' or 'hallmarks' of creative teams and individuals in music videos. As Railton and Watson have urged, the danger of auteurism is not the search for hallmarks *per se*, but the search only for hallmarks of one creative individual in the film; the risk of obscuring the role of music, performance and other creative personnel (2011: 68). Perhaps the most famous example of the collision of the two production cultures is articulated in Noel Gallagher's voiceover to the collected videos on his DVD (Oasis, *Time Flies . . . 1994–2009*, 2010). It is represented again by John Hardwick in his video the *'Ballad of the Mighty I'* (2014) for Gallagher's band High Flying Birds, with a young pretentious wannabe-Italian film director counterpoised to the serious musician who wants to play live.

Notes

1. P. Romhanyi, personal communication, 7 November 2016.
2. P. Romhanyi, personal communication, 7 November 2016.
3. P. Romhanyi, personal communication, 7 November 2016.
4. P. Romhanyi, personal communication, 7 November 2016.
5. N. Goffey, Dom & Nic personal communication, 9 February 2016.
6. N. Goffey, Dom & Nic personal communication, 9 February 2016.
7. S. Beckett, personal communication 11 August 2016.
8. J. Nava, personal communication, 12 December 2016.
9. D. Gent, personal communication, 27 October 2016.
10. D. Gent, personal communication, 27 October 2016.
11. D. Gent, personal communication, 27 October 2016.
12. D. Gent, personal communication, 27 October 2016.
13. R. Curtis, personal communication, 25 April 2017.
14. *Daily Star*, 14 May 1992, as quoted in WIZ, personal archives.
15. J. Nava, personal communication, 12 December 2016.

7 DISTRIBUTION

How have British music videos been distributed in the fifty-year period since 1966? Existing scholarship focuses overwhelmingly on MTV (Denisoff 1991, Kaplan 1987, Marks and Tannenbaum 2012, Austerlitz 2007, Banks 1996). Even Andrew Goodwin's *Dancing in the Distraction Factory*, with the declared ambition to tell the story not of American music video but of British music video, dedicates two chapters to MTV (Goodwin had relocated to the USA during the writing of the book). This has led to a widespread public perception that music videos throughout the 1980s and 1990s were synonymous with MTV, and that MTV was the main viewing platform for British youth. But this is not supported by the evidence on television distribution and audiences. In this chapter, I detail the changing distribution of music videos in Britain between 1966 and 2016. I present evidence about the uniquely British television and home entertainment formats through which British audiences have engaged with video since the 1970s; and I then move on to suggest some ways in which authorship and genre have altered in the YouTube era, based on the experiences of directors, producers and commissioners working in the industry in 2016.

Television

In the 1960s, promotional clips were pre-recorded inserts made for youth- and music-focused television shows. They were made when a band wasn't able to appear live on the show. The mimed studio performance inserts for *TOTP*

(BBC 1964–2006) were usually filmed on a Wednesday. They were recorded on film or Ampex (Smith 2019: 6), and often commissioned by band management. One of the earliest examples is the Moody Blues' '*Go Now*' (1964) clip (Smith 2019: 7–8). Peter Whitehead quickly became a creative innovator in the field, and it was during this era that landmark pop promos for The Kinks, The Who, Pink Floyd, the Dave Clark Five, The Animals, The Beatles and Manfred Mann were made.

The BBC's attitude towards pop promos and music videos appears to have been mixed. The corporation disliked them because it could not categorise them as programmes or adverts. On either definition, they were inadmissible. As programmes they were inadmissible because the BBC was a producer, not a broadcaster who purchased independently produced programmes (like ITV). As adverts they were inadmissible because the BBC was a charitable organisation funded from public money through the licence fee, and was not permitted to advertise. The default rule was therefore that an artist-supplied promo should not be used to promote the single climbing up the charts, but must only be used if the single had already achieved chart success and if the artist was unavailable for the scheduled *TOTP* studio recording.

Fryer, in his study of music television in Britain from the 1960s to the mid-1980s, has found evidence that in the 1970s the BBC increased its screening of videos both on *TOTP* and the Saturday-morning shows. He cites Halliwell (1986: 840) describing *TOTP* as 'another outlet for pop videos' (Fryer 1997: 156). This was caused by a shift in BBC policy to support new music in the show, 1977–85. It meant the show would present a band before the band had climbed up the charts (normally, a band would only appear after this). A clip might also be used if the band didn't want to mime for the main studio recording.

In 1979, *TOTP* was securing viewing figures of 19 million (*The Guardian* 2004). Nigel Dick describes the process when he recounts commissioning videos for Stiff Records towards the end of the decade, although by this point, record labels had begun to employ pluggers to promote videos directly to television producers. With the successful broadcast on *TOTP* of '*Video Killed the Radio Star*' (Russell Mulcahy, 1979), '*Pop Muzik*' (Brian Grant, 1979) and '*I Don't like Mondays*' (David Mallet, 1979), showing a video became more standard. But there were caveats. The video had to meet *TOTP*'s definition of an acceptable video. The producers initially refused to broadcast Kate Bush's '*Running Up That Hill*' (David Garfath / Kate Bush, 1985) and '*Cloudbusting*' (Julian Doyle / Kate Bush, 1985) because they lacked synchronised vocal performance. There were rows behind the scenes. Labels would threaten, 'If you don't show this video, we won't let our other band who are likely to be number one appear on the show.' Fryer believes that filmed inserts, controlled by the artist, were rare prior to the explosion of video in Britain in the mid-1980s. Occasionally, videos such as David Bowie's '*John, I'm Only Dancing*' (Mick Rock, 1972) were banned because they were seen as potentially subversive for the intended teen audience. Frankie Goes to Hollywood's *'Relax'* (Bernard Rose, 1983) video was banned for its homosexual content (Fryer 1997: 164).

In the late 1970s, possibly the most important screening platform for British audiences was *TISWAS* (ITV 1974–82), a kids' TV show created by ATV which aired on Saturday mornings. In 1978, episode 7 of series 5 of *TISWAS* (TX 21/10/78), for example, showed videos of Dr Feelgood's *'Down at the Doctor's'*, Elton John's *'Part Time Love'*, The Boomtown Rats' *'Rat Trap'* (David Mallet, 1978) and The Moody Blues' *'Driftwood'* (*TV.com* n.d.). The videos were often the main feature of a guest voting segment, so stimulated debate about the merits of the new artistic medium, particularly those videos targeted at kids. The videos of Madness, directed by Stiff founder and MD Dave Robinson and strongly targeted at a British audience of schoolkids, were ideal. *TISWAS* had a large audience, especially of the impressionable youth demographic age group who could purchase the promoted singles at their local record store on Saturday afternoon. In marketing terms, the smaller the gap between exposure and an opportunity to purchase the advertised product, the greater the likelihood of the purchase being made. *TOTP*, screened midweek, had no such narrow gap. As a consequence, pluggers would wrestle to get their videos onto the producers' list for *TISWAS*. By contrast, other music shows on the BBC such as *The Old Grey Whistle Test* (BBC2 1971–88) vehemently preferred live performance from bands and consistently turned up their noses at music video.

During the 1970s and 1980s, bands increasingly refused to conform to the BBC's rigid guidelines for mimed studio performance on the show, because it undermined their authenticity. For post-punk bands, miming on a stage surrounded by awkward, fawning teenagers with pre-set camera moves introduced by radio DJs lacking credibility was not the way they wanted to be perceived by their fans, and was not always right for the attitude or genre of the song they were promoting. Malcolm McLaren, following this line of argument, was apparently angered by the appearance of the Sex Pistols performing 'Pretty Vacant' in 1977. This led to the rise of independently produced clips being made by artists' management companies and sent to the BBC instead.

There were two cases where the bands insisted videos were sent to *TOTP* for this reason: Queen's *'Bohemian Rhapsody'* (1975) and UB40's *'Red Red Wine'* (1984). The video for 'Bohemian Rhapsody' was filmed, edited and mixed live by Bruce Gowers at Elstree studios, where Queen were rehearsing for their tour, because the band didn't think the song would be credible if they were seen to mime to it in the *TOTP* aesthetics of the time (Roseman 2010). When the BBC refused to screen *'Red Red Wine'* on *TOTP* because of its 'unsuitable content' (alcohol, violence), an angered band insisted their management say they were out of the country; the BBC relented and screened the video.[1] The music video in Britain developed, then, as a way for artists to be in charge of their own television performance because the uncreative, bland and homogeneous way in which the multi-camera studio teams on shows like *TOTP* presented their mimed performances damaged their authenticity. (*The Old Grey Whistle Test* and, subsequently, Jools Holland's *Later* avoided this problem by allowing bands to perform live.) If miming was to be done, it had to be done in a creative way that endorsed the artists' authenticity.

With the exception of *TOTP* and the Saturday-morning kids' shows, however, Britain's music video industry was mainly an export industry until the late 1980s. In the 1960s the key market was North America. Broadcast listings for the *Ed Sullivan Show* (CBS 1948–71) in the 1960s reveal that both The Beatles and the Dave Clark Five (the British pop acts who appeared most frequently) supplied a number of clips on tape and film, while *Shindig!* (ABC 1964–6) frequently represented British acts *in absentia* on tapes acquired from *TOTP* or *Ready, Steady, Go!* Videos were also screened on *Popclips* for the Nickelodeon cable channel in 1977, which Michael Nesmith of the Monkees had been involved in setting up (Austerlitz 2007: 29). In his autobiography, Roseman claims to have been involved in setting up HBO's influential *Video Jukebox* (1981–6), a series of thirty-minute episodes that showcased music videos from popular artists of the time such as Duran Duran, David Bowie and the Human League.

During the late 1970s (and before the MTV network debuted), HBO was already airing one or two promo clips as fillers in between their feature films and other series. These short clips also carried the *Video Jukebox* moniker. When *Video Jukebox* premiered as a half-hour series in December 1981, HBO was reaching more households than MTV (which had been launched only four months earlier), so for about a year, until MTV caught up to HBO's subscriber count, a video that aired on *Video Jukebox* may have received more exposure there than it would on MTV. The series had no host until September 1985; this may have been an inspiration for the presenterless format of *The Chart Show* in Britain, launched in 1986.

But Europe was also important. Smith reports that European television channels were keen to screen British music videos: the continental European pop show, West German Radio Bremen's *Beat-Club* (Erstes Deutsches Fernsehen 1965–72), showcased some videos which the BBC had deemed unsuitable for *TOTP*, such as Peter Whitehead's political promo for the Rolling Stones' '*We Love You*' (1967). Whitehead's innovative promo for Eric Burdon and The Animals' '*When I Was Young*' (1967) was sold to Dutch television for £45. The Kinks' self-made social comment promo for '*Dead End Street*' (1966), also rejected by *TOTP*, was subsequently shown on the French TV show *Bouton Rouge* (ORTF 1967–8) in early 1967, and Belgian television's *Vibrato* on 8 March 1967 (Smith 2019: 534). The same year, *Beat-Club* screened Peter Goldmann's videos of '*Strawberry*

Fields Forever' (1967) and '*Penny Lane*' (1967) in *colour* (Smith 2019). By 1979, British record labels were making promos for single releases as a standard procedure and sending them to Europe.[2] But Roseman reports that Japan was also starting to screen British promos on popular music television shows in the late 1970s (2010).

When MTV launched in 1981, its main content was British. British Producer Kris P. Taylor moved to New York in 1980 to pursue a career in photography, and witnessed the birth of MTV first-hand. She found herself gravitating to music because 'all the English bands were playing there: Adam and the Ants, Human League, OMD, Depeche Mode, The Police. And then Boy George, Culture Club, Eurythmics.'[3] She took a job in the PR department of Island Records placing British videos for British artists in US clubs such as the Ritz. Prior to the launch of MTV, Taylor explains that,

> the biggest outlet for videos was actually clubs – dance clubs – and there were probably forty or fifty around the country. And then small TV channels. And then MTV was launched in August 1981. And it was just so exciting. We just couldn't wait for this when it was announced, we were going to have a cable channel that would play music videos all day long. And they played an Island video, The Buggles' '*Video Killed the Radio Star*'. I didn't really have anything to do with that but then after that I used to hand-deliver the videos to MTV when they arrived.[4]

When MTV launched on 1 August 1981 with the British video for '*Video Killed the Radio Star*', it had a contract only to air in New York and it had very little content to screen. Geralde Casale reports that, as a result, 'they played the same ten videos all day long': Rod Stewart videos (which British producer John Roseman was making), David Bowie videos (which British producer Scott Millaney was making), '*Video Killed the Radio Star*' (directed and produced by David Mallet and Scott Millaney), and the Vapours' '*Turning Japanese*' (Russell Mulcahy, 1980) (Prato 2011: 42). For Bob Pitman, 'the risk we took was, we'll launch with 200 videos. It ain't enough to have a network, but if we work, the record companies will make more videos' (Prato 2011: 38).

In his office on Golden Square in London's Soho, British producer Scott Millaney received a phonecall from Bob Pitman, asking: 'Are you that guy who's making loads of videos in the UK that the BBC has banned?' When Millaney replied 'Yes,' Pitman said: 'Put those tapes in a suitcase and get on a flight to New York: I need them.'[5] Siobhan Barron, who launched production company Limelight with her directing brother Steve, remembers taking commissions directly from MTV and mediating between the British record labels and MTV to secure the budget and negotiate a release date.[6] British labels were ahead of the game: A Flock of Seagulls' Mike Score recalls that the band's album *A Flock of Seagulls* (1982) was 'sitting on the shelf waiting for something to happen' when 'Clive Davis, who owned Jive Records, which we were on, came to us and said, "We're going to do a promo clip, because there's a new company called 'MTV' and they're looking out for promos from new bands"' (Prato 2011: 46).

Because of the BBC's stranglehold on television and the fact that the UK only had two terrestrial channels and no cable or satellite yet, many British videos from the early 1980s were rarely or never viewed by British audiences on British television sets. Contrary to the amount of focus on MTV in British scholarship, MTV was not widely viewed in the UK until much later, because cable and satellite were not widely available. It wasn't until the mid-1990s that MTV made any significant inroads in the UK. In 1992, for example, it had only achieved a 1.6 per cent viewing share, and this was an all-time high (BARB 2016, cited in Smith 2017: 13). By 1999, this had fallen to 0.4 per cent (although this was offset by an increase in viewing of the other MTV channels, such as MTV2), less than the audience for Discovery that year (0.5 per cent) (ITC / BARB 2001, cited in Chalaby 2002: 189). One of the reasons MTV wasn't especially popular in the UK, even when cable and satellite were more widespread, was because from the late 1980s onwards MTV USA offered a large amount of US music, and MTV Europe a lot of Eurotrash. British videos for British bands were mainly available on the British music television shows.

All of this changed with the launch of Channel 4. MTV attracted so much attention in the USA when it launched in 1981 because it was so distinctly different from mainstream TV. It did not have that edge in the UK from November 1982 onwards, when Channel 4 launched. MTV's raucous voice of popular music culture by youth, about youth and for youth was, by contrast, achieved in the UK with the launch of *The Tube* (C4 1982–7) in 1982. It was dynamic, youth-authored, *authentic* music programming for television. That was part of the founding vision for Channel 4, and a driving motivation for the music commissioning of the channel.

The Tube was followed by the launch of *The Chart Show* (Channel 4 1986–8 and ITV 1989–98), which delivered a British version of what scholars such as Goodwin, Grossberg and Kaplan were celebrating as so unique in MTV: dedicated postmodern programming of the video clip. *The Chart Show* was even more radical than MTV because, like *Popclips*, it did not have a presenter. So whilst MTV was available in the UK in the 1990s, it was not widely watched, because not all households received cable or satellite and because other British-born video shows secured much higher viewing figures. *The Chart Show* replaced radio as the platform for breaking new British artists to new British bands for a period in the 1990s. Whilst today it is tempting to attribute this to the dominance of the visual, it was also because back in the 1990s there was no equivalent to Radio 6. It was possible to secure airplay on the radio for established bands and TV time for established bands, but breaking new bands was the focus of the record industry in the 1990s, which had money to spend on this whilst it reaped the dividends of CD sales of back catalogues.

During the 1990s, British television audiences were primarily consuming music videos through *The Chart Show* and *Live and Kicking* (BBC1 1993–2001), and to a lesser extent the ITV programme *SM:tv* (Blaze / ITV 1998–2003). *Live and Kicking* was a morning children's magazine programme which, like *TISWAS*, featured a voting segment for Video of the Week. According to the BBC, the show's popularity was at its peak during the 1996/7 series presented by Zoe Ball and Jamie Theakston, when it regularly had 2.5 million viewers. This later fell, and by 2001 ITV's competitor Saturday-morning show, *SM:tv*, was attracting 1.8 million against *Live and Kicking*'s 0.8 million (Wells 2001).

Aware of its weak footprint in the UK, MTV launched MTV UK in 1997. However, within a few years of the number of British households subscribing to MTV beginning to rise, MTV decided to drop music video programming as the content for its main channels. This was partly a result of deep problems within the organisation. It coincided with the decision to axe *The Chart Show*, leading to the collapse of the captive audience in Britain and an increasingly fragmented audience for music videos. It is conventional to describe the death-toll of music videos as 1998, when *The Chart Show* was axed and MTV announced that it would change its programming from music videos to reality shows. Crisis meetings between the Music Video Producers' Associations in London and LA were held. Commissioners ceased automatically to make videos for the first three single releases from an artist's album, and MTV ceased its regular main-channel broadcasts of music videos. After the events of 9/11 in New York and widespread fears about a global recession, the record labels put a brake on spending. Budgets for low- to middle-range established artists were cut back. Spending on videos for new artists was stopped, because none of the channels were screening new artists; budget was reserved for established international acts who were still guaranteed to get airtime on MTV. VH1 had largely moved away from screening new music videos by this time, too.

British music video then reinvented itself in grime on Sky's Channel U (subsequently Channel AKA). Today synonymous with Wiley, Skepta and label BBK, grime emerged in 2002 when garage was on the wane and Wiley made 'Eskimo' (some called it Eski-beat) – although it wasn't until 2004 that grime received mainstream chart success with Lethal Bizzle's *Forward Riddim* (2004), a year after Dizzee Rascal had won the Mercury Prize for *Boy in da Corner* (2003). Founded in 2003 by Darren Platt, Channel U was distinct from mainstream channels because it showed videos by unsigned artists. Five years earlier *The Chart Show* producers might have rejected these grime videos because of their lo-fidelity quality and lack of production value. MTV would have rejected them because they did not address a 'universal' (aka US) audience in their themes and iconography. But screening videos addressed to a distinctively British and often specifically London audience, was no problem for the Channel U producers. Because production of music videos had dropped, they were short of content, and the low quality of many videos was no bar to broadcast.

The aesthetic that emerged in grime videos is Britain's twenty-first-century punk. It originated for practical reasons. Roony Keefe, creator of the seminal *Risky Roadz* DVD series in 2004, describes it as a DIY style, 'birthed from wanting to get something done, and making it happen, regardless of budgets or camera quality' (Hancox 2017). When grime started in the early 2000s, digital cameras had not been widely adopted and smartphones didn't exist. The music could only be heard on pirate radio, which – being illegal, and with the stations constantly having to move location to evade the authorities – was hidden from view. Grime artists didn't have access to budgets or film production companies, so they began using home camcorders.

Grime was a refreshing antidote to the postmodern hyper-real and high-end Golden Era music videos of MTV and *The Chart Show* of the late 1990s. Grime videos showed, as Hancox says, 'a vision of the British capital dominated not by Big Ben and Buckingham Palace, but brutalist tower blocks, chicken shops, off-licences, bus stops and bored teenagers mucking about on council estates' (Hancox 2017). The references of grime videos were very real. Videos such as the Mitchell Brothers feat. Kano, '*Routine Check*' (2005), took issue with the Metropolitan Police Force's use of the stop and search law to harass young Black men, and advised what to do if stopped. Others articulated serious themes through comic lyrics and imagery, such as Jammer's '*Murkle Man*' (2005) and Bearman's '*Brown Bear Picnic*' (2005). When grime became a little more mainstream and successful, the artists reined it back in 2014 with a number of influential videos that reclaimed the earlier DIY aesthetic and authentic video, such as Skepta's '*That's Not Me*' (2014) and '*It Ain't Safe*' (2014), shot on an old VHS camera on the Tottenham estate where he grew up) and Wiley's '*On a Level*' (2014), which featured the main grime MCs: Wiley, Stormzy, Novelist and Giggs.

Home Video

The era in which music videos functioned as an industrial advertising product was very brief: from the late 1970s to 1984. A television commercial was something a brand funded itself and paid a fee to a broadcaster to transmit, hoping to recoup those costs latterly from sales. Bob Pittman argued that MTV would only start to pay licence fees to the labels if and when music videos ceased to sell records: 'We clearly sell records for them. We have a nice symbiotic relationship with the record industry, and we don't want to change it' (Sanjek 1996: 646, Banks 1996: 45). But labels were starting to view music videos as an industrial product through which they could earn revenues from copyright, not as commercials. They were short *television programmes* for which broadcasters should pay. A 1984 report commissioned by the UK record industry stated that a music video should be defined as a visual work 'initially intended to stimulate sales of a single play record'; but '[i]t is a fallacy that record companies make video solely for promotional purposes . . . the increasing opportunities for commercial exploitation make it possible for record companies to see some, albeit very small at present, return on their investment' (Fisher 1984: 1). The report suggests a number of routes to increase commercial exploitation of video and raise revenues, such as domestic VHS sales and licensing of videos to airlines for in-flight viewing. By 1984, individual labels had started to charge licence fees (Banks 1996: 65) through the newly established Video Performance Limited (VPL), sister company to the MCPS (Mechanical Copyright Protection Society), PPL (Phonograph Performance Ltd) and PRS (Performing Rights Society). Block annual deals were made with the major TV networks – MTV, BBC and ITV.

In addition to licensing fees, record companies began to make money from music videos by selling them (on compilation or single-artist VHS tapes or, more recently, DVDs) via high-street shops such as HMV and Virgin Records. In 1984, Dave Laing wrote that,

> In Britain, there are now some 300 'long-form' music videotapes available to buy or rent. These are programmes with running times of anything above the average audio album length of 40 minutes. They account for some 5 per cent of the available catalogue of pre-recorded videocassettes. Of the 300, over half are simply films of live concerts and only about 18 per cent can be said to be 'original' long-form videos. The remainder consist of compilations of the short one-song music videos or re-releases of television shows. (Laing 1984: 79)

VHS sales were, in part, a way of avoiding the cultural gatekeepers at *TOTP* and MTV. In the early 1980s, Sheffield art–music–film collective Cabaret Voltaire started a VHS distributor in Sheffield called Doublevision, 'a short-lived but seminal hub of guerrilla film-making and mixed media mischief' (*Fact* 2011). Factory Records had also launched a VHS distributor, called FCL. Cabaret Voltaire had been making experimental sound and vision works informed by Dada, Burroughs and Gysin since the early 1970s, and in 1979 had collaborated with director Peter Care on an avant-garde short film entitled *Johnny Yesno*, which appears to have been their first release on the newly launched Doublevision VHS label in 1982. Throughout the early 1980s they continued to release pioneering mediatised performance videos through Doublevision. The central feature of *'Sensoria'* (Peter Care, 1984) was, for example, a landmark technique wherein the camera would appear to traverse gravity and spin in an unusual and dramatic arc.

British artists began to release video albums in the early 1980s as well. A video album was a compilation of videos united by a concept and sometimes woven together through an overarching narrative linked to the album, for which inserts were filmed. It was a medium through which artists could speak directly to their fans and to their audience, bypassing BBC producers, gatekeepers and preservers of the status quo. It suited the record labels, who were trying to maximise opportunities for commercial revenues from music video and long-form associated content (Kuhn 2002). Many of these video albums were directed by the leading British music video directors of the era, and included videos which were not broadcast on British TV or released to accompany individual single releases. Soft Cell's *Non-Stop Exotic Video Show* (1982) was directed by Tim Pope at GLO Productions as a companion release to their debut album, *Non-Stop Erotic Cabaret*, and was issued on VHS, Betamax and Laserdisc. Elton John's *Visions* (1982) contained videos all directed by Russell Mulcahy with input from Keith Williams, and was released on VHS and RCA's CED (Capacitance Electronic Disc) video disc in 1982 (to accompany the album *The Fox*).

Arena (An Absurd Notion) was a video album released by Duran Duran's label, PMI, on VHS in March 1985. It was based around a concept concert video filmed during the course of Duran Duran's 1984 *Sing Blue Silver* North American tour. Instead of releasing a straight concert video, Mulcahy added a storyline and surreal elements that are interwoven with footage of the band performing on stage. Arena included Mulcahy's long-form video for *'The Wild Boys'*, which was originally planned as a teaser for a full-length feature film of the same name based on William S. Burroughs' 1971 novel *The Wild Boys: A Book of the Dead*. However, that film was never made. In 1988, Eurythmics released a video album titled *Savage* to accompany their 1987 album of the same name. Most of the videos were directed by long-term collaborator Sophie Muller, and followed Annie Lennox's character of a frustrated housewife-turned-vamp. Lennox would go on to make another thematic video album for her 1992 solo album *Diva*, again directed by Muller.

Some of these were retrospectively distributed video compilations, rather than works preconceived as video albums: Kate Bush's *The Hair of the Hound* (1986) and its successor *The Whole Story* (1987) were both video compilations released on laserdisc and VHS. The Rolling Stones' *Video Rewind* (1984), released on VHS and laserdisc, was a compilation of video clips recorded between 1972 and 1984, although instead of presenting unrelated videos it used a framing story directed by Julien Temple featuring Wyman and Jagger. Bananarama's *'The Video Singles'*, released by Channel 5 in 1987, was a compilation release of four videos from the *True Confessions* album. Matt Johnson's account of the rationale behind The The's video album *Infected* (1986) gives insight into the format. Johnson explained that he came to the video album idea after reaching a 'crossroads' in his career. 'Having not played live for three and a half years and having such a low profile – for instance not having my picture on my sleeves – I decided to raise the whole stakes of the thing and risk becoming known a lot more as a personality' (Pye 1986: 13). Peter Christopherson, Mark Romanek and Tim Pope were three of the directors brought on board with a £350,000 advance from CBS records. The completed film was premiered at the Electric Cinema in West London, and screened on Channel 4 in 1986, followed by a showing on MTV. It was shown at independent cinemas across the world and released on VHS video early in 1987. It has never been released on DVD.

One of the first compilation DVDs released by the music industry was Björk's 1998 *Volumen*. Record labels soon caught up by releasing collected editions for other artists, but the post-2001 exploitation of music video back catalogues on DVD and Blu-Ray (such as those released recently for The Beatles and Pink Floyd) was not included, so this chapter now moves on to look at the impact of the internet in Britain.

Internet

The British music video production industry made a gradual transition to digital in the early 2000s. For the purposes of this essay, I date the digital distribution period from 2006, when YouTube was purchased by Google – for it was during the two years from 2006 to 2008 that the record labels grappled most overtly with the challenge of how to use the internet effectively as a promotional platform in the way that TV shows had used music video. Could the old model of a music video be transferred onto this model? The challenge to the old model had in fact begun much earlier, when *The Chart Show* was axed, when The Box changed its programming and when MTV decided that its main channels would broadcast mostly lifestyle content, providing airtime only for fully established artists. What was gone was the era in which TV could be used as radio had been in the 1950s: to break new and unknown artists. What had gone was a *captive audience*. In fact, the disappearance of the captive audience did not happen overnight; it was a graduated absence, consisting of a series of steps that transformed viewers from 'passive' recipients of broadcasting by an elite of planners into active creators of, and searchers for, content online: from the addition of Channel 4 to the portfolio of linear TV channels that disrupted and splintered the audience, to the use of the remote control on the TV, which made channel-hopping easier, to the wide uptake of multiple new channels on satellite and cable, including MTV's additional specialist channels. The old model of music video, like the old model of television advertising, relied upon a captive audience. When that captive audience dissolved into the ephemera of YouTube, the old model stopped working.

How have genres of music video been affected by digital? Everyone interviewed felt the performance genre had declined since YouTube. Video commissioner Carrie Sutton explained: 'How many performance videos have already been done? How do you make a performance video that people want to watch and how do you make it different?'[7] How can a performance video stand out from the vast array of archive band performance footage that's already on the internet? Videos such as Don Letts and The Clash's '*London Calling*' or Joy Division's '*Love Will Tear Us Apart*' would no longer stand out. The authorial sincerity of performance videos such as '*Unfinished Sympathy*' and '*No Surprises*', which worked so well on broadcast television, don't work on the internet, which almost requires an ironic authorial tone.

Instead, the internet appears to prioritise the spectacle. Hot Chip's '*Over and Over*' (2006) illustrates this postmodern excess. Directed by Nima Nourizadeh, it shows the band performing in front of a green screen with tracking points for CGI to be imposed at a later date. This footage is intercut with shots of storyboards and other elements in the filmmaking process. The video is authenticating itself by placing itself in the tradition of pastiche and self-parody, revealing all the inner tricks of the trade of the filmmaking apparatus. It is beyond postmodern because it knows it is postmodern. Another is Disclosure's '*Grab Her*' (Emile Sornin 2014), which mines from the British comedy television series *The Office* (BBC 2001–3). Produced at Riff Raff and directed by Sornin, a French director, the video begs the trick film question, 'how did they do that?' As well as postmodern pastiche, both films foreground Tom Gunning's novelty of the spectacle and confirm his thesis that in the age of YouTube, novelty and spectacle attract (1990a).

But the internet has also arguably seen an increase in post-punk, DIY authenticity. Some of the changes are a result not of the internet *per se*, but what has been called the 'democratisation' of production that has taken place in Britain. Whereas in the 1960s and 1970s, film production equipment could (in the main) only be accessed at art school or by working in the industry, by the 2000s the same forces that made grime videos for Channel AKA possible made all genres of video possible. Cheap digital cameras, home computers, editing software and iPhones democratised film production. Artists could produce and distribute their own videos without record labels. Blunt's '*Mersh*' (2016) illustrates this. The video features nothing more than three minutes of Blunt sitting on a couch in a red T-shirt and red Polo hat, with a white girl in shades sporting a sweatshirt that says MIAMI, sharing a joint and occasionally rapping while a red light strobes.

Carrie Sutton believes Spike Jonze's video for Fatboy Slim's '*Praise You*' (1998), commissioned by John Hassay at Skint, was 'prescient of the YouTube era'. Although it was released in 1998, 'you'd think it was a YouTube video, playing with that very low-fi idea "was it real or was it not real". "Praise You" was one of the first videos that was made in a different way and connected in a different way. You'd think Jonze saw it coming.'[8]

The rise of non-commissioned lyric videos and mash-ups initially met with legal action by the labels. But since 2016, when revenues from unofficial videos outstripped revenues from licensing official videos because the labels successfully negotiated deals with Google and YouTube for a percentage of advertising income (Eastwood 2014), the labels have encouraged them. When a pop act releases a new song, they'll make a vertical video (optimised for viewing on smartphones), a lyric video (a label response to the flurry of lo-fi fan-made vids on YouTube), an official video and often a 'making of' video to boot. 'Lyric videos are becoming increasingly complex,' says Sony's vice-president of creative, Mike O'Keefe.

> Fans want an immediate representation of the track, then the official video creates another spike of excitement. We did a highly stylised performance of George Ezra singing the songs for his recent lyric videos, while Dua Lipa's lyric video for 'One Kiss' had an Instagram feel, which also went down incredibly well. (Haider 2018)

Initially the problem was of how to break a new artist on the internet amidst so much traffic. There was a nostalgia for the gatekeepers and filters of broadcast television. But then two releases produced a model to show labels how videos could be used to promote artists. The first was not British: OK Go's video for *'Here It Goes Again'* (2006), featuring an intricate dance routine performed on eight treadmills, turned the band into an international act when it went viral and was named Most Creative Video by YouTube in 2006. The second was made by a creative agency team and production company in London with a French director: Cadbury's *'Gorilla'* advert (2007), though not a music video, was produced by a music video company and visualised a British track. *'Gorilla'* became a canonised model for what could be achieved with an entertaining and novelty visual effect wrapped around a 'how did they do that?' question. But, unlike *'Here It Goes Again'*, *'Gorilla'* evoked emotion and brought a historic track by a British artist (Phil Collins) back to life. Video commissioner Carrie Sutton calls it the 'click on' effect: when enough users like or tag others, a clip goes viral. To be compelling, a video needs to have an element of novelty – which could be an intensely pleasurable element, a nostalgic element, a comedic element or an effect.

It is arguable that the internet has facilitated a simpler narrative, more influenced by photography than feature films. Jon Hopkins' *'Open Eye Signal'* (2013) is an important work by Aoife McArdle in which very little happens. It is a narrative without drama. McArdle has described it as 'a singular, hypnotic journey that's almost endless' (Minsker 2013). It is an eight-minute-long road movie with a difference; it charts the journey of a lone skateboarder through the awesome landscapes of the American West to the soundtrack of Hopkins' epic track. What appears to be the start of a narrative, as the skateboarder jumps onto his board and heads off, turns out to be simply about the increasingly existential, occasionally surreal journey itself. Things happen, but they are neither caused by the lead actor nor do they have an effect on the lead actor – they are seemingly inconsequential. So the narrative defies the generic rules of mainstream US film drama.

This absence of dramatic structure and the foreground of the photographic paradigm are also evident in the photographic genre and the GIF. The video for Mount Kimbie's *'Before I Move Off'*, released in late 2010, was made up of hundreds of fast-moving photographs. When sequenced together, these photographs generate a stream-of-consciousness story of life. One hundred and fifty-one of the images were uploaded via Mount Kimbie's Facebook, so they could be appreciated individually. London-based photographer and filmmaker Tyrone Lebon took all of the photographs.

But our interviewees felt the traditional model of commissioning a high-end video for a major international artist would persist, because of the continued examples of artists for whom that model works. In Britain, One Direction were an example of a pop band led very much by video. Their video for *'Best Song Ever'* (2013), commissioned by Mike O'Keefe in the London offices of Sony, broke the then Vevo twenty-four-hour record with 12.3 million views. Sony artists Little Mix are also video-led. O'Keefe explained that in the internet age, all artists are international; there are no more local music genres for whom they commission targeted genre videos.

> Videos are still very important, and they're the worldwide calling card for an artist. So if you want to break a band across the world: make a really good video that resonates everywhere; that will be the job fifty per cent done; the artists have all got to go out there and do promo and TVs and all the rest of it, but it's really important. I mean, we want everyone to be international these days. I've just shot the video for Little Mix's 'No More Sad Songs'. The track's already been out four weeks, five weeks. When they dropped the video, the video got like five million views in twenty-four hours and it shot up iTunes, it shot up the sales chart.[9]

Since my interview with O'Keefe, the chart regulations have changed. From July 2018, the UK singles charts have included online views of music videos on YouTube and other video sites. That reflects the industry's recognition of those sites in music consumption and appreciation.

Some interviewees stressed the greater creative freedom of the internet's reduced regulation (the impact of British Board of Film Classification (BBFC) certification has barely been felt). 'MTV had all these rules where you couldn't do this, you couldn't do that, you couldn't smoke, you couldn't drink, you couldn't mutilate toys. It was relentless. I still have a huge pack at home of the rules.' For Sutton there is more artistic space to create something arresting, unusual or controversial on the internet.

> Now it's the opposite, so when an artist is, musically, referring to something very visceral and very real and very gritty and traumatic or a moment of violence in their lives, we say let's go with it, let's reflect that in the visuals, if it needs to be hard-hitting we'll make something hard-hitting because there aren't those rules now.[10]

The internet has also allowed more business freedom for alternative production models. Sutton notes that, increasingly, production companies are investing in music videos as short film showreel pieces to develop the portfolios of their directors. When a video is financed from other sources, filmmakers can retain their moral rights and copyright. Klein's *'Marks of Worship'* (Akinola Davies, 2016) illustrates this. It was an independently produced video rather than a commissioned video, and the copyright lay with the director, Akinola Davies. In an interview, Klein explains,

> Akin basically wanted to do a video for 'Marks of Worship' and I was like 'Really? "Marks of Worship" is not even a song!' I just wanted to make something that was really nice, me and my family and friends just having a great time and just being excellent, and that was it. We were listening to Rihanna and Vybz Kartel while we were shooting the video. [laughs] It was kind of a mess. (Saed 2016)

This model is not entirely new. Both Peter Whitehead in the 1960s and Derek Jarman in the 1980s approached musicians with a co-producing deal and retained copyright in their films. Liz Kessler confirms that music video has always been an industrial product, subsidised by other sectors of the entertainment industry through the reduced fees paid to crew and creatives. Since the 1980s, companies have invested in videos or raised finance from other sources from time to time to kick-start the career of individual directors, or stimulate a change of career or genre for a director. The rewards from such an investment come later when the director – it is hoped – generates income from advertising or TV.

Whilst Gunning is perhaps right to stress the revival of the novelty spectacle of content on YouTube, in Britain, the novelty spectacle of music video predated the internet. As Sherril Dodds observed, the 'arresting images' of New

Order's *'True Faith'* (Philippe Decouflé, 1987) video encouraged repeated viewings (Dodds 2001, 2004: 56). *'True Faith'* illustrates the imperative to deliver something bold and visually compelling without sacrificing intellectual content or artistic authenticity. Because director Philippe Decouflé was an esteemed artist, the band were not selling out with an irrelevant gimmick. When Chris Cunningham's video for Leftfield feat. Afrika Bambaata, *'Africa Shox'* (1999), was commissioned at the end of the 1990s, I remember sitting in the office of Mark Conway, label manager at Higher Ground, a semi-indie within Sony, with Cunningham, being given the brief. Conway explained that he was looking for a video concept which was intellectually interesting enough to warrant repeat viewings and analysis on Radio 4, but also captivating, compelling and entertaining enough to win the kids' vote on Saturday-morning TV.

Videos such as Dean Blunt's *'Mersh'* and the Fat White Family's *'Touch the Leather'* (Roger Sargent, 2014/16), illustrate the tendency of filmmakers to iron out dramatic structure when creating content to be viewed online, in favour of simplicity and repetition. The way that videos hail and hook viewers online is different to captive television. But repetition and flatness, whilst found in excess online in K-pop and the GIFs built into K-pop videos and memes, are not new. A sample look at the early videos of Devo and Talking Heads, such as *'Once in a Lifetime'* (Byrne / Basil, 1981), illustrates the pre-existence of that aesthetic. Like the later internet videos, they are simple, use repetition and do not have a dramatic developmental structure. The difference lies in the business of the screen. The superimposed insets of *'Once in a Lifetime'* would not work on YouTube or mobile because of the plethora of other content floating around on the screen, such as banner ads.

The idea that the internet functions like radio has found some currency in the British music video industry recently. YouTube is the world's second-largest search engine and third most visited site after Google and Facebook. In 2018, 95 per cent of the most watched videos were music videos. The point made by some, such as Liz Kessler, however, is that there is no evidence that these music videos are actually being watched rather than used as background radio. It is worth remembering that the same was said in some quarters of MTV in the early days. Weird Al Yankovic has recalled: 'Even if I wasn't actively watching, MTV would always be playing in the background, kind of like "video wallpaper"' (Prato 2011: 42). People had MTV parties in which MTV would be playing (aka 'streaming') in the background.

Mike O'Keefe at Sony says the data that Sony collects do not support this theory. When I asked him whether he thought music videos are heard, not seen, on YouTube, he replied:

> I don't know, maybe they do, but if they were going to do that why wouldn't they just put the lyric video on or the track? And then you

would imagine that the views would all balance out because it's just about the music but they don't seem to . . . Spotify streams, and Shazam, and obviously look at everything that happens on iTunes, but if you look at the business side of things lyric videos get, I don't know, say 10 per cent of views, other bits of content get 10 per cent of views, but the main official video still gets 80 per cent of the interest.[11]

In Britain, the fifth generation of video directors has emerged: amongst them Daniel Wolfe, Us, Aoife McCardle and Holly Blakey. But directors such as Jamie Thraves, Sophie Muller and WIZ continue to shoot videos too.

One view is that the potential for parody and pastiche has vastly increased. Reynolds argues that since the year 2000, media content has been increasingly 'flat' and there has been a 'deficit' of newness (2008: 405). In music history, he argues, the innovative '60s and '90s 'were each followed by a period of going-in-circles (the seventies and 2000s respectively)' (2011: 428). Since 2000, the music industry has seen 'potent musical intellects engage in a restless shuffling back and forth within a grid-space of influences and sources, striving frenetically to locate exit routes to the beyond' (Reynolds 2011: 427). It is also tempting to argue that the internet has increased the postmodern temperature of commissioned music videos.

Authors such as Holt have argued that the US trend of producing video albums, such as Beyoncé's *Lemonade* (2016), represent a wave of music becoming 'more visual' (2011). The internet age may have seen a more innovative visual aesthetics emerge in the USA, but the evidence I've presented thus far demonstrates that British innovation pre-existed the internet in the '60s, '70s and '80s. The experimentation of the video era with distribution outlets such as Doublevision is a key aspect of this overlooked history. As Sean Cubitt has argued, 'Cabaret Voltaire's *Sensoria* is an indicator of the transitional phase between pop video and the art sector' (Cubitt 1991: 89–90). But the 'transitional phase' to which Cubitt refers has been less a chronological period than a zone in which ongoing conversations between groups of practitioners engage.

Most British audiences viewed music videos on Channel 4 until the late 1990s, when The Box and MTV were more widely subscribed to, and subsequently on Channel U. In retrospect, many of the early cultural studies academics were not asking the question 'why music video?' but 'why MTV?' If we rephrase the question to ask 'why music video?' and try to tease out the distinctive story of British audiences and musicians, we cannot avoid the relationship between British art schools and the popular music industry, shifts in television distribution patterns and the democratisation of film technology. The 2000s have seen even more of a shift towards art, with the video by Us for Benga's '*I Will Never Change*' being featured in the Saatchi Gallery, and Chris Cunningham's videos exhibited at the Anthony d'Offay Gallery, the Royal

Academy of Arts and the Venice Biennale. But the 2000s have also seen a return to the DIY aesthetic of early punk in grime and YouTube content. It is to the subject of art that I turn next.

Notes

1. B. Rose, personal communication, 26 October 2016.
2. N. Dick, personal communication, 3 April 2017.
3. K. Taylor, personal communication, 2 December 2016.
4. K. Taylor, personal communication, 2 December 2016.
5. S. Millaney, personal communication, 12 April 2018.
6. S. Barron, personal communication, 22 April 2017.
7. C. Sutton, personal communication, 16 November 2016.
8. C. Sutton, personal communication, 16 November 2016.
9. M. O'Keefe, personal communication, 2 April 2016.
10. C. Sutton, personal communication, 16 November 2016.
11. M. O'Keefe, personal communication, 2 April 2016.

8 ART, COMMERCE AND AMERICA

In this chapter, I examine the differences between American and British videos from 1966 to 2016. I will begin by examining the impact Britain is thought to have had on the US music video industry through the first, second and third so-called 'British Invasions' of pop music. Then I will move on to look at distinctively British tendencies in music video, particularly in the pre-2000 period, drawing together the findings of the previous chapters.

INFLUENCE: FIRST, SECOND AND THIRD BRITISH INVASIONS

The argument underlying this book is that what we now call the music video began in a social, artistic and industry sense in London in the 1960s; the US music industry adopted it after seeing British videos on TV and realising in the mid-1980s that music videos were the most effective marketing method of the age to make money from music. They adopted the British style, mixed it with their own Hollywood musical style, higher budgets and superior slick effects, set designs and polished post-production, and served it back to the British as a US invention. As MTV was transformed from a small station transmitting only in New York into a *high-end corporate marketing model*, the world took note. But if the distinctively '80s music video began life in the UK, why was that, and what were the consequences of that?

In 1964, over 80 per cent of records sold in the USA were British. The concept of the 'British Invasion of America' was allegedly coined by CBS news anchorman Walter Cronkite to describe this. It's said to have begun in

February 1964, when The Beatles first appeared on the Sunday-night variety programme *The Ed Sullivan Show* (CBS 1948–71). When British bands weren't willing or able to travel to the States to perform live to meet demand from TV shows like this, they would send a video instead. The role of music video in the first British Invasion can be illustrated by the Dave Clark Five, an English group formed in 1957. Originating in North London, the band was promoted as the vanguard of a Tottenham Sound (as distinct from Liverpool's Mersey Beat sound). Of the British Invasion groups, they were the first to have a major US tour and the second to appear on *The Ed Sullivan Show* (two weeks in March 1964, following The Beatles' three weeks in February 1964). They made eighteen appearances on the show in total, more than any other group of the British Invasion.

Video and film played a key part in the Dave Clark Five's creative endeavour. In 1965, the band released *Catch Us If You Can*, directed by John Boorman (released in the USA as *Having a Wild Weekend*). In 1966, Clark produced and directed an original 35mm promo for the track 'Nineteen Days', which premiered to over 70 million viewers on *The Ed Sullivan Show* on 20 November 1966 (Collins 2018: 111). It was one of the first instances of non-performance footage being included in a promo clip, and one of the earliest boy band promos – selling a male band through sexualised imagery targeted at the female gaze. The video, which shows the band mucking around playing water sports, was made because the band did not want to go back on tour. In January 1967, the group formed its own film company, Big Five Films, to make low-budget features and documentaries. Through the company, in 1966, Dave Clark produced a promotional film titled '*Hits in Action*', which incorporated the footage and clips he had made and used to promote previous singles. It was distributed internationally in cinemas in front of the James Bond film *You Only Live Twice* (1967). Clark says he happened upon the idea of promotional clips whilst watching commercials on TV.[1]

What was singularly significant about this work was that it was authored by the artist, Dave Clark himself. Ray Davies had similarly conceived and directed the video for The Kinks' '*Dead End Street*' (1966) himself. In this new era, visual culture rivalled rock culture. Artists were increasingly writing their own material and defining their own visual identity – and authenticity – through films devised by themselves, executed in collaboration with directors. Dave Clark also insisted on a reversionary clause in the group's contract with record company EMI, which allowed him to claim ownership of all their recordings after the initial period of licence, including the rights to his promotional clips (Collins 2018: 27). So whilst 1966 marks the end of the British Invasion because the dominance of the British bands was starting to wane, it also marks the beginning of the authentic, authored art-school promotional clip that would dominate Britain for the next fifty years.

In 1981/2, most of the videos aired on MTV were either entirely British or were videos of US artists made by British filmmakers. The second British Invasion, or what Goodwin calls the first phase of MTV (1981–3), was distinctively different because it was *led by video*. It was an invasion of British video, not of British music. British music sold in the USA because the videos were played on MTV, not vice versa. In 1964, demand for British artists had been led by live tours, radio and live TV appearances. Promotional clips were supplied only in response to pre-existing demand – usually a direct request from a producer for the artist to appear on a show. But in the second Invasion, bands like Duran Duran sold records in the USA because they had played on heavy rotation on MTV. When they arrived in a state to tour, they could tell whether MTV had already launched in that state by whether or not they were recognised on the street. Bands whose music sold in the USA because of their videos include David Bowie, Eurythmics, Culture Club, Duran Duran, the Human League and Bananarama. In the account of the early years presented by Prato (2011), David Bowie's videos are cited more often than others as the most memorable and popular with VJs.

The domination of the US market by British producers in the '80s was only possible because British businesses had set up shop there. British production company MGMM set up an office in New York, then headquarters of MTV and the centre of the music business, to facilitate its directors Brian Grant, David Mallet and Russell Mulcahy to make videos for US artists and labels. The production company Limelight, founded in Soho in 1979, set up offices in Los Angeles in the 1980s for Steve Barron and his sister to work from. The Oil Factory, founded in 1985 and home to WIZ, Jamie Thraves and Sophie Muller, opened an office in LA in 1989. Black Dog Films had a sister company in LA, operating with the Ridley Scott Associates Family. Propaganda Films had offices in London, LA and New York, incorporating Satellite Films. The subsidiary benefit to the British companies was that it gave them access to Hollywood for directors with feature-film ambitions. Not all of the first generation of specialist British music video producers set up in the USA – GLO Productions (run by Gordon Lewis), Midnight (run by Michael Hamlyn, representing Julien Temple amongst others), Aldabra (run by Tim Bevan) and John Roseman Productions (representing Mike Brady and Duncan Gibbons) did not; instead, these companies drew up partnership agreements with LA-based production companies for joint representation. In the music industry, production companies act as talent agents as well as production companies, with exclusive deals to represent and produce for named directors in specified territories; this differentiates them from feature and television production companies.

In 1977/8, producer Jon Roseman reports taking *'Bohemian Rhapsody'* (1975) director Bruce Gowers to set up in Los Angeles, only to find that there was not a single production company making music videos in the city. Steve Barron confirms that the USA had no equivalent body of specialist production companies and post-production companies. Roseman says he had to fly British directors out to the USA from the UK to shoot 'anything that moved, including Ambrosia, April Wine, George Benson, Debbie Boone . . . Alice Cooper . . . Van Morrison . . . Supertramp, Van Halen and the Kinks' (2010: 94). Barron was hired by Michael Jackson's team after the manager saw that Barron's video for the Human League's *'Don't You Want Me'* (1981) on MTV had led to the track reaching number one in the US charts; it convinced him of the power of music video to sell records, and the skill of Barron as a director (Prato 2011: 147). Lacking US directors and production companies to produce the work, American labels hired British directors to work with many of their major international artists in the first six years of MTV. Brian Grant directed the Olivia Newton-John video for *'Let's Get Physical'* (1981); Steve Barron directed Michael Jackson's video for *'Billie Jean'* (1983); and Arlene Phillips choreographed Tina Turner's *'Private Dancer'* (1984), Whitney Houston's *'How Will I Know?'* (1985) and Houston's *'I Wanna Dance with Somebody'* (1987).

In his autobiography, Roseman wrote that he 'spent a long weekend at home trying again to figure out what was wrong with America and their antipathy to music videos'. He reached the conclusion that 'unlike Britain, there was no *Top of the Pops* or morning kid shows that would churn them out'. Record labels in the USA were very rarely commissioning videos because there were so few places to screen them in the 1970s. By contrast, '[t]he record companies in the UK saw them as an integral part of promotion and supplied them for free to any TV station who wanted them' (Roseman 2010: 104). This problem was only partly solved when, in 1981, HBO began to screen *Video Jukebox*, and then MTV was launched. MTV was initially only in New York, and it would be at least six years before US labels had a cluster of specialist US production companies and American directors.

Andy Morahan, who conceived and directed the epic *'November Rain'* video for Guns N' Roses (1991/2) – a video described by Austerlitz as a 'music video folly' (2010: 35) – explains the transition that he witnessed:

> After MTV started, people thought, 'Oh this is a great marketing tool, another great way of selling records' . . . MTV was exploding, it wasn't wallpaper like it is now, it was a cultural event: you would get a Friday night world premiere. The Americans in a way were slower than the English to cotton on to [music videos]. But boy, once they cottoned on to it, they took it to a whole other level. The pressure of being commissioned to do a video in America became a lot bigger. People in England were still having fun and experimenting with it. But from the USA you'd get calls from the MD's office virtually saying, 'We've got this artist and if you don't make a f***** good video I'm going to cut your legs off.' It became a much bigger thing, because America does that. It became

about bums on seats and money. Suddenly everybody wanted a piece of the action, and they wanted to do it brilliantly.[2]

From the late 1980s onwards, the USA embraced the medium. It developed an infrastructure of production companies specialising in music video along with a much stronger trade association than the UK had ever had (the MVPA), and an array of directors such as David Fincher, Mark Romanek and Spike Jonze. That explosion led to the escalation of American video budgets through the 1990s to the $3–4 million level: the aspirational videos directed by Hype Williams and Paul Hunter. This in turn created a tension, with British filmmakers feeling resentful that British labels were not spending equivalent budgets; as a result, Britain felt to some like the poor cousin of the USA.

But the overly slick, big-budget industrial apparatus that the USA created in the 1990s ultimately backfired when *authenticity* reared its head in the third and final invasion of the USA by British artists.

The third British Invasion arose from this crisis of authenticity in US R&B videos prompted by UK grime. On 4 December 2009, British newspaper *The Financial Times* ran a piece titled 'Boom Times for Black British Musicians'. Unlike American R&B, grime hadn't produced an escapist music video genre depicting a fantasy rich lifestyle. British grime artists had instead created a video genre about the very real places they came from: the genre abounds with neighbourhood anthems. Talking about the sudden interest from the USA, Skepta said in 2015: 'They have to come on my wave . . . I understand the objective now, and like, I ain't going to fucking America to shoot a video. They need to come to the roads with me' (Hancox 2017). The moment was marked by Drake's performance at the 2015 Brit Awards, for which he had seemingly all the UK's grime MCs join him on the stage, following which he announced that he was signing to Skepta's British record label, BBK. With US artists such as Pharrell spearheading collaborations with UK grime artists, it appeared to some observers that the British grime scene was lending some much-needed realism and authenticity to a music video genre that, in the USA, had gone too far in the direction of selling wealth as an aspirational dream. The video for Skepta's '*It Ain't Safe*' (2014) was shot on location on the Tottenham estate. In search of the early aesthetic of grime, the 2010s witnessed a resurgence of VHS-looking videos, not only in grime but in other pop music genres in search of authenticity and attitude. It was a salutary reminder that authentic music wasn't about the money – it was about the street, and about *keeping it real*.

THE CONDITIONS FOR BRITISH POP PROMO CREATIVITY

If music video was developed firstly in the UK, why was that, and what were the consequences of that, and why did it have a greater relationship with 'authenticity'? As always, the research cannot supply all the evidence, but it did generate some initial ideas about the necessary conditions for the high levels of productivity and innovation in British music videos throughout the 1960s, '70s and '80s. A number of possible factors stood out.

British art schools

The first factor is the role of the art school. Its contribution to economic growth in the creative industries has also been analysed by Banks and Oakley (2016) in light of changes in higher education since the 1980s. The state-funded art schools, many founded in the nineteenth century, offered the prospect of social and economic mobility for marginalised youth and tended to be seen as the working-class alternative to university. As Frith and Horne have argued, the art schools created 'stars' and musicians who were into visual media (1987). They cited Dave Laing's *One Chord Wonders* (1985), which suggested that 'nearly a third of punk rock musicians had been students of some kind and most of these had in fact studied art' (cited in Frith and Horne 1987: 127). Of the 1960s bands who pioneered music videos, Dave Clark, Ray Davies (The Kinks), Roger Waters and Nick Mason (Pink Floyd) went to the Hornsey College of Art; Paul McCartney and John Lennon (The Beatles) went to the Liverpool College of Art; Syd Barrett went to Camberwell School of Art; and Pete Townsend (The Who) went to Ealing Art College.

To these artists, the pop promo wasn't a marketing tool but an extension of their creativity, as their enthusiasm for embracing the new format illustrated. The promo shot on the beach featuring a mannequin made by Pink Floyd for 'Arnold Lane' (Derek Nice, 1967), for example, was written by Syd Barrett, who had studied painting at Camberwell. According to Nick Mason, a promo wasn't needed because *TOTP* wouldn't transmit promos unless in lieu of an act unable to travel to the show to perform live; but the band 'convinced' their manager that they needed a promotional film for it, and, since Derek Nice was the only film director they knew, asked him to direct it. An alternate promo was made shortly afterwards. Later leading video artists who went to British art schools included Freddie Mercury (Ealing Art College), Stuart Goddard / Adam Ant (Hornsey College of Art) and Jarvis Cocker, PJ Harvey and M.I.A. (Central St Martins). Many of the creative relationships and ensuing artistic album covers have recently been documented by Mike Roberts (2019) in his book *How Art Made Pop and Pop Became Art*.

But the film directors also came to music video through British art schools: Peter Whitehead, Derek Jarman (Slade), Godley and Creme (Manchester and Birmingham), Tim Pope (Hornsey and Ravensbourne), Andy Morahan (Central St Martins), Sophie Muller, Storm Thorgerson and Jamie Thraves (RCA); all of who were equally affected by the experimental culture. The art schools, in the words of Banks and Oakley, 'walked an uneven path between utility and ornament; between the purely pragmatic necessities of serving local industry and the desire of teachers and students to move beyond such "narrow" instrumental concerns' (2016: 4). These directors did not learn their craft or earn the right to direct by climbing the official trade union ranks. Shynola got their first computer to make '*Guns Blazin*" (1998) at art school. Richard Heslop made his '*7 Songs*' video at the London College of Printing (now LCC, the London College of Communication), using LCC's equipment, and Annabel Jankel and Rocky Morton made '*Accidents Will Happen*' (1979) and launched their animation company Cucumber – celebrated for pushing the boundaries of filmmaking with innovative combinations of animation, CGI and live action – after graduating from West Surrey College of Art and Design. In the words of Frith and Horne,

> Art schools place constant emphasis on experimental practice, but also preserve art's traditions, teach the established art techniques against which students are expected to rebel. Art school students have usually accepted the challenge, showing a healthy disdain for the demands of the past – except that is for the romantic demand that being an artist means living as an artist. (Frith and Horne 1987: 35)

British VFX and post-production industry

The second factor is the role of post-production. In Britain, music video was an R&D sector for post-production; the nascent post-production companies were mainly located in Soho alongside music video production companies, film labs and record stores (Caston 2019a). Rushes, for example, founded in 1977 (and closed in 2017), was a leading UK post-production house founded at the same time as the music video industry started to grow in Soho. It was famous for its music video work and had done the pioneering post on Dire Straits' '*Money for Nothing*' (Barron, 1985). It launched the Rushes short film festival and was the first in the UK to acquire a Rank-Cintel URSA (replaced with a Thomson Spirit) and a C-Reality Telecine, as well as being the first to adopt a Discreet (now Autodesk subsidiary) and Flame compositing suite. Many of the creative innovations of VTR, MPC, Molinaire, Framestore and The Farm were developed in collaboration with music video directors, who would be given 'reduced rate' overnight access to their facilities in exchange for allowing the post house creatives to experiment with new techniques, train junior creatives and trial new software. Acutely aware that in a three-minute silent video a director could not secure a viewer's attention by means of a dramatic plot turn or clever dialogue, many of those directors relied instead on post-production techniques to communicate ideas. Film and video artists, not based in the cluster with all the networking opportunities that Soho offered, lacked the opportunity to access post-production.

British moral rights and sales culture

The third reason was authenticity. The idea of artistic works as an extension of an artist's personality that could not be alienated is a powerful and deep-seated part of European (and British) creative culture, discussed in the chapter on authorship; this played no small part. Whereas in the USA, music videos were happily produced as alienated 'works for hire', in the UK, as a result of the European moral rights culture, British music videos were adopted more often within a production culture which saw them, *qua* 'creative works', *as an expression of one's own personal philosophy and identity*. When Austerlitz writes that '[m]usic videos are consumer products . . . simultaneously the casing for an agglomeration of consumerist lifestyle choices, and themselves the commodity which they advertise' (2007: 3), he describes primarily the music videos of the USA. In Britain, music video has very rarely been used by artists or labels to sell 'consumerist lifestyle choices'. The British aversion to music video as marketing is evident in British videos that parody established US genres, such as Chris Cunningham's '*Windowlicker*' for Aphex Twin (1999). It is no accident that most of the companies (and directors and producers) who directed music videos in Britain were also directing television commercials, from Steve Barron to Jonathan Glazer – because British commercials similarly rejected the US marketing trope. From the 1960s onwards, British agencies developed a soft sell aesthetic, distinct from the hard sell developed by US agencies of the 1950s (Fletcher 2008, Nixon 2013, Bernstein 1986, Garrett 1986). In campaigns for products such as Hamlet cigars and John Smith beer, British advertising agencies and productions drew, like the satirical videos described above, on comedy, pastiche and irony.

Blocked career entry points in film and television

The fourth factor is that career entry points were blocked. The music video industry may be a curious instance of supply driving demand. As Grossberg has suggested (1993), the release of youth-oriented music films in the 1970s contributed to a rise in the number of young people seeking careers as film directors. But film was expensive. Aspiring directors couldn't pick up an iPhone. The cost was not just the cameras and lights, but the stock, processing and Steenbeck hire. Entry to the industries was very closely regulated by the trades unions, and it was extremely difficult to get a union card. School leavers and graduates sought unconventional routes. But in the late 1980s, as independent feature film companies such as Goldcrest and Palace went bust and fully funded features were replaced by deferred payment pictures, opportunities were limited. Some sought funding from the BFI and Arts Council of Great Britain, but funding was highly competitive, especially when it was restructured in the 1980s. Music video offered a way forward. In an interview with then Institute of Contemporary Arts director Gregor Muir, video director John Maybury explained that he only took work as a music video director in order to access expensive celluloid filmmaking equipment and props for feature films that he couldn't access elsewhere; he described the decision as selling his 'soul to the devil' (Maybury 2012).

A British Style?

In this section, I look at video examples of a British style which haven't already been discussed in previous chapters as distinctively British in terms of dance, authorship or experimentation. The discussion focuses mainly on videos from Disc 5 – titled 'Wit' – of the DVD Boxset.

Many of the distinctive features of these videos arose from the production culture of Soho constituted and moderated by the video commissioners, and from the music subcultures of British artists. The labels held assumptions – often based on information fed back to them by 'pluggers' (in-house or out-of-house agents such as Anglo Plugging, who acted as distributors, placing videos on channels and shows like *The Box* and *Live and Kicking* in the UK) about what kinds of videos the editors of TV shows would play and wouldn't play, what kinds of videos fans wanted to see and what kind of strategy to run as a result. For example, the video for The Prodigy's *'Smack My Bitch Up'* (Jonas Åkerlund, 1997) was commissioned and produced with the knowledge that it would probably be banned from broadcast and that the publicity accruing from this could not only secure greater market reach than a safer commission but also the best kind of publicity to authenticate a marketing strategy for a band that shouldn't be 'marketed' in the first instance. Having videos 'banned' in the 1990s was often regarded as a positive result when it would serve to further authenticate a band. Small and / or independent labels would often use experienced freelance commissioners (such as John Moule, who regularly commissioned for Mute Records) who could bring this depth of experience to the job, rather than asking a junior member of staff to commission. The semi-independents would sometimes ask their parent label's in-house video commissioner to commission: Leftfield's *'Afrika Shox'* (1999), for example, was commissioned by Mike O'Keefe, head of video at Sony.

Throughout the '80s and '90s, the major labels would have a separate video commissioning department in London and LA or New York. In interviews for this book, video commissioners Mike O'Keefe (Sony), Trudy Bellinger (EMI), Dilly Gent (Parlophone), Carrie Sutton (Chrysalis) and Carole Burton-Fairbrother

(Virgin) confirmed that for international acts, the domestic video department might commission a different video or re-edit a video made for another market. In the London office of Virgin, Carole Burton-Fairbrother predominantly commissioned videos for artists on the UK repertoire. She confirms that throughout her career, Virgin treated the USA and UK as 'two very distinctive markets', often requesting more performance shots of the bands for videos of UK acts destined for the US market, or asking one of the US offices to commission the video: 'In the US it was so much more about the image of the artist. They wanted performance-based videos with lots of artist close-ups. Nothing quirky. More formulaic and generic.'[3] Nick Egan agreed: in the USA, 'it was all about the artist. In UK it was more about the concept and that's why Chris Cunningham came out of the UK.'[4] Carrie Sutton reported that when commissioning for a US release at Chrysalis, she would ask the director to include US iconography rather than British iconography (basketball rather than netball, desert rather than lush green hills).

For example, when Creation Records released Oasis's second album, *What's the Story, Morning Glory?* (1995), it was planned to be a crossover album that would break the band globally; but the USA was a hard market to crack for a British indie band, and the band had a troubled record in working with directors. For *Definitely Maybe* (1994), their first album, Creation had hired directors with a background in photography and documentary (Nick Egan, Corinne Day and Mark Szaszy) to create a non-mediatised look that the band felt was more authentic to their cultural roots. For *What's the Story*, Creation wanted directors who had a track record in selling artists in the USA through more mediatised videos – but who were also English, and could hopefully respect the band's musical heritage whilst appealing to an international audience. Jake Scott, who had already directed R.E.M.'s acclaimed video for '*Everybody Hurts*', released in 1993, and on the back of that had launched his production company Black Dog in LA (a subsidiary of Ridley Scott Associates), was hired to direct the first release, '*Morning Glory*' – although in the end, that wasn't released in the USA. Success came with Creation's hiring of British director Nigel Dick, an extremely experienced pair of hands who had begun his career at Stiff Records in London before moving to LA to launch Propaganda Films. He had directed Band Aid, Tears for Fears and Def Leppard. Dick directed the videos which contributed to breaking Oasis worldwide: '*Wonderwall*' (1995), '*Don't Look Back in Anger*' (1996) and '*Champagne Supernova*' (1996), although in his famed narrative to his DVD collection, Noel is not appreciative of those efforts and reserves his less negative comments for the work of director / photographer Egan.

Nonetheless the British directors Dick, Egan, Jake Scott and Andy Morahan were frequently hired by London offices to make US videos for the UK repertoire because they were perceived to understand both markets – by which was meant the audiences, the broadcasters and the musicians themselves, who hailed from often very different musical traditions. Jake Nava was also hired throughout the 1990s as a British director who could work with both markets, as was his brother, Emil Nava. Andy Morahan summarised the benefits:

> Well, it was nice being an English director . . . we had the best of both worlds, we were making two kinds of videos. We had Prefab Sprout, Aztec Camera, fantastic kinds of people, British artists. That would never have flown in America.[5]

It was less common for American directors to be brought to London to work with UK acts. The exception was Spike Jonze, because he brought to London an irreverence, an enthusiasm for breaking the rules and mixing up the genres. He disliked 'slick' and 'polished', and favoured messy, DIY and all those seminally 'English' traits. It is significant that Morahan says 'British artists', because it suggests that the roots of the experimental artistic production culture in Britain lay not with the filmmakers but with the artists themselves, their record labels and managers.

The assumption was that a British-style video wouldn't work in the USA. Of course, there were examples which disproved this – foremost Chris Cunningham's *'Come to Daddy'* (1997), which broke all of the criteria but went on heavy rotation on MTV after being selected by the programme *12 Angry Viewers* (MTV 1997–8). It was for that reason that very experienced commissioners such as Carole Burton-Fairbrother knew that if they were commissioning from an experienced and / or talented director with a 'gut instinct' for the medium, and for particular bands and their fans, they shouldn't issue a specific brief but should give them carte blanche to produce something unpredictably and often inexplicably 'brilliant' that could take off. It was easier to say this in the 1990s, however, when video departments knew that if a video bombed, they had enough budget to commission an alternative version; but that open brief lies beneath many of the videos in the landmark collection.

What are the traits of British music video? One is a tendency to use video as social and political critique. The Specials' video for *'Ghost Town'* (1981), directed by Barney Bubbles, a graphic designer who created album covers, illustrates this. It was filmed during the night and early morning of 27/8 June 1981, just a few months after the Brixton Riots happened in April 1981. The video showed footage of the bass player Panter driving the band around London in a 1962 Vauxhall Cresta, intercut with POV shots of semi-derelict areas in the East End and the deserted streets of the financial district of the City of London. It addressed Britain's urban decay, unemployment and class divide, and to many it spoke of the policies of the Thatcher government. Jerry Dammers came up with the central idea, which Bubbles adapted

(Gorman 2008: 147). With his graphic design background, Bubbles seems to deliberately obscure any separate sense of a director's authorship.

Another example is the video for UB40's *'Red Red Wine'* (1984). The band had named themselves UB40 after the document issued by the UK government's Department of Employment, called the Unemployment Benefit Form 40, which unemployed British workers were required to submit when applying for benefit. Released in the second term of Thatcher's government, the video presented in letterboxed black and white a story of an ordinary young working-class builder who heads to the pub, where his wages are stolen, his girlfriend leaves, he gets kicked out of his flat and finds himself homeless and alone in the gutter. According to Bernard Rose, the director of the video, the BBC refused to screen the video on *TOTP* because of its violence and alcohol-related content. But the band liked the video so much that when the track reached number one in the UK charts they left the country, duplicitously claiming other promotional responsibilities when invited by the BBC to play live on the show. In those days, *TOTP* had a policy of screening either a video or a live performance of the number one track. The video reflected the band's origins and identity, Rose recalls. 'It was kind of documentary, it was very naturalistic. It was expressionistic but it was still in a pub, people drinking, getting drunk, falling in the gutter. It wasn't glamorous.'[6]

The Chemical Brothers *'Believe'* (2005) focused on the alienation of British working-class life. It was filmed at the MG Rover Longbridge plant in Birmingham, which had just been shut down, and dealt directly with the social, political and psychological fallout of long-term automation for workers. The video follows a paranoid factory worker terrified of the automated assembly robot he operates, imagining that he is being chased by one of the machines. Of shooting in Longbridge, the directors, Dom & Nic, said, 'The workers were fantastic because they knew it was closing' and 'the location gave so much to the film . . . the feeling of grimy factory and really big robots that felt like dinosaurs'. The idea 'came from the music to start with, the little sounds that sounded like a robot; and the lyrics as well', so it was not an idea developed separately by the team. Yet it had the same focus on isolation, alienation and the 'hallucinatory element that had been running through The Chemical Brothers videos we had done'.[7] *'Believe'*'s focus on alienated urban life is not dissimilar to Chris Cunningham's video for Leftfield featuring Afrika Bambaata (*'Afrika Shox'*, 1999), which portrayed the embattled Black man staggering through New York as his limbs fell over – a film which was not conceived by Cunningham to document US racism, but which invites that interpretation.

Others are explicitly political. The artist / filmmaker / activist M.I.A. has made consistent use of her videos as tools of artistic political expression. Her video for *'Boyz'* (2007) is a flash-filled sensory onslaught that pays little regard to video conventions of the time in order to visualise the political point regarding masculinities underlying M.I.A.'s lyric. *'Born Free'* (M.I.A. / Romain Gavras, 2010) presents a dystopian, graphic and terrorising vision of ethnic cleansing and gun violence taking place in parts of the world at that time. *'Bad Girls'* (M.I.A. / Romain Gavras, 2010) elicited mixed reactions, with some claiming it propagated Arab stereotypes and others claiming the video confronted women's rights in Saudi Arabia. *'Double Bubble Trouble'* (M.I.A., 2014) drew on the VHS lo-fi aesthetic of grime in its portrait of gun and knife crime in South London. Director WIZ has created many political videos for British artists: in the Manic Street Preachers' *'If You Tolerate This Your Children Will be Next'* (1998) he presents the idea that if people fail to take responsibility for the political consequences of their actions, they will lose their identity. In The Chemical Brothers' *'Out of Control'* (1999), WIZ depicts a Mexican conflict between government and the Zapatista Army of National Liberation, a revolutionary group that appeared during the 1990s. Kasabian's *'Club Foot'* (2004) is dedicated to Czech student Jan Palach, who set himself on fire in 1969 in protest against renewed Soviet suppression of Czechoslovakia. Dizzee Rascal's *'Sirens'* (2007) shows Dizzee being chased by fox hunters on horses, who pursue him through his house and then onto the streets. At the end of the video he is trapped in an alleyway, killed, and his blood smeared on the hunters' faces.

But British music video directors have also tended to tackle issues with humour and irony, particularly when targeting the music industry itself. In Julien Temple's video for Judas Priest's *'Breaking the Law'* (1980), centred on a bank heist, the bank staff look threatened when the band use electric guitars (rather than guns) to force an entrance; in an almost comic-strip-style parody of the TV cop series genre, the cashier's glass cracks. When it turns out the band have broken into the bank to liberate a locked-up gold disc of Priest's album *British Steel* (1980), the video functions as a metaphor for the tyranny of the record industry. 'You don't know what it's like!' screams Halford, taking the gold disc to his driver in his waiting convertible. Traktor's video for Basement Jaxx's *'Where's Your Head At'* (2002) also takes a pop at the music industry: a dark critique of the way that record labels turn their artists into monkeys. Us's video for Wiley's *'Numbers in Action'* (2011) also exposes the apparatus behind music videos. At the end of his video for Noel Gallagher's High Flying Birds, *'Ballad of the Mighty I'* (2014), experienced director John Hardwick allows Gallagher his final damning critique of the entire music video business in a parody of a young, pretentious video director who mistakenly calls him Liam. In the boxset category 'Pop Will Eat Itself' there are further examples of videos commenting on the marketing apparatus of the medium, from Russell Mulcahy and the Buggles' *'Video Killed the Radio Star'* (1979) to Steve Barron and Dire Straits' *'Money for Nothing'* (1985), Michel Gondry and Thomas Dolby's *'Close But No Cigar'* (1992) and Chris

Cunningham's and Aphex Twin's '*Come to Daddy*' (1997). Losey and Benstock's stop-animation video featuring Tilda Swinton for Orbital's '*The Box*' (1996) was influenced, according to Losey, by the film *The Man Who Fell to Earth* (Nicholas Roeg, 1976), and was intended to capture the intense sense of alienation of Swinton's character from the mediatised world. In the case of 'The Box', the effects were created entirely in camera.[8]

Far from selling stars, British artists and directors declothed them. British videos took every opportunity to declothe the star, demonstrate her imperfections, expose her ordinariness, idiocy, incompetence, fragility or downright meanness . . . they celebrated the anti-hero, and if there wasn't one, they turned their main artist into one. Mat Kirkby's video '*Witness the Fitness*' (2001) presents Roots Manuva as the loveable rogue, the bum, the failure and the underdog who steals from primary school kids. In his video for Basement Jaxx's '*U Don't Know Me*' (2005), Kirkby has Queen Elizabeth turn out to be a naughty rogue who likes boozing, eating kebabs, provoking fights with bouncers and then fleeing the police. In Sophie Ellis Bextor's line-dancing video '*Murder on the Dance Floor*' (2001), Muller has Bextor turn out to be the loser and cheat. In Ledwidge's video '*Crying at Airports*' (1998), far from winning the competition, Whale's national Swedish synchronised team are the much-parodied losers. In '*Supreme*' (2000) Vaughan Arnell and Robbie Williams present a tribute to British Formula One driver Jackie Stewart in which the rival driver competing for the 1970s F1 World Championship 'Bob Williams' (played by Robbie) crashes his car, makes a surprise recovery, and ultimately loses the title when he gets diarrhoea before a race and is unable to appear at the starting grid due to getting locked into his caravan. British videos parodied wealth, beauty, femininity and masculinity, and especially targeted the icons of celebrity, power and success. None of this fits Goodwin and Vernallis's dictum, based largely on American videos, that music videos must *sell the star*.

A third distinctive tendency of British music videos lies in experimentation and VFX. Carole Burton-Fairbrother felt that within Virgin, the videos 'coming out of the UK were edgy and more original, less formulaic'.[9] Many of these examples were examined in Chapters 2 and 3, and the boxset is full of examples that substantiate Carole's argument. But the point touches on a topical issue in current scholarship on music video, where music video has time and again been singled out for its foregrounding of the spectacular (Hayward 1990: 127, Mundy 1999). Hayward argues that the orientation towards formal novelty and surprise is not only a product of the early self-conscious evolution of the new industrial product (1990: 126), but also an inherent characteristic of the medium. He writes that 'it is unlikely that the exploratory-experimental project of music video will eventually "arrive at", and thereby *deliver*, a stable form' (1990: 127) because it has evolved after the 'high period of classic Hollywood Realist Cinema' and in the era of television with its plurality of narrative and realist forms, textual bricolage, and the age of advertising, trailers and programme packaging (1990: 127). Hayward makes an extremely important point about the constant impact of changing platforms on the rules of the music video form – a point on which I will pick up in the final chapter. Here, I want to stress the importance of distinguishing between types of eye-catching, impressive visual characteristics of music video: those arising from low-cost post-production and camera effects, which have dominated in the UK, and those arising from high-cost production values of chorus line, studio sets, lavish locations and costumes, which have dominated in the USA.

The European trick film tradition may be connected to the fact that British videos have tended to exploit low-cost in-camera and post-production FX. There is no doubt that the non-formulaic use of novelty effects has been greater in the UK than the USA, and I believe this is in no small way due to the integration of post-production and video production in the Soho cluster, art school experimentation and the resistance to video as a marketing tool. But where US music videos drew heavily on the musical genre for their exposition, it is arguable that the British drew by contrast on the trick film genre (1898–1908) which foregrounded novelty effects. 'Trick novelties', as the British often called trick films, received a wide audience in the UK, with Robert W. Paul and Cecil Hepworth among their practitioners. Throughout its chameleon existence, music video in Britain has always tended towards the spectacular, from the pioneering videotape effects of '*Bohemian Rhapsody*' (1975) to the ramping of Radiohead's '*Street Spirit*' (1996). It is no accident that Carole Burton-Fairbrother was the first to commission music videos from Michael Gondry and Jonathan Glazer early on in their careers. The visual effects used for '*Close But No Cigar*' (1992), '*Money for Nothing*' (1985) and '*Where's Your Head At*' (2002) were all cutting-edge techniques in the early and experimental stages of being developed in the London post-production houses of Soho.

The fourth domain of difference applies specifically to the '70s and '80s, before the USA adopted the artifice of music video. As Carter Ratcliff (1983) and others have noted, David Bowie's performance work seems rooted not only in the Romantic notion of art that Frith and Horne observed as an aspect of art school culture (1987) but the avant-garde performance tradition rooted in the second decade of the twentieth century. Like Wilde, Bowie was eager to experiment with gender, sexuality, orientalism and self-invention. He saw no distinction between art and commerce. Mercury, Lennox and Bush also seemed to be cut from the 'aesthetics of self invention' (Waldrep 2016): they were pop musicians who took the idea of the image and of the self as art to new heights. The notion of the self as work of art, and of fashion (aka 'dressing up') as a route to social critique and change, may well have roots in glam rock, punk, Carnaby Street and New York – but they may also have deeper roots in British cultural traditions which have not yet been fully probed. With the cross-dressing of British pantomime and the 'dressing up' of children's television series *Mr Benn* serving as examples, British artists of the late '70s and '80s were exposed to more than just glam rock. Mr Benn, created by David McKee, was a character who appeared in an animated children's series (BBC 1971). In each episode, Mr Benn – wearing a black suit and bowler hat – would leave his house at 52 Festive Road to visit a fancy-dress costume shop. The moustachioed, fez-wearing shopkeeper would invite him to try on an outfit (caveman, spaceman, wizard, zookeeper, cowboy, pirate). Newly attired, Mr Benn would exit the shop through a magic door to the world of his costume, where he would have an amazing adventure; he'd always return back through the magic door to normality afterwards. More than a few British videos from the '80s bring Mr Benn's adventures to mind; but was this another way to avoid selling the star as a real person? Another way of servicing Britain's anti-star culture – by dressing the star up as someone else?

Counterflows

At the beginning of this chapter I made the bold claim that the USA learned the art and craft of music video from British producers and musicians. It's a highly problematic statement, and I must now lay down some clarifications and corrections. When I argue that the UK taught the USA music video, I mean corporate USA; amongst American subcultures in music, fashion and film, there have been more radical alternatives to the massive marketing model of music video used by the big record giants. The videos of Nine Inch Nails, who frequently collaborated with Peter Christopherson in London, Weezer, the Beastie Boys, The White Stripes, Foo Fighters, Soundgarden, REM and Elbow all contain examples of more authored, visual works which defied the American corporate culture of selling stars – but they remained *in a minority*.

The first correction regards the genres of music that enabled the pioneering British videos. The relationship between the USA and the UK has not been a one-way flow of influence, as the research of Perone (2009) and Philo (2014) demonstrates. When the first British promos were produced and exported to the USA in the 1960s, there was already a kick-back to the dominance America was felt to have held in the 1950s. Scholars have rightly pointed out that bands like The Beatles and the Rolling Stones were largely remediating American music brought to the UK by US artists touring Britain in the 1950s and 1960s. Bands such as The Kinks and the Small Faces, however, did not appropriate the US songs of labels such as Motown; they were hostile to what Blake has called 'sonic Americanisation'. They 'saw themselves as guardians of British musical culture' (Blake 2004: 149–50). But there is no doubt that the flow and influence of music, fashion and film in these years was mutual and often ran through complex subcultural connections, rather than the mainstream channels which might have been evident on television in the 1970s and 1980s. The genres of music which, in Britain, laid the conditions for non-performance experimental and conceptual videos throughout the 1980s and '90s, had at least some roots in the USA. As Lawrence has shown, contemporary disco dancing emerged out of African American social dance, the rise of the discotheque and the New York gay scene (Lawrence 2009: 201). Before it was exported to Europe, 'house' was the name given to varied dance forms that developed in New York City and Chicago clubs during the 1970s (Sommer 2009).

The second correction regards visual artists in the USA. Presenting the 1980s era as a one-way flow of influence from Britain to the USA obscures the pioneering work of artists such as Toni Basil, Devo and Talking Heads, who made innovative videos with postmodern irony. Toni Basil was a key creative figure in avant-garde music videos of the later 1970s and early 1980s. American band Devo had much more in common with experimental avant-garde British bands of the era and were making videos long before MTV, with '*Secret Agent Man*' in 1976 (directed by Chuck Statler) and their cover of '*I Can't Get No Satisfaction*' in 1978, which brought them mainstream attention after their live appearance on US TV (Cateforis 2004). Their earlier videos were shot on celluloid and projected at their live gigs. Yet the fact that Toni Basil reports that she hadn't heard of Devo until David Bowie told her about them (Prato 2011: 320) illustrates the sheer scale of the cross-cutting influences between the USA and the UK, particularly in the late 1970s, when transatlantic travel had been made more accessible by cheap flights from airlines such as Freddie Laker. The Talking Heads video for '*Once in a Lifetime*', co-directed by Toni Basil, was released in February 1981 – also before MTV was launched. It showed David Byrne against a white cyc, doing a slightly weird robotic dance with graphics behind him and clips of religious rituals.

There are other instances of British artists influenced by US videos. Whilst I have argued that the video concept album of the early 1980s was a British phenomenon, Annie Lennox has said that the *Savage* and *Diva* video albums were inspired by Blondie (of whom Lennox was a huge fan), who made a video album for their 1979 LP *Eat to the Beat* that contained a combination of straight performance and more conceptual clips. Moreover, scholars are still debating the influence of the pioneering TV series *The Monkees* (NBC 1966–8); whilst Matthew Stahl (2002) argues that the Monkees project was influenced by Richard Lester's 1964 film *A Hard Day's Night*, there are striking similarities between the image presented of The Monkees in those two TV series and some of the clips made by The Dave Clark Five discussed in this chapter. The format of the *Monkees* TV show was, arguably, a model used by Simon Fuller for the S Club 7 project decades later for CBBC and BBC1.

The third point regards the demise of domestic audiences in the YouTube era. Our research project looked a fifty-year period during which media platforms were profoundly transformed by a shift from national to global audiences (although when MTV was still broadcasting music videos, it moved away from that global model to a model based on delivering locally targeted product to its myriad subsidiary channels). In the digital period it makes much less sense to talk of a distinctive British audience because music videos are distributed not through domestic broadcasters but global platforms such as YouTube and Vevo, for whom making different national versions would make no sense. It is easier to identify a British style in the period up to the 1990s than it has been since the early '00s. Moreover, in this same period, travel between the two production centres of LA and London has not only vastly increased but the two production centres have accumulated at least thirty years of working together. Even in the 1930s, when Britain was making musicals and musical shorts, as Mundy points out, there was a constant transatlantic flow of people, which facilitated an ongoing exchange of ideas and technical expertise. But that flow was hastened in the 1970s by cheap flights to New York, and since 2000 the exchange of ideas has been intensified by the internet. By 2016, Los Angeles and London shared much more knowledge about each other's production and aesthetic styles and had collaborated on many more projects – to the extent that today it makes sense to speak of a shared production culture between London and LA.

The fourth point regards grime. Since the third British Invasion of grime, and in the wake of Obama's presidency and the rise of the American far right, the USA has embraced the protest video on a scale not previously witnessed in music videos. This may in itself also be a result of the greater freedom of the internet (where there are no conservative gatekeepers of TV shows). During the years 2015–17, American artists have used video as self-expression and to articulate political viewpoints that have been excluded from mainstream politics. Since 2016, there have been significant authored ironic, political works such as Childish Gambino's *'This is America'* (Hiro Murai, 2018), Pussy Riot's *'Make America Great Again'* (Jonas Åkerlund, 2016), Joey Bada$$' *'Land of the Free'* (Joey Bada$$ and Nathan Smith, 2017) and Kendrick Lamar's *'Alright'* (Colin Tilley and The Little Homies, 2015). The USA has edged towards a culture in which video is more a medium of artistic expression than a method of selling songs. Since leaving Destiny's Child, Beyoncé has consistently used her music videos to give voice to political issues, as the videos for *'Formation'* (Melina Matsoukas, 2016) and her collaboration with Jay-Z on the video for *'Apeshit'* (Ricky Saiz, 2018) demonstrate. Protest videos were released only occasionally in the age of MTV – for example, Public Enemy's *'Fight the Power'* (Spike Lee, 1989), and TLC's *'Unpretty'* (Paul Hunter, 1999).

In saying this I do not mean to understate the immensely progressive impact of MTV screening the early Janet and Michael Jackson videos on TV. The USA has also embraced a more diverse choreographic culture recently in the work of Wendy Morgan and Ryan Heffington, who choreographed the movement for Maddie Ziegler in Sia's acclaimed video for *'Chandelier'* (Daniel Askill, 2014). Just because work is slick, polished and high-production, that does not mean it cannot also be radical, oppositional and deliberately political: for in gender representation, after early inroads from Christina Aguilera's *'Beautiful'* (Jonas Åkerlund, 2002) and Lady Gaga's *'Born This Way'* (Nick Knight, 2011), US videos and directors have embraced gender fluidity with increasing confidence, humour and artistry, as shown by the videos for Janelle Monáe's *'Pynk'* (Emma Westernberg, 2018), P!nk and Channing Tatum's *'Beautiful Trauma'* (The Golden Boyz, 2017) and Charli XCX's *'Boyz'* (Sarah McColgan/ Charli XCX, 2017).

A long-prevailing view in British scholarship on British popular music is that authenticity is compromised by marketing in pursuit of sales (Perone 2009). But as Waldrep shows in his work on Bowie (2004, 2016), that hasn't been the case with British music video artists. British videos have also been fuelled by the notion of a romantic artist who herself is an artwork, and for whom the video is art. For artists such as Bowie, there was a way to unite art and commerce without selling out: authenticity was not incompatible with commerce. The fact that British artists have tended not to want to use video as a marketing tool for their celebrity status does not mean that they haven't wanted to use it as a means to make money.

NOTES

1. D. Clark, personal communication, 23 August 2018.
2. A. Morahan, personal communication, 10 May 2016.
3. C. Burton-Fairbrother, personal communication, 15 January 2016.
4. N. Egan, personal communication, 28 October 2016.
5. A. Morahan, personal communication, 10 May 2016.
6. B. Rose, personal communication, 26 October 2016.
7. D. Hawley, Dom & Nic personal communication, 9 February 2016.
8. L. Losey, personal communication, December 4, 2017.
9. C. Burton-Fairbrother, personal communication, 15 January 2016.

9 CONCLUSION

The time has come to reflect on the other, broader academic issues raised in this work. Much of what has been presented in this book supports the analytical framework established by the first generation of cultural studies scholars, particularly that published by Goodwin (1993) and Aufderheide (1986) on the relationship between sound and image. Goodwin argued that each of the music components of a track (tempo, rhythm, arrangement, harmonic development, acoustic space and lyrics) could or would be related to elements of the visual track created: the tempo, for example, might be reflected in the speed of the camera movement, the editing in the action depicted or the visual effects, whilst rhythm might be echoed in the 'pulse' of images. A large number of videos produced in Britain during the period 1966–2016 beautifully illustrate Goodwin's argument: from The Cure's *'Close to Me'* (Tim Pope, 1985) and The Art of Noise's *'Close (to the Edit)'* (Zbigniew Rybczyński, 1984) to the syncopated heartbeat of Massive Attack's *'Teardrop'* (Walter Stern, 1998). However, a huge number of the videos examined in this study can't be explained by Goodwin's model. Whilst minimalist videos such as Mount Kimbie's *'Before I Move Off'* (Tyrone Lebone, 2010), Toy's *'Lose My Way'* (Joe Morris, 2012), Wiley's *'On a Level'* (Skepta, 2014) and Dean Blunt's *'Mersh'* (2014) contain some minor elements of syncopation, they are absent of many of the more complex elements identified by Goodwin, yet they somehow succeed as videos because *they are doing something more complex than simply 'visualising a song'* as Goodwin theorised *or 'selling a star'* as Vernallis wrote. That is because they are platform-sensitive. *'Lose my Way'* works on YouTube, but

CONCLUSION

probably would have been rejected by the producers of *The Chart Show* and MTV if it had been made in the 1990s. However, this isn't to reject Goodwin's model, because it remains the best available useful theoretical framework to serve as a starting point for a language of *music video critical appreciation.*

In Britain, what kind of video has been commissioned depends on the extent to which it is perceived to authenticate the artist by the artist, management and marketing department. A video for one of the UK's then most successful bands once ended up in court because the band decided in the middle of filming that the video was *inauthentic*. The artist was from Manchester. The acclaimed director didn't know much about the cultural and artistic values of the Manchester music scene. A very large sum of money was lost and two major entertainment multinationals went to court. Why did that happen? Because the label's view of what kind of video would authenticate the band was substantially different to the band's. For another more recent example of this disjuncture, see Tim Nash's account of making the video for Wiley's '*Wearing My Rolex*' (Kim Gehrig, 2008): *White People's Vision* (Somesuch Stories, n.d.). Director Kim Gehrig went on to make Wiley's award-winning '*Cash in My Pocket*' (2009) after that tense experience, but Wiley refused to grant us permission to use that video in our landmark collection, nominating other videos in preference.

It is difficult to appreciate how this authentication works from the point of view of commissioners, managers, artists, directors and producers without understanding genre – which is their stock in trade. As Railton and Watson argue, '[v]ery little work exists that has attempted to use genre as a way of understanding music video' (2011: 43). Here, I've proposed a vocabulary basic in industry practice. Within the industry, people talk about three types of video (format), and then use the concept of genre to denote either film and television genres or music genres. The concept of 'heavy metal videos' or 'rock videos', for instance, denotes the kind of video usually commissioned for an artist being marketed in the heavy metal music genre: it might be a horror narrative, for example. Commissioners will also talk about genres specific to music video but not allied to any particular music genre: the 'going for a walk' genre, sports genre or reverse narrative genre. To draw up a complex aetiology of music video genres is possible in theory, but in practice would involve interviewing more commissioners than consulted in this project, because it's the commissioners who deal in genre on a daily basis. When directors pitch a genre, they will do so after careful consideration about what associations it will trigger in the audience and whether it will authenticate or discredit a band's image, and the commissioner will do the same.

When I first began teaching music videos to students, I did so by presenting them with a selection of (anonymised) genuine pitch treatments and asking them to role-play in seminars from the perspective of artist, director and commissioner to see which video would be selected – before playing them the eventual commissioned video. Judging what is going to be perceived as authentic by a band is not as easy as it sounds. Artists often struggle themselves when presented with a number of written pitches. Artists also change their minds. So do label managers. For every dozen videos that have been successfully commissioned since the 1990s, there are probably over one hundred rejected treatments and more than a handful of disputes in post-production about what was promised but not delivered.

Whilst there haven't, as far as I am aware, been any published contributions on cycles and genres named as such in the scholarship on music video, some authors have produced useful and insightful pieces identifying common themes and traits in relation to larger trends in marketing, technology and broader cultural and artistic trends: Austerlitz on music video 'follies' (2010) and Strøm on animation videos (2007), Sherril Dodds on dance videos (2009a), Gregory on boy bands (2019), Richardson on the audio-surreal (2011), Fowler on Scratch videos (2017) and a growing literature on girl groups (Leach 2001, Dibben 2002, Leonard 2017, Fenster on country and western videos (1993), Piggford 1997, Warwick 2013). This sits alongside recent scholarship focusing on individual directors as auteurs: Vernallis and Ueno (2013) on Floria Sigismondi, Adams (2014), Leggott (2016) and Lockwood (2017) on Chris Cunningham, Beebe on Gondry, Spike Jonze and Hype Williams.

Scholarship since Google purchased YouTube in 2006 (which I take as the date on which the digital era began) has tended to focus heavily on the argument that music video is a specific medium *here to stay* (e.g. Railton and Watson 2011), populated by a host of individual auteurs and a larger number of failure-directors / genre-directors of which an urgent process of canonisation is needed. The distinction between auteur directors and others is echoed by work from an artists' film and video paradigm identifying film directors and film works that meet the innovation and auteur criteria necessary to fulfil laudable work within the art film paradigm (e.g. Donnelly 2007b, Rogers 2013). I hope the discussion that I have presented here shows that in British music video at least, isolating supposed auteur directors from the context of genre cycles in which their works are produced risks obscuring the very nature of the music video medium. The evidence presented in this book suggests absolutely that Railton and Watson are right to argue that the film auteur paradigm is problematic because 'the formal, generic and commercial imperatives of music video make it much less likely that a director will have the desire, or more precisely the opportunity, to develop a distinctive visual signature' (2011: 68). Yes, there might be evidence of an individual style, but what is really fascinating is how directors are able to service that in the interests of creating a film which voices the artist in some way. Music videos are not simply films of directorial expression. In order to excel in the medium of music video, directors need expertise in genre borrowing; they need to have mastered the skills not only of imitation but appropriation, homage, satire, parody and pastiche, but most of all, they need to understand music: music traditions, music subcultures, identities and music marketing.

The research undertaken for the book also suggests that where scholars discuss or attribute causation to individuals in music video production, they should take into account the wide range of what's known in the industry as 'happy accidents' rather than intentional effects, and the actions of many figures other than directors. Apart from the artists themselves, a collaborative approach to authorship enables scholars to appreciate the substantial creative role of video commissioners in the selection and negotiation of treatments and directors, as well as label managers and executive producers, production designers, costume designers and make-up artists. But in particular, this book has shone a light on the work of music video editors. The role of the editor in music video is much more significant than has previously been acknowledged. In British music videos, it has been the editor who ensures that the relationship between the soundtrack and the picture track works – as much as, if not more than, the director, who ensures that the core idea authenticates the band's music and identity. The editor is the person who syncs the shots, makes the cuts and interprets the rhythm of the live action to mirror (or not) the rhythm of the music. I hope that the case studies in Chapter 3 expand and enrich our understanding of the types of editing deployed in the British industry since the mid-1960s, which vary greatly from the models repeatedly put forward by scholars such as Vernallis (2001 and 2007) and Korsgaard (2017). Taking a collaborative view is consistent with the work of Guat (1997), Livingston (1997), Murray (2014) and Sellors (2007, 2010) on film creation as collaborative.

Why videos look the way they do (to answer the initial questions posed by Goodwin and other scholars of music videos) is not just a result of decisions made by directors, producers and editors. It's also a result of larger economic and technological trends in the film and television industry. The research conducted for this book has shown that part of the reason for the very considerably pioneering use of post-production effects in British music video is because the industries developed in an integrated fashion in the same cluster in Soho, London, from the early 1970s in particular, with music video functioning as the R&D sector for the screen industry as a whole. The significance of post-production effects in video production in the UK has been recognised by scholars such as Fetveit, who argues that since the late 1990s there has been an 'aesthetic of mutable temporality' in music video in which the 'initial temporality of body movements as performed for the camera are partly over-ruled and controlled in the post-production process' (2011: 161). The effect is that 'the editing coheres with the song's mood the way it evolves, and with the deeper emotional logic of the song' (2011: 163) – citing as examples videos post-produced in London, such as the Rolling Stones' *'Like a Rolling Stone'* (Michel Gondry, 1997), Radiohead's *'Street Spirit'* (Jonathan Glazer, 1996) and Portishead's *'Only You'* (Chris Cunningham, 1998) as examples. This is an area worthy of more research, and, for that reason, the names of the editors are given in the credits for the landmark boxset along with the telecine operators (colourists), VFX artists and post-production companies (where known), to enable future historians of music video to identify patterns and themes in the work of these post-production teams.

The major ambition of this book has been to rectify a widespread apprehension that the music video originated with MTV. As such this book contributes to the scholarship re-evaluating the relationship between the UK and USA in popular music (Horn 2009, Miller 2000, Blake 2004, Campbell et al. 2004b, 2004c). Whilst scholars such as Austerlitz (2007) recognise that 1960s pop promos contained many key precedents for the later US boom, the view persists in scholarship today that, while the first videos can arguably be traced back to the beginning of the last century, they really came into their own during the 1980s due to the launch of MTV (Burns and Hawkins 2019: 1). The evidence considered in this book simply doesn't support that assertion. Not only did music videos exist as a cultural form before then, but an industry with a distinctive value chain, specialised production chain and threefold format typology of performance / concept and narrative video matured in London in the 1970s well before MTV was launched. The distinctive cinematographic and editing style that would be mimicked throughout the 1980s in the USA was well established, rooted and crystallised in Britain by 1979. Pop promos were screened in Europe on domestic music television, prime-time entertainment and children's television shows from the mid-1960s onwards, increasingly so in the 1970s. Britain may have been a small market in comparison to the USA, with a smaller volume of sales achievable in comparison to the USA, but it was nevertheless an important domestic market to access through *The Chart Show* and *TOTP*. Domestic audiences across the world viewed music video on TV stations and programmes other than MTV.

It has also been possible to identify some distinctive features of British music videos during the fifty-year period from 1966 to 2016. In this period, videos in Britain have been characterised by a drive not to celebrate, not to advertise and not to sell the star – a hugely different sentiment to the USA. This, in combination with DJ-led electronic music, laid the conditions for non-performance conceptual videos. The street origins and anti-establishment ideology of punk and grime have led many artists to reject the mediatised constructions of video and find in the media a way to construct an authentic visual form. A predisposition, acquired in part from British art schools, to intentionally break the rules, combined with an act of necessity, of having been excluded from formal training by the trade unions, which led to a tendency to accidentally break the rules. This in turn combined with the fertile growth of post-production companies in the same socio-geographical cluster of Soho, leading to a huge steer towards

CONCLUSION

experimentation and innovation in the 1980s and 1990s – a steer which has declined in recent years, as British video artists have sought minimalism and developed a preference for in-camera effects. Throughout the entire fifty-year period, music videos in Britain have offered a vehicle for people excluded from and stigmatised by mainstream media to talk to other groups of people outside their immediate subcultural group and music community. I have given examples of The Specials and UB40 commenting on Thatcher's Britain, of the videos fighting against homophobia and HIV in 1984/5, and of M.I.A.'s videos today. In the early 2000s, grime artists used Sky TV to communicate radical alternatives and objections to the institutionally racist structures of education, policing, employment and social justice against which they were struggling.

In addition to these traits, until the mid-2000s, British musicians and labels have been more experimental than the USA in dance, collaborating with choreographers from modern dance to produce realistic, dramaturgical, surrealist and expressive modes of choreography. This may in part be a result of the extraordinary, boundary-crossing work of British and European choreographers, including but not limited to Akram Khan, Matthew Bourne and Wayne McGregor (Anderson 2008, Cabitza 2015). Many of the videos examined in this book challenge the dominant binary distinction between 'masculine' and 'feminine' genders. British artists have upstaged, inverted, challenged, mocked and ridiculed gender as a code of performance since the late 1970s. As such, they don't conform to the portrait of women as objectified sex objects claimed by many scholars in the field. But these findings support and extend arguments put forward by scholars in relation to androgyny and camp styles in the performances of individual artists such as Annie Lennox (Piggford 1997, Rodger 2004), PJ Harvey (Gardner 2016), Mick Jagger and Freddie Mercury (Whiteley 1997b, 2013a) and Björk (Dibben 2009), as well as Hawkins (2017), Coates (1997) and Dibben (2002).

Remediation

In recent years, this literature has been joined by a considerable body of work looking at what I'd call 'digital music video', which I define as video produced since the launch of YouTube in 2005 and its purchase by Google in 2006. A new chapter in scholarship has opened up with enquiries into how music video has changed in the age of the internet (Hearsum and Inglis 2013, Vernallis 2010, 2013a, 2013b, Korsgaard 2013, 2017). Korsgaard endorses Tom Gunning's view that music video has returned to the origins of film with a reimagining of the 'cinema of attractions', and suggests that music video is a digital format that remediates (2017). In the 1980s music video was widely theorised as postmodern by the likes of Kaplan and Goodwin. For Jameson, postmodern artists 'operate as *bricoleurs*, recycling previous works and styles'. Postmodern art *is* pastiche because, 'all that is left is to imitate dead styles, to speak through the masks and with the voices of the styles in the imaginary museum' (Jameson 1985: 115). The idea of music videos as postmodern has largely been shelved, however, by the music video scholars of the digital era as an overreaction to the 'flow' of MTV in the 1980s (Keazor and Wübbena 2010, Aust and Kothenschulte 2011, Korsgaard 2017, Railton and Watson 2011).

Instead, scholars today argue that music illustrates the theoretical model of 'remediation' by Bolter and Grusin (2000). For Korsgaard, 'music video fundamentally functions through acts of remediation: music video only represents something new to the extent that it reworks the traditions outlined above'. Korsgaard argues that '[i]t is precisely by incorporating, modifying, and transforming the aesthetic techniques of previous practices that music video attains its special audiovisual configurations' (Korsgaard 2017: 24). I hope that this study has shown that, on the contrary, British music video artists and filmmakers often heralded something very new in the post-production techniques and aesthetic styles they pioneered. The R&D function of British music video has been at the heart of its influence and impact on television commercials, feature films and television drama – all of which have adopted techniques pioneered in video.

That point notwithstanding, British music videos have always remediated narratives and styles from other cultural and artistic forms from the very start. The Who remediated English slapstick for their collaboration with Michael Lindsay-Hogg, '*Happy Jack*' (1966). In his video for The Animals '*When I Was Young*' (1967), Whitehead 'remediated' newsreel-style footage of World War II. The Kinks' '*Dead End Street*' (1966) remediated the cinematic style of the silent era, trick film (in the magical disappearance of the revived corpse), a Dickens-style narrative, and photographic realism (in the montage). In their video '*We Love You*' (1967), the Stones and Peter Whitehead remediated footage from recording sessions along with segments that re-enacted the 1895 trial of Oscar Wilde, with Jagger, Richards and Marianne Faithfull respectively portraying Wilde, the Marquess of Queensberry and Lord Alfred Douglas. Music video has always recycled and referenced, and that is partly because pop music has always recycled and referenced. Appropriation and citation are intentional characteristics of the form which place music and artists within film and music traditions so as to anchor their cultural value and authenticity for target audiences. Intertextual referencing, citation and appropriation do not occur in a vacuum. They are social acts which occur in a real social context.

The fact that remediation appears to have increased since 2006 may be because music videos are so prominent online. But this may not be because of any supposed internal logic of music videos. The internet needed content. From the start, there was a shortage of content online; media corporations seeking to exploit the opportunities offered by the new digital platform looked in their back catalogue to see what could be recycled. Music corporations exist to recycle product, as do all media companies. As Gillian Doyle points out in her seminal *Understanding Media Economics* ([2002] 2013), media corporations make relatively little money from the first cycle of a product; much larger revenues accrue from second, third and subsequent exploitations. The job of media corporation directors is to seek and find opportunities for these secondary and tertiary cycles. In the case of music videos, record labels prepared the way for this by ensuring that all the rights to videos were held and managed by music rights collection agencies, not by film or acting collecting agencies. In Chapter 8, I looked in detail at this intellectual property arrangement as legal and financial ownership. Record labels were quick to insist not only that directors and producers signed away their copyright and moral rights, but that all performing actors and extras signed clearances for 'all media, in perpetuity and throughout the universe' rights. Actors' contracts were not regulated by Equity and would not have been acceptable either to Equity or to the mainstream sectors of television drama, feature films or television commercials, where actors were placed on time and geography-specific buyouts with residual payments payable for any additional exploitation.

How Do We Think about Music Videos?

One of the key questions in entering this research project was how to define music video. In Chapter 2, I defined it as a value chain: *Promos and music videos are short films commissioned and released by record labels for mass audiences; they comprise a copyrighted synchronised picture and audio track in which a percentage of the royalties accrue to the recording artist or record label and are generally, but not always, produced out of house by independent production companies or sole traders working from home.* In so doing, I rejected a textual analysis-based definition of music video of the kind advanced by Korsgaard as a 'family resemblance' (2017), preferring to look not solely at the textual traits which are evident on YouTube, but to look underneath at the industry arrangements which are not immediately obvious from the text. A music video is a commissioned work with an underlying formal rights exploitation agreement.

Defining a music video as an industrial value chain tells us that a significant amount of the digital content which forms part of the online presence of British music is not music video, fan mash-ups and lyric videos (unless those videos are formal commissioned lyric videos by the labels) among them. There is a surprisingly broad consensus in the literature that user-generated content (UGC) should be treated as music videos (e.g. Korsgaard 2017: 19, Perrott 2019). But this is not consistent with the way record label commissioners such as Mike O'Keefe talk about music video. For a label, UGC is relevant digital content which impacts the way that a marketing department invests in and commissions official music videos; labels monitor it and try to anticipate it when they plan their marketing strategy for an artist. For sure, authors such as Perrott are careful to distinguish between 'official' and 'unofficial' videos, using the language that is presented on YouTube to discriminate between the two. It would not be possible to narrate the story of the music video industry without reference to these non-commissioned videos, because the way that they work to package music for consumers and listeners has displaced the official video and has contributed to budgets in the UK; but mash-ups and fan videos are as much, if not more, a result of the rise of participatory culture on YouTube (Burgess 2008). YouTube has always oriented its services towards content sharing, including the sharing of mundane and amateur content, rather than the provision of high-quality video, as Burgess and Green demonstrate (2009). There remain many questions about how we define and analyse them (Karpovich 2007, Prior 2010, Vernallis 2013a, 2013b).

The *sine qua non* of the music video is the collaboration between the artist and the filmmaker. If that hasn't taken place (as it hasn't in a fan mash-up or an unofficial lyric video), it's not a music video. It's a film that someone has made using a published song without clearing the rights to use the song first. That phenomenon is fascinating and is worthy of a study in itself, as is the record labels' response to it (initially taking the videos down; now endorsing them, because the labels have negotiated advertising revenue). But they aren't music videos. As a historian of music video, what specifically interests me is the collaborative endeavour between all of the creatives involved on the music industry side and the film industry side in the creation of commissioned videos – and that is absent from non-commissioned, fan-authored works. 'This is America' (2018) came from a long-standing collaboration between rapper / actor Donald Glover and director Hiro Murai, including the acclaimed series *Atlanta*. Some of the best British music videos have come from such collaborations: David Mallet and David Bowie, Sophie Muller and Annie Lennox, Robbie Williams and Vaughan Arnell, The Chemical Brothers and Dom & Nic, Chris Cunningham and Aphex Twin, Spike Jonze and Fatboy Slim, Andy Morahan and George Michael, Peter Christopherson and Nine Inch Nails, Jake Nava and Beyoncé. In the course of those long-standing collaborations, the filmmakers have reached a deeper understanding of the artist and the issues that I discussed in Chapter 2.

Defining a music video as a value chain in which there is a contract between the artist and filmmaker to assign a synchronisation licence for the video in exchange for commercial rights (usually throughout the world, in perpetuity and all media) enables us to accept into the definition videos commissioned by labels with considerable freedom and very few creative constraints on the directors. For example, the trilogy of films '*The Queen Is Dead*', '*There Is a*

Light That Never Goes Out' and '*Panic*', commissioned by The Smiths (1986), were credited to Derek Jarman, although whether Jarman or their cameramen directed them is contested. Another recent example is the *Valtari Mystery Film Experiment*, in which Sigur Rós gave a dozen filmmakers the same budget and asked them to create whatever came into their heads when they listened to songs from the band's forthcoming album. The video for 'Ekki Múkk' conceived by British director Nick Abrahams (2012), featuring Aidan Gillen, was one of these, and it is included in our collection as an example of a different kind of commissioning. Another example is Klein's '*Marks of Worship*' (2016), directed by Akinola Davies: a borderline case, because Davies retained the rights but a synchronisation licence was granted by the label, and the video was made in collaboration with the artist, Klein, who appeared in the video. There are, I'm told, more examples of this kind of approach daily, as production companies and directors invest their own funds into a music video because of the sense of mutual benefit if the video turns out well – as a film for the director's portfolio helping to attract further work, and as a video for the artist stimulating further exposure and appreciation.

Whilst British music videos have long been part of record labels' marketing activities, they are not adverts or television commercials, and never have been. Yet still, in 2011, Railton and Watson in their otherwise commendable and valuable book on music videos argue that 'all music videos are first and foremost a commercial for an associated but distinct consumer product' (2011: 2). A positive step forward would be to stop referring to videos as advertising, because they work on a completely different business model from television commercials and advertising and their *raison d'être* is not a straightforward product (the song). British music videos have been part of the broader apparatus for selling and distributing music that the twentieth century yielded. In his seminal *The Art of Selling Songs: Graphics for the Music Business, 1690–1990* (1991), Kevin Edge presents an overview of this history. The book was a companion to an exhibition of the same name held at the Victoria & Albert Museum between February and June 1991. Edge points out that for most of the history of the music business, music has had to be sold without its core characteristic of sound. As sheet music, or as vinyl, it manifests as a silent product in the shops. Packaging played more than a substantial role in the communication of information about the product. Edge surveys all kinds of commercial graphics used to sell music, from title pages and frontispieces and scores of sheet music in the earliest decades of music sales, to concert posters, programmes and press adverts, to vinyl record sleeves and CD inlays in the penultimate decade of the twentieth century. Packaging is part of the activity of marketing music, if we take 'marketing' to describe the action or business of promoting and selling products and services.

Music video is like packaging, rather like the album cover. Unlike the album cover, it includes sound. Music video was the first kind of packaging used by labels which *included* the core characteristic of sound. It evolved because television happened. In the 1950s and 1960s, the target audience started to encounter music not just on the radio or in the record store, but on the telly. During the 1960s and 1970s, the number of shows on TV screening music videos grew. In the 1980s they grew more, and the music industry's successful exploitation of the CD format led to a boom that funded the growth of music videos. But the 1980s also saw a decline in vinyl sales – and *covers*. It is not insignificant that British music video grew out of the ashes of the vinyl album cover, which had previously been a significant artistic enterprise for graduates of British art schools. Seeing music video in this context, it makes sense that Storm Thorgerson oversaw Pink Floyd's visuals work, and it makes sense that Peter Christopherson, who began in graphic design, ended up in music video, as well as Mick Rock and Stéphane Sednaoui, with their backgrounds in music portrait photography. Graduates of art schools who might previously have concerned themselves with making innovative and often political covers for albums from the 1980s onwards went into making music videos instead of, or in addition to, their covers work. The close relationship between videos and album covers continued throughout the 1980s and 1990s. Imagery from the video for Godley and Creme's '*Cry*', for example, was used as the album cover for their 1987 *Changing Faces*, and Sophie Muller's video for '*Why*' used the album cover image from Annie Lennox's *Diva* (1992).

Like album covers, music videos are commercial film art made for hire, film art which is not owned by the originators or created under free conditions. This places it low down the hierarchy of screen arts alongside advertising, corporate video and all industrial film (Caston 2019b). It is a commissioned art – rather like architecture or graphic design. Like album covers, videos draw on different genres: some are more closely attuned to a concept, others focus on identity; some are portraits, others are cartoons or graphic designs; some deploy the talents of famous artists (Andy Warhol's cover for the Velvet Underground), others do not. Behind the scenes there are many parities between the history of album covers presented by Jones and Sorger (2006) and the history of British music videos. Jones and Sorger describe the tensions between bands, marketing departments and graphic designers, the differences between labels, and the tendency for major labels to want to feature bands on a cover – and indeed for bands to want to be featured on the cover – with the most pioneering album covers being made early on in a band's career, when the band and label were typically more willing to take risks (Jones and Sorger 2006: 84–5). The album cover was 'part of the purchased product and . . . a permanent possession', whereas CD covers and audio-cassette covers weren't; they had 'the same inherent function as other types of product packaging such as soap or spaghetti' (1999: 90).

The vinyl album cover answered the question: 'How will consumers notice (an) album in a store?' (Cusic 1996: 52). In the digital online world, there are no sales clerks, no store CDs or vinyl and no all-around visual displays. The digital music video today answers the question: 'How will consumers notice music online?' *Notice* is a crucial word, because the kind of browsing that people once did in record stores isn't duplicated online. The 2019 International Federation of the Phonographic Industry (IFPI) music report showed that in 2018 streaming revenue grew by 34 per cent and accounted for almost half (47 per cent) of global revenue, driven by a 32.9 per cent increase in paid subscription streaming. But we know that most of the revenue accruing to record labels from 'music-related video content' is from advertising, not from music video licences or any evidence of 'caused' music sales (sales arising from exposure to a music video). Current research indicates that most music consumers search for content in a focused, deliberate way online, based on recommendations from friends, music groups and lists. They aren't passively waiting for music content to be served to them by the editors of *TOTP* or *The Chart Show* or the VJs of MTV. That is one of the reasons that advertising has experienced such difficulty with the online world, because it doesn't have a captive audience of the kind it could rely on in the TV era. Music videos have to work very hard in this environment to have anywhere close to the impact they had on linear TV. Heads of music video and marketing at record labels know that all kinds of visual content, from live gig footage to fan videos, can help to increase audio exposure to songs. Sometimes, very rarely, an official music video will capture the zeitgeist and be shared, but the label expectation for that is low unless they have an artist who is already a superstar, like Beyoncé, or unless they can get an extremely accomplished music video director – or, ideally, both.

If we think about music videos as album covers, a universal model that explains the relationship between the rhythm and timbre of the song and the pacing of the visuals is unnecessary – because just as all album covers vary in the visual genres on which they draw, and vary according to the way that they will be displayed in a record store, all music videos will vary depending on the brief given to the makers about the context in which they are viewed (and on the maker's expert understanding of how that platform is best exploited). The apparatus and artefacts for selling music change over time, because the ways in which fans appreciate and consume music have changed, from the music hall to the retail outlet to streaming today. In the same way that we shouldn't equate music videos with MTV, we shouldn't equate music videos with YouTube, tempting though it is. There are many delivery platforms other than YouTube and mobile phones. There will be a day when the internet is superseded by a new platform. Like album covers, music videos are subject to larger financial and technological shifts in the industry of the kind identified by Edmond (2014). Piracy has been the endemic blight of the music industry. It has twice caused a major shift in productivity in the industry – in the 1970s, audio-cassette piracy, and in the 1990s/2000s, internet piracy – with very substantial implications for label marketing.

Relationship to British Screen Industries

How does this research on British music videos relate to existing scholarship in film and television studies? Darley argues that music videos are part of a 'distinct lineage' of works which has been 'less theorised', 'less lauded' and existed on the margins in comparison to narrative feature films and television (2002: 37), stretching back to the spectacular entertainments of the late eighteenth century and the nineteenth century. Darley includes computer games, certain films and some music videos in which the 'surface' and spectacle take priority. Korsgaard shares this ambition, and cites the work of Peeters (2004) on the spectacular in music video to support his case. Trick film was one of the most popular film genres watched in music halls during the period 1898–1908; it deployed mainly in-camera effects such as slow motion, fast motion and multiple exposure, as well as editing FX such as the substitution splice. Historians such as Gunning have argued that much of the pleasure of viewing trick films resided in the pleasure of experiencing the novelties themselves. The significance of post-production and in-camera effects is broadly consistent with my earlier comments. I have argued that British films have tended to foreground spectacle and effects more than US videos. This is in part a result of the art school effect, the artist's film and video tradition, the trick film and the incredible innovation of the UK's (or Europe's) VFX industry based in Soho. However, where in the 1960s the effects were in-camera, in the 1980s and 1990s, as London's post-production industry grew, they were increasingly post, and in the 2000s, there has been a rebellion against post FX and a preference for in-camera effects of the kind realised in the London Grammar video.

The collection of music videos analysed here sits within a burgeoning corpus of scholarship dedicated to documenting the post-war history of British film culture and film production. It is also relevant to the shift towards pleasure amongst filmmakers and audiences in Britain in the 1970s (e.g. Harper and Smith 2012). It confirms the argument of Grossberg (1993) that, with films such as *Tommy* (Ken Russell, 1975), Pink Floyd's *The Wall* (Alan Parker, 1982), *Jubilee* (Derek Jarman, 1978) and *Quadrophenia* (Franc Roddam, 1979), 'youth music films began to compete with rock culture and even threaten to displace it as the voice of youth in the 1980s and 1990s' (1993: 198). The analysis of dance videos presented here is consistent with John Mundy's (2007) work showing that British musicals were, in comparison with US musicals, less slick, less polished and lower budget, and addressed specific cultural issues: 'British musicals both drew upon and articulated important and distinctive aspects of British national identity, including contentious issues of social class, regionalism, attitudes to youth as well as gender' (Mundy 2007: 8) – and with a larger body of work on film, music and television in Britain (Donnelly 2002a, 2002b, 2005, 2007a, 2007b) and British artists' videos (Curtis 2006). The section on authorship also ties in well with Holly Rogers' recent work on artists working with videotape, where she ventures the potentially useful concept of the artist–composer to capture the work of artists such as Björk, who express their ideas through both film and music (Rogers 2013: 1). However, to progress, still more work is needed on the underlying organisations and networks that bridge the very differing production cultures of film and music, which have resulted in such successful creative collaborations between 1966 and 2016.

With an approach that focuses solely on individual directors, the risk is that 90 per cent of the content will be judged inadequate for a canon, and it wouldn't be the first time this has happened to audiovisual archives. I would suggest that music videos are considered as a type of commercial film art and marketing by record labels. In the larger picture of moving image heritage, music videos fall within what archivists would categorise as commissioned *industrial films*. Industrial films constitute a vast body of films in the British National Film Archive which have been largely neglected by scholars. They do not count as 'free art' in the definition of Marcuse in the 1930s, which forms a crucial constituent part of the paradigm within which British film studies has operated since the 1970s; and, as a result, very little of the archive has been analysed by academics. In the introduction to their collected edition on industrial film, Hediger and Vonderau (2014) write: 'In terms of output, industrial and commissioned films are definitely among the most prolific formats or genres in film history.' But 'little scholarship has been devoted to this corpus of films', because they are not suitable 'raw material for the production of academic auteur criticism', which continues to dominate film studies. Hediger and Vonderau conclude that

> one cannot but agree with collector-archivist Rick Prelinger, a pioneer in the field of industrial-film research, when he states that, 'it would be a great leap forward for cinema studies if we were able to avoid the auteur theory this time'. (2014: 10)

Free art 'transcends its social determination and emancipates itself from the given universe of discourse and behaviour while preserving its overwhelming presence' (Marcuse 1978: 6). Viewed through a paradigm in which they lack the prestigious conditions of the 'autonomous' or 'free' art for which auteur theory is suitable, music videos lie at the base of Britain's cultural hierarchy of screen arts (Caston 2019b).

However, still more work is needed on the relationship between the different parts of the screen industries to appreciate the broader trends affecting productivity in each zone within what I term the larger ecology. Elsewhere I have argued that the British music video industry functioned as an R&D sector for post-production effects and talent development (2019b). The British directors discussed in this book used mise-en-scène and post-production rather than dialogue in their films. Many were not initially funded by the BFI, which, up until the late 2000s, preferred to recruit directors from a TV soap opera and theatre background, because it was argued that this talent development stream alone affords the greater requisite experience in directing dialogue. However, since Film4 and Warp Films entered the market, music video directors such as Glazer, who used post-production effects, music and mise-en-scène rather than dialogue to communicate 'story', 'character' and 'mood', have been funded to make features with a noticeable impact on film styles. Simon Frith may be right that the only way forward is to conduct more ethnographies of the kind that have been conducted in music (2019) and early on in the history of film (Powdermaker 1950).

Tom Gunning has suggested that in terms of film, 'the two ends of the twentieth century hail each other like long-lost twins' (2003: 51). I regret that there was neither time nor space in the chapter on distribution to examine the impact or innovation of British music videos on smartphones, although this would be a worthy topic for follow-on research. The small screen is no new thing to the musical short, as Andrea Kelley (2015) has shown in her historical documentation and analysis of the US 'Soundies' of the 1940s. There has been a recent interest amongst scholars in vertical music videos for the mobile (Dibben 2014, for example). It would be interesting to compare the vertical music video genre and audience experience (sociologically) with those of the early Soundies: the Panoram movie machine, a jukebox cabinet containing a screen on which patrons could watch three-minute musical films, one number for every ten cents, launched in 1940 (Herzog 2004). I think there are also interesting questions about the audience experience of watching videos online, and the extent to which filmmakers have changed how they make videos for these.

Archive preservation is a necessity if this research is to take place. Music videos are part of Britain's screen heritage, yet very little of this heritage is being preserved for British audiences outside the well-known collections of artists famous for their videos such as The Beatles, Pink Floyd and Radiohead. The British Library has a collection of VHS viewing copies donated by the Musicians' Union. Having already received the videotape collections of Oil Factory when it closed (the work of Sophie Muller, WIZ and Pedro Romhanyi), the BFI has now received a donation of the entire personal film and video archive of British video director Steve Barron, and is hoping to receive a donation from Jamie Thraves. The film and video archive of pioneer Peter Whitehead has been taken in by De Montfort University. Until the early 2000s, many of the label masters were held at post-production houses for duplication prior to broadcast. With label buyouts and mergers, some have been lost. EMI is unusual in having preserved its archives in a systematic way, and when the videos were digitised in the late 1990s, donated most of its PMI master videotapes to the BFI National Film Archive. Dave Clark owns and holds all the master tapes and reels for the Dave Clark Five's videos, and these are apparently held in warehouse space just outside London. Keith Macmillan is said to hold all of the original master tapes of *The Chart Show* in another warehouse. Vanderquest, tasked by the industry to provide copies for commercial outlets, holds copies of a vast amount of these videos, but at £100 plus per video, the price is too expensive for research.

A key research question which has not yet been investigated is why certain regions and / or nations have been successful in developing constellations of filmmaking talent passionate about music and making music videos (above and below the line) at some points in history and not others. Above the line, France and Sweden are two notable examples. France has produced Michel Gondry, Jean-Baptiste Mondino, Romain Gavras and Stéphane Sednaoui. Sweden has produced Jonas Åkerlund, Johan Renck, Johan Camitz (who directed the Spice Girls' '*Wannabe*'), Jonas Odell and Lasse Hallström (who directed many videos for Abba). Whilst often maintaining homes and production company representation in the countries of their birth, most of these directors have secured representation and production agreements to work in London and Los Angeles simultaneously. Investigation into the legal and financial arrangements between the film and music industries would be crucial in helping to understand their significance.

The pop promos and music videos that have formed the subject of this study are part of a larger industrial product in Britain: musical shorts. Musical shorts are popular short-form content produced through an intentional collaboration between artist and filmmaker which are platform-neutral. What distinguished the post-1966 short was the practice and ideology of the filmmaker as auteur. They retain their popular appeal in a music hall, at a cinema, on TV, on YouTube and on your mobile. Because they are short, they are chameleon-like and flexible and can be packaged up in a variety of ways. Because of their adaptability, musical shorts will rise to the fore at experimental periods in the expansion of a new media platform whenever content is lacking. In the year 1935, there were 912 million admissions to British cinemas, so music shorts were shown at the cinema. In the 1980s and 1990s, Britain's mass audience was watching content on TV, so musical shorts were broadcast there as music videos. Today the mass audience is online, and that is where the videos have gone. Music videos are a category of mediated performance or musically edited content which will manifest wherever the largest audience is found. The record labels had the foresight to anticipate this when they set talent buyouts to include 'all media, throughout the universe, in perpetuity'.

APPENDICES

I Primary Sources

Personal communications

Interviews (face to face and phone)

Interviewers: Emily Caston (EC), Justin Smith (JS), Mimi Haddon (MH), Rowan Aust (RA).

Beckett, Steve (MH), 11 August 2016. Phone interview.
Bedford, Piers (JS), 11 October 2017. Oxfordshire.
Bellinger, Trudy (EC), 23 October 2016. Santa Monica, CA.
Benstock, Jes (RA), 7 December 2017. London.
Bernard, Natricia (EC), 1 February 2016. London.
Bixler, Litza (EC), 3 March 2016. Phone interview.
Blakey, Holly (EC), 1 February 2016. London.
Brunaro, Anna (MH), 23 September 2016. Phone interview.
Burton-Fairbrother, Carole (EC), 15 January 2016. London.
Chivers, Steve (EC), 8 June 2018. Phone interview.
Clancey, Julia (EC), 24 October 2016. West Hollywood, CA.
Clark, Dave (JS), 23 August 2018. Phone interview.
Crome, John (JS), 8 February 2016. Rockbourne, Hampshire.
Dick, Nigel (EC), 3 April 2017. Los Angeles, CA.
Dom & Nic (EC), 9 February 2016. London.
Egan, Nick (EC), 28 October 2016. Hollywood, CA.
Farrell, Aidan (EC), 15 March 2018. London.

Gent, Dilly (EC), 27 October 2016. Santa Monica, CA.
Grant, Brian (MH), 11 January 2017. Phone interview.
Heslop, Richard (EC), 17 September 2015. London.
Howie, Niven (EC), 1 December 2016. London.
Kearns, Tony (RA), 12 December 2017. London.
Kessler, Liz (EC), 1 March 2019. Phone interview.
Kubaisi, Tareq (EC), 24 January 2018. London.
Landay, Vince (EC), 30 October 2016. Santa Monica, CA.
Langridge, Helen (EC), 4 May 2017. London.
Larthe, Juliette (EC), 19 January 2016. London.
Lindsay-Hogg, Michael (JS), 30 June 2015. London.
Lole, Cynthia (EC), 31 May 2017. London.
Losey, Luke (RA), 4 December 2017. London.
Mathieson, John (EC), 8 January 2018. London.
Medak, Peter (JS), 9 July 2016. Phone interview.
Millaney, Scott, and Grant, Brian (EC), 12 April 2018. London.
Miller, Daniel (EC), 31 March 2015. London.
Morahan, Andy (EC), 10 May 2016. Phone interview.
Mulcahy, Russell (EC), 29 October 2016. West Hollywood, CA.
Muller, Sophie (EC), 19 April 2018. London.
Nava, Jake (EC), 13 December 2016. Phone interview.
O'Keefe, Mike (EC), 2 April 2016. Santa Monica, CA.
Roberts, Paul (EC), 1 February 2016. London.
Romhanyi, Pedro (MH), 7 November 2016. Phone interview.
Rose, Bernard (EC), 26 October 2016. CA.
Shadforth, Dawn (EC), 12 February 2016. London.
Shadforth, Dawn (MH), 17 November 2016. Phone interview.
Sillis, Aaron (EC), 22 September 2015. Phone interview.
Singh, Vic (JS), 7 February 2017. London.
Sutton, Carrie (EC), 16 November 2016. London.
Talamo, Nigel (MH), 10 November 2016. London.
Taylor, Kris (EC), 2 December 2016. London.
Thomas, Jeff (EC), 5 April 2017. Santa Monica, CA.
Thraves, Jamie (EC), 10 November 2014. Phone interview.
Totty, Ben (EC), 16 January 2016. London.
Wells, Mike (EC), 7 March 2018. Phone interview.

Interviews (email)

Barron, Siobhan, 22 and 25 April 2017. Emails.
Cameron, Angus, 17 March 2016. Email.
Curtis, Russell, 25 April 2017. Email.

Kessler, Liz, 22 February 2019. Email.
Lindsay, Tom, 23 May 2017. Email.
Pope, Tim, 24 September 2018. Email.
Whitehead, Peter, 1 October 2015. Email.

Email queries

The following industry people answered research queries relating to the landmark collection and to production credits assisted in the identification of masters and versions of masters: Vaughan Arnell, Siobhan Barron, Steve Barron, George Belfield, Otis Bell, Tom Bird, Cindy Burnay, Mary Calderwood, Angus Cameron, Sarah Chatfield, Russell Curtis, Ray Davies, Rob Dickens, Katie Dolan, Matthew Fone, Marisa Garner, Kevin Godley, Nick Goldsmith, Brian Grant, Phil Griffin, Rosie Hacket, John Hardwick, Kai Hsuing, Georgia Hudson, Amanda James, Tom Jobbins, Geoff Jukes, Tony Kearns, Mat Kirkby, Julia Knight, Ringan Ledwidge, Don Letts, Tom Lindsay, Mike Lipscombe, John Madsen, David Mallet, John Maybury, Aoife McArdle, Scott Millaney, Huse Monfaradi, Sophie Muller, Tim Nash, Jake Nava, Mike O'Keefe, Fiz Oliver, Dania Pasquini, Tim Pope, Róisín Murphy, Martin Roker, Pedro Romhanyi, Robbie Ryan, Jake Scott, Don Searll, Shynola, Carrie Sutton, Julien Temple, Hannah Turnbull-Walter, Peter Whitehead, Adam Whittaker, David Wilson, Daniel Wolfe, Piers Bedford, Tom Bird, Caswell Coggins, Anton Corbijn, Russell Curtis, Suzy Davis, Robin Dean, Ged Doherty, Pete Dyson, Matt Forrest, Jamie-Rose Fowler, Marissa Garner, Kevin Godley, Nick Goldsmith, Brian Grant, Neil Grigson, Robert Hales, Kai Hsuing, Georgia Hudson, Amanda James, Garth Jennings, Pat Joseph, Daniel Kleinman, Thomas Kuntz, Julia Knight, Joe Lancaster, Phil Lee, Rob Legatt, Don Letts, Keith Macmillan, David Mallet, Maria Manton, John Maybury, Nakkas Mickael, Maria Mochnacz, Huse Monfaradi, Joe Morris, Andy Orrick, Dania Pasquini, James Rosen, Gail Sparrow, Don Thomas, Laura Tunstall, Louise Whiston, Ed Wise.

Focus group participants

Animation Focus Group: 19 June 2015, British Library (Foyle Room), London: Justin Smith, Emily Caston, Richard Barnett, David Knight, Maria Manton, Tim Hope, Jennifer Roberts.

Experimental and Artists' Video Focus Group: 17 September 2015, British Film Institute, London: Emily Caston, Justin Smith, Mark Evans, Richard Heslop, Will Fowler, Gary Thomas, Liz Kessler, Ewan Jones Morris.

Dance Focus Group: 30 October 2015, British Film Institute, London: Emily Caston, Justin Smith, Mark Evans, David Knight, Florence Scott-Anderton, Arlene Phillips, Holly Blakey, Dan Curwin, Dylan Cave.

Authorship Focus Group: 12 November 2015, British Film Institute, London: Emily Caston, Justin Smith, Mark Evans, Florence Scott-Anderton, Keith Negus, Dave Laing, Andy Linehan, Paula Hearsum, Marketa Uhlirova, Dylan Cave.

Editing Focus Group: 26 November 2015, British Film and Video Council, London: Adam Dunlop, Art Jones, Tony Kearns, Julia Knight, Tom Lindsay, Dawn Shadforth, Emily Caston, Justin Smith, David Knight, Mark Evans, Florence Scott-Anderton.

Industry panel meeting participants

10 April 2015, 8 May 2015 and 13 May 2015: Foyle Room, The British Library, London: Adam Dunlop, Art Jones, Astrid Edwards, Barnaby Laws, Cynthia Lole, Dan Curwin, David Knight, Dawn Shadforth, Dominic Leung, Dougal Wilson, Fran Broadhurst, Henry Schofield, James Hackett, John Hassay, John Moule, John Stewart, Juliette Larthe, Liz Kessler, Tom Lindsay, Max Giwa, Phil Tidy, Richard Barnett, Richard Skinner, Sasha Dixon, Svana Gisladottir, Tareq Kubaisi, Tom Russell, WIZ, Jake Polansky.

4 December 2015: Eliot Room, British Library Conference Centre, The British Library, London: Fiz Oliver, Ben Totty, Holly Blakey, Jamie Thraves, Katie Dolan, Martin Roker, Mary Calderwood, Andy Morahan, Adam Dunlop, Art Jones, Astrid Edwards, Barnaby Laws, Cynthia Lole, Dan Curwin, David Knight, Dawn Shadforth, Dominic Leung, Dougal Wilson, Fran Broadhurst, Henry Schofield, James Hackett, John Hassay, John Moule, John Stewart, Juliette Larthe, Liz Kessler, Tom Lindsay, Max Giwa, Phil Tidy, Richard Barnett, Richard Skinner, Sasha Dixon, Svana Gisladottir, Tareq Kubaisi, Tom Russell, WIZ.

20 December 2016: British Film Institute, Stephen Street, London: George Barber, Fraser Kent, Fiz Oliver, Dom & Nic, Hannah Turnbull-Walters, Angus Cameron, Adam Whittaker, Brian Grant, Ian Roberston, James Marrs, Jamie Thraves, Jane Third, Julia Knight, Kate Kotcheff, Matthew Fone, Nathan Killham, Nathan Richards, Matthew Clyde, Martin Sullivan, Nigel Talamo, Niven Howie, Ollie Weait, Paul Roberts, Sally Llewellyn, Scott Millaney, Steve Barron, Tom Jobbins, Toby Tremlett, Toby Tobias, Adam Dunlop, Art Jones, Astrid Edwards, Barnaby Laws, Cynthia Lole, Dan Curwin, David Knight, Dawn Shadforth, Dominic Leung, Dougal Wilson, Fran Broadhurst, Henry Schofield, James Hackett, John Hassay, John Moule, John Stewart, Juliette Larthe, Liz Kessler, Tom Lindsay, Max Giwa, Phil Tidy, Richard Barnett, Richard Skinner, Sasha Dixon, Svana Gisladottir, Tareq Kubaisi, Tom Russell, WIZ, Neil Grigson.

Facebook research group: 'Fifty Years of British Music Video',
29 September 2015–

Trudy Bellinger, Liz Kessler, Jake Polansky, Joel Marcus, Taichi Kamura, Lucy Nolan, Will Oakley, Sally Lewellyn, Faith Holmes, John Pardue, Tom Lindsay, Fi Kilroe, Robin Dean, Rich Skinner, Niven Howie, Tracy Bass, Benny Trickett, Angus Cameron, Kris P. Taylor, Tarequ Kubaisi, Tom Jobbins, Helen Neal Massey, Leila Sarraf, Cara Brady, Faser Kent, Phil Barnes, Kate Start, Neil Grigson, Mike O'Keefe, Juliette Larthe, Clare Clarkson, Claire Neate-James, Martin Roker, Sarita Allison, Otis Bell, Carrie Sutton, Jeff Thomas, Line Postmyr, David Knight, Ewan Jones Morris, Adam Dunlop, Alison Carter, Ninian Doff, James Hackett, Sally Heath, Astrid Edwards, Joe Guest, Keith Hide, Sally Campbell, Fiz Oliver, Rick Wollard, Wayne Holloway, Elizabeth Flowers, Katie Swain, Lana Topham, Huse Monfaradi, Simon Coull, Daniel Millar, Pete Chambers, Sarah Chatfield, Bona Oradwue, Angus Hudson, Arlene Philips, Roisin Murphy, Denise Larkin, Brian Grant, Matthew Clyde, Tom Harding, Oleg Poupko, Alex Panton, Rubin Mendoza, Nathan Richards, Katy Lynne, Susan Silverman, James Rose, Peter Care, Justin Pentecost, Nick Taylor, Linda Russell, Marcus Domleo, Richard Heslop, Vincent Landay, Mark Gibbons, Caroline Bottomley, John Hassay, Rachel Jillions, Davida Janet Eisner, Nick Morris, Ian Roberson, Steve Giudici, Rob Lumb-Mercer, Paul Flattery, Adam Lockhart, Dan Sherwen, Howard Greenhalgh, Perry Joseph, Dave Robinson, Aoife McArdle, Mark Hasler, Jane Skinner, Maggi Townley, Nick Burgess-Jones, Bruce Ashley, Justine White, Jolyon Bateman, Philip Dupee, James Mackay, Jamie Grant, Gregg Masuak, Helen Whiting, Orson Nava, Martin Goodwin, John Keeling, Marie McGonigle, Ollie Weait, Kate Kotcheff, Marcelo Anciano, Matthew Alden-Morris, Sara Rollason, Barnaby Laws, Paul McKee, Andrew Clarkson, Johnny Donne, Fredrik Bond, Andy Hylton, Rikki Finegold, Toby Tobias, Andy Picheta, Joe Dyer, Nigel Talamo, Mark Murrell, Hannah Turnbull-Walters, Christopher Ranson, David Amphlett, Wayne Imms, Doug Nichol, Tony Kearns, Christopher Hughes, Michael Geoghegan, Pete Nash, Louise Knight, Adam Whittaker, Ben Totty, Fran Broadhurst, Andy Morahan, Laura Boyd, Paul Roberts Househam, Mike Lipscombe, Holls Therese.

II Listing and Film Credits for Landmark Special Edition Boxset

Below are listed the full credits for the landmark special edition boxset *Power to the People: British Music Videos 1966–2016, 200 Landmark Music Videos* PAL. Region 2. Discs: 6. Thunderbird Releasing. Released 5 March 2018. Run time: 900 minutes. ASIN: B077YDJVN6.

Disc 1: Performance

1/ Band Performance

Rolling Stones 'It's Only Rock N Roll (But I Like It)' (1974) 5:21. D: Michael Lindsay-Hogg, DoP: Martin Bond, Ed: David Crossman (2" videotape).

The Clash 'London Calling' (1979) 2:15. D: Don Letts, DoP: John Metcalfe (16mm). Commissioned by CBS Records.

Joy Division 'Love Will Tear Us Apart' (1980) 2:29. D: Stuart Orme, DoP: Peter MacKay. Commissioned by Factory Records.

Siouxsie and the Banshees 'Happy House' (1980) 2:53. D and DoP: Piers Bedford, P: Verity Roberts, Ed: Gordon Grimward.

The Cure 'Close to Me' (1985) 3:57. D: Tim Pope, P: Lisa Bryer, DoP: Chris Ashbrook, Ed: Peter Goddard, Col: Mike Udin.

Stone Roses 'Fools Gold' (1989) 4:22. D: Geoff Wonfor.

Oasis 'Cigarettes and Alcohol' (1994) 5:12. D: Mark (Alex) Szaszy and Corinne Day, P: Will Waller, DoP: Dan Landin, Ed: Simon Hilton / Joel Marcus. PC: 4D Productions. Commissioned by Dick Green for Creation Records.

Duran Duran 'White Lines (Don't Do It)' (1995) 5:38. D: Nick Egan, P: Kirsten Syme, DoP: Martin Coppen, Ed: Nicholas Weyman-Harris. PC: Satellite Films (35mm). Commissioned by Parlophone.

Reef 'Place Your Hands' (1997) 3:38. D: David Mould, DoP: Dan Landin, Ed: Russell Icke. PC: Partizan. Commissioned by Mark Richardson for Sony Music.

Blur 'Song 2' (1997) 2:00. D and Ed: Sophie Muller, P: Rob Small, DoP: John Lynch, Art: Clare Clarkson, Col: Tom Russell @ VTR, Post: VTR. PC: Oil Factory. Commissioned by Dilly Gent for Parlophone.

Oasis 'All Around the World' (1998) 7:46. D: Valerie Faris and Jonathan Dayton, DoP: Max Malkin, Ed: Eric Zumbrunnen, Post: various including Paul Vester. PC: Dayton-Fairs Productions. Commissioned by Scott Spanjick for Epic New York.

Manic Street Preachers 'If You Tolerate This Your Children Will Be Next' (1998) 5:37. D: WIZ, P: Niki Amos, DoP: Tom Ingle, Ed: Gary Knight @ Final Cut, Col: Tareq Kubaisi @ VTR. PC: Oil Factory (35mm). Commissioned by Mike O'Keefe for Sony Music.

Supergrass 'Pumping on Your Stereo' (1999) 3:29. D: Garth Jennings, P: Nick Goldsmith, DoP: Igor Jadue Lillo, Ed: Dominic Leung, Col: Tareq Kubaisi @ VTR, Puppets: Jim Henson. PC: Hammer & Tongs. Commissioned by Dilly Gent for Parlophone.

Moloko 'The Time Is Now' (2000) 4:31. D and Ed: Dominic Leung, P: Hammer & Tongs, DoP: Denzil Armour-Brown. Commissioned by John Chuter for Echo Records.

Arctic Monkeys 'The View from the Afternoon' (2006) 4:44. D: WIZ, P: Benedict Cooper, EP: Paul Fennelly and Toby Hyde, DoP: Daniel Landin, Ed: Tom Lindsay @ Metropolis, Col: Tom Russell @ Prime Focus. PC: Factory Films (35mm). Commissioned by John Moule for Domino Records.

Hot Chip 'Over and Over' (2006) 3:56. D: Nima Nourizadeh, P: Grade Bodie, DoP: Ben Moulden, Ed: Dan Sherwen, Col: Kai van Beers at VTR, Post: Ali Burnett at Red / Smoke and Mirrors. Commissioned by Katie Griffiths and John Moule for EMI Records.

The Horrors 'Sheena is a Parasite' (2007) 1:49. D, DoP and Ed: Chris Cunningham, P: James Wilson, Post: Golden Square. Commissioned by Ross Anderson for Loog Records.

Vampire Weekend 'A-Punk' (2008) 2:18. D: Garth Jennings, P: Nick Goldsmith, Ed: Dominic Leung. PC: Hammer & Tongs. Commissioned by Phil Lee for XL Recordings.

Wild Beasts 'Brave Bulging Buoyant Clairvoyants' (2008) 3:58. D: OneinThree, P: Tamsin Glasson, DoP: Dan Trapp, Ed: OneinThree, Col: James Bamford @ The Mill, Post: The Mill. PC: Colonel Blimp. Commissioned by Bart McDonagh for Domino.

Toy 'Lose My Way' (2012) 4:28. D, P, DoP and Ed: Joe Morris. PC: Brass Moustache. Commissioned by Heavenly Records.

Arctic Monkeys 'Arabella' (2013) 4:38. D: Jake Nava, P: Benedict Cooper, DoP: Dion Beebe, Ed: Julia Knight. PC: Believe Media (35mm). Commissioned by Jonny Brandshaw for Domino Records.

King Krule 'A Lizard State' (2014) 4:34. D: Jamie-James Medina, P: Audrey Davenport, DoP: Tim Sidell, Ed: Spencer Campbell, Col: Nat Jencks. PC: Forever Pictures. Commissioned by Phil Lee for XL Recordings.

2/ Vocal Performance

Godley and Creme 'Cry' (1981) 4:01. D: Kevin Godley, P: Lexi Godfrey, Ed: Roo Aiken, Post: Carlton TV.

Sinéad O'Connor 'Nothing Compares 2 U' (1990) 5:09. D: John Maybury, DoP: Dominique LeRigoleur.

Massive Attack 'Unfinished Sympathy' (1991) 4:03. D: Baillie Walsh, P: Mark Wightwick, DoP: John Mathieson, Art: Leigh Bowery, Col: Soho 601. PC: Limelight. GB1209050400.

Björk 'Big Time Sensuality' (1993) 5:04. D: Stéphane Sednaoui, P: Line Postmyr, Ed: Craig Wood, Col: Tom Russell @ VTR. PC: Propaganda. Commissioned by Paul McKee for One Little Indian.

Radiohead 'No Surprises' (1997) 3:53. D: Grant Gee, P: Phil Barnes, DoP: Dan Landin, Ed: Jerry Chater, Col: Tareq Kubaisi @ VTR, Post: Sean Broughton @ Smoke and Mirrors. PC: Kudos. Commissioned by Dilly Gent for Parlophone.

Coldplay 'Yellow' (2000) 4:32. D: James and Alex, DoP: Richard Stuart. Commissioned by Faith Holmes for Parlophone.

Elton John 'I Want Love' (2001) 4:51. D: Sam Taylor-Wood.

The Streets 'Fit But You Know It' (2004) 4:08. D: Dougal Wilson, P: Tim Cole, DoP: Dan Bronks, Ed: Suzy Davis. PC: Colonel Blimp. Commissioned by Cara Brady for WEA / London Records.

Bat for Lashes 'What's a Girl To Do?' (2007) 2:54. D: Dougal Wilson, P: Matthew Fone, DoP: Matias Montero, Ed: Joe Guest, Col: Jean Clement for MPC. PC: Colonel Blimp (16mm with 35mm Anamorphic lenses).

Dan Le Sac vs Scroobius Pip 'Thou Shalt Always Kill' (2007) 3:29. D, P and Post: Nick Frew, DoP: Jim Phillpot, Ed: Jake Roberts. Commissioned by Mike Salmon.

FKA twigs 'Water Me' (2013) 3:23. D: FKA twigs and Jesse Kanda, P: Juliette Larthe and Shimmy Ahmed, DoP: Sy Turnbull. PC: Prettybird UK. Commissioned by Young Turks.

Wiley 'On a Level' (2014) 3:31. D: Skepta.

Disc 2: Concept

1/ Concept Featuring Band

Manfred Mann 'The Mighty Quinn' (1968) 2:55. D and Ed: John Crome, DoP: Ray Orton and Nick Nolan. PC: Eyeline (16mm). Commissioned by Gerry Bron for Fontana.

Eurythmics 'Sweet Dreams (Are Made of This)' (1983) 3:22. D: Dave Stewart, Chris Ashbrook and Jon Roseman, P: Dave Stewart and Jon Roseman, DoP: Chris Ashbrook, Ed: Bill Saint. John Roseman Productions (35mm). Commissioned by RCA Records.

Cabaret Voltaire 'Sensoria' (1984) 4:00. D: Peter Care.

Duran Duran 'The Wild Boys' (1984) 4:14. D: Russell Mulcahy, P: Chrissie Smith, DoP: Tony Mitchell, Ch: Arlene Phillips, Ed: Tim Waddell. MGMM (35mm). Commissioned by Parlophone.

The The 'Infected' (1986) 5:05. D: Peter Christopherson, P: Fiz Oliver, DoP: Adam Rodgers, Ed: Philip Richardson.

My Bloody Valentine 'To Here Knows When' (1991) 4:48. D: Angus Cameron, P: Fiona Adams, DoP: Sam Montague, Ed: Nigel Simpkiss. PC: Popata (16mm and Super 8). Commissioned by Creation Records.

Leila K 'Ça plane pour moi' (1993) 3:24. D, DoP and Ed: Richard Heslop, P: Kim Mnguni. PC: Oil Factory.

PJ Harvey 'Down by the Water' (1995) 3:45. D: Maria Mochnacz, P: Ana San Martin, DoP: Seamus McGarvey, Ed: Tony Kearns. PC: Nemesis Films. Commissioned by Pinko for Island Records.

Tricky 'Black Steel: In the Hour of Chaos' (1995) 3:51. D and Ed: Mike Lipscombe, P: Steve Williams, EP: Geoff Folkes, DoP: Kate Stark, Post: Cinesite (Eve Rambourn on Flame). PC: Media Lab (S16mm). Commissioned by Pinko for Island Records.

Massive Attack 'Karmacoma' (1995) 4:26. D: Jonathan Glazer, P: Nick Morris, DoP: Steve Keith Roach and Tim Maurice Jones, Ed: Rick Lawley, Col: Sean Broughton. Commissioned by Carole Burton-Fairbrother for Virgin Records.

Therapy? 'Diane' (1995) 4:38. D: WIZ, P: Kim Mnguni, DoP: Dan Landin, Ed: Struan Clay, Col: Tareq Kubaisi @ VTR. PC: Oil Factory (35mm). Commissioned by Robin Dean for A&M Records.

Radiohead 'Street Spirit' (1996) 4:21. D: Jonathan Glazer, P: Nick Morris, DoP: Tim Maurice-Jones, Ed: John McManus. PC: Academy. Commissioned by Dilly Gent for Parlophone.

McFly 'Room on the 3rd Floor' (2004) 3:23. D: Si and Ad, P: Laura Kaufman, DoP: Daniel Bronks, Ed: Mark Alehin @ Boomerang. Post: ShinyEye. PC: Academy. Commissioned by Liz Kessler for Island Records.

The Ting Tings 'Shut Up and Let Me Go' (2008) 2:54. D: Alex and Liane, P: Charlotte Woodhead, DoP: Will Bex, Ed: Amanda James, Col: Rushes. PC: Factory Films. Commissioned by John Hassay.

Radiohead 'House of Cards' (2008) 4:33. D: Blip Boutique (James Frost and Mary Faggot), P: Dawn Fanning, Technical Director: Aaron Koblin, Ed: Nick Wayman-Harris. Post: The Syndicate. PC: Zoo Films.

Coldplay 'Strawberry Swing' (2008) 4:20. D: Shynola, P: Margo Mars, DoP: Aaron Platt, Post: MPC. PC: Black Dog / RSA. Commissioned by Kirsten Cruickshank.

Klaxons 'Twin Flames' (2010) 3:31. D: Saam Farahmand, P: Fenella Sanderson, DoP: Dan Bronks, Ed: Gus Herdman @ Trim, Post: Blind Pig @ Absolute. PC: Partizan. Commissioned by Emily Tedrake.

London Grammar 'Wasting My Young Years' (2013) 3:30. D: Bison, P: Liz Kessler, DoP: Matyas Erderly, Ed: Vid Price, Col: Mark Vincent. PC: Academy A+. Commissioned by Caroline Clayton for Ministry of Sound.

2/ Pure Concept

23 Skidoo 'Kundalini' (from the film *7 Songs*) (1982) 5:09. D, P, DoP and Ed: Richard Heslop. Baptist Pork Entertainments (found video footage and 8mm and 16mm film).

LFO 'LFO' (1991) 3:59. D and P: Jarvis Cocker, Filmmakers: John Foxx, Penny Downes, Paul Plowman, Gary Smith. Commissioned by Warp Records.

Autechre 'Second Bad Vilbel' (1995) 4:44. D: Chris Cunningham, P: Mary Calderwood and Cyndi Rhoades, DoP: Charles Teton, Ed: Nick Spencer. PC: Activate. Commissioned by Steve Beckett for Warp.

Tricky 'Overcome' (1995) 3:45. D: Mike Lipscombe, P: Will Oakley. Commissioned by Pinko for Island Records.

Howie B 'Music for Babies' (1996) 6:08. D: Run Wrake. Commissioned by Cynthia Lole for Polydor.

Future Sound of London 'We Have Explosive' (1996) 4:04. D: Run Wrake.

Melting Pot 'Something Is Wrong' (1996) 5:28. D, P, DoP and Ed: Dawn Shadforth (Canon Hi8).

Coldcut and Hexstatic 'Timber' (1997) 4:45. Video Art: Stuart Warren Hill and Robin Brunson. Stock footage from Greenpeace. Part of the Natural Rhythms Trilogy, produced with Greenpeace.

All Seeing I 'The Beat Goes On' (1998) 4:02. D and Ed: Dawn Shadforth, P: Phil Tidy, DoP: Rob Hardy, Col: Dom at Rushes. PC: Image Dynamic Productions (16mm). Commissioned by Phil Howells.

Massive Attack 'Teardrop' (1998) 4:56. D: Walter Stern, P: Laura Kanerick, DoP: Dan Landin, Ed: John McMannus @ OBE, Col: Tareq Kubaisi @ VTR, Post: Sean Broughton @ Smoke and Mirrors. PC: Academy (35mm). Commissioned by Carole Burton-Fairbrother for Virgin Records.

The Avalanches 'Frontier Psychiatrist Version 1' (2001) 4:37. Dir: Tom Kuntz and Mike Maguire, P: Richard Weager, DoP: Jake Polonsky, Ed: Tony Kearns. PC: Propaganda Films. Commissioned by Richard Skinner for XL Recordings.

UNKLE 'Eye for an Eye' (2003) 6:28. D: Ruth Lingford and Shynola. PC: Oil Factory.

Gnarls Barkley 'Crazy' (2006) 2:59. D: Robert Hales, P: Coleen Haynes, Ed: Ken Mowe. PC: HSI Productions. Commissioned by Cathy Pellow for Atlantic Records.

FKA twigs 'How's That' (2013) 3:35. D: Jesse Kanda. PC: Prettybird. Commissioned by Young Turks.

Rudimental feat. John Newman 'Feel the Love' (2013) 3:54. D: Bob Harlow, P: Sarah Tognazzi / Gaetan Rousseau, DoP: Steve Annis, Ed: Leila Sarraf. Commissioned by Dan Curwin. PC: Somesuch.

Benga 'I Will Never Change' (2013) 2:00. D: Us (Chris Barrett and Luke Taylor), P: Liz Kessler, DoP: Matt Fox, Ed: Vid Price, Col: Mark Horrobin. PC: Academy. Commissioned by Daniel Millar for Sony Music.

Pinkunoizu 'Moped' (2013) 4:53. D, P, DoP and Ed: Ewan Morris Jones. Commissioned by Full Time Hobby.

Disc 3: Dance

Elton John 'I'm Still Standing' (1983) 3:13. D: Russell Mulcahy, P: Jackie Byford, DoP: John Metcalf, Ed: Roy Andrews, Ch: Arlene Phillips. PC: MGMM (35mm). Commissioned by Rocket Records.

Kate Bush 'Running Up That Hill' (1985) 4:58. D: David Garfath, Co-D: Kate Bush, DoP: Phil Meyheux, Ed: David Gardner. PC: Paul Weiland (35mm).

New Order 'True Faith' (1987) 4:08. D and Ch: Philippe Decouflé, P: Michael H. Shamberg (35mm). Commissioned by Factory Records.

Fine Young Cannibals 'She Drives Me Crazy' (1988) 3:38. D, P and Ch: Philippe Decouflé, DoP: Darius Khondji (16mm).

The Prodigy 'Out of Space' (1992) 4:01. D: Russell Curtis, Ed: Bluey Durrant.

Beverley Knight 'Made It Back' (1998) 3:28. D: Jake Nava, P: Nick Landin, EP: Emily Caston, DoP: Simon Chaudoir. PC: The End (35mm). Commissioned by Dilly Gent for Parlophone.

Basement Jaxx 'Red Alert' (1999) 4:00. D and Ed: Dawn Shadforth, P: Anna Brunoro, DoP: Rob Hardy, Ch: Litza Bixler, Col: Dom @ Rushes, Post: The Mill. PC: Black Dog / RSA (16mm). Commissioned by Richard Skinner for XL Recordings.

Aphex Twin 'Windowlicker' (1999) 10:34. D and Ed: Chris Cunningham, P: Cindy Burnay, DoP: James Hawkinson, Ch: Vincent Patterson, Col: Ben Eagleton @ Rushes, Post: Glassworks. Black Dog / RSA (35mm). Commissioned by Warp Records.

Blur 'Music Is My Radar' (2000) 5:01. D: Don Cameron, P: Jo Allen, DoP: Alex Barber, Ch: Blanca Li, Ed: Nick Wayman Harris, Col: Adrian Seery, Art: Dan Betteridge. PC: Tsunami.

So Solid Crew '21 Seconds' (2001) 5:23. D: Max and Dania, P: Simon Poon Tip, DoP: Greg Copeland, Ed: Claudia Wass. PD: Bullet (35mm). Commissioned by Relentless Records.

Kylie Minogue 'Can't Get You Out of My Head' (2001) 3:47. D and Ed: Dawn Shadforth, P: Cindy Burnay, DoP: John Mathieson, Ch: Michael Rooney, Col: Frank Voturier at MPC, Post: Red. PC: Black Dog / RSA (35mm). Commissioned by Faith Holmes for Parlophone.

Moloko 'Familiar Feeling' (2003) 3:56. D: Elaine Constantine, P: Hannah Sherlock, DoP: Richard Mott, Ed: Ivan Cullens, Col: Frank Voiturier @ MPC. PC: Point Blank. Commissioned by Róisín Murphy.

Basement Jaxx 'Hush Boy' (2006) 3:53. D: Phil Griffin, P: Kate Phillips, DoP: Greg Copeland, Ch: Paul Roberts, Ed: Dan Robinson @ Cut+Run, Col: Kai Van Beers at VTR, Post: Smoke and Mirrors. PC: Alchemy. Commissioned by Phil Lee for XL Recordings.

Arctic Monkeys 'Brianstorm' (2007) 3:01. D: Huse Monfaradi, P: Kat Armour-Brown, DoP: Fredrik Callingcard, Ch: Natricia Bernard, Ed: Sam Sneade, Col: Tareq Kubaisi. PC: Black Dog / RSA (35mm). Commissioned by John Moule.

Duffy 'Rain on Your Parade' (2008) 3:33. D and Ed: Sophie Muller, P: Rob Small, DoP: Simon Chaudoir, Ch: Natricia Bernard, Col: Tom Russell. PC: Factory Films (16mm). Commissioned by Ross Anderson.

The xx 'Islands' (2009) 2:49. D: Saam Farahmand, P: Ben Sullivan, DoP: Will Bex, Ch: Supple Nam, Ed: Tom Lindsay, Post: Munky at Trim. PC: Partizan. Commissioned by Young Turks.

Radiohead 'Lotus Flower' (2011) 5:02. D and P: Garth Jennings, DoP: Nick Wood, Ch: Wayne McGregor, Ed: Leila Sarraf. Commissioned by LX Recordings.

Atoms for Peace 'Ingenue' (2013) 4:32. D: Garth Jennings, P: Helen Power, DoP: Nick Wood, Ch: Wayne McGregor, Ed: Dom Leung. PC: STK Films.

The Feeling 'Boy Cried Wolf' (2013) 5:20. D: L. J. Scott, P: Kristyna Sellnerova, DoP: Davey Gilder, Ch: Arthur Pita and Edward Watson, Ed and Col: Jimmi Phillips. PC: Little Yellow Jacket. GBZA41301078. Commissioned by Faye Purcell at BMG Rights Management.

Chase and Status 'International' (2014) 4:12. D and Ed: Taichi Kimura, P: Tina Pawlik, DoP: Dan Stafford-Clarke, Ch: Holly Blakey.

Jungle 'Time' (2014) 3:34. D: Oliver Hadlee Pearch, P: Corin Taylor, DoP: Adam Scarth, Ch: Holly Blakey, Ed: Max Windows, Col: Julien Biard @ Finish. PC: Colonel Blimp. Commissioned by Phil Lee for XL Recordings.

FKA twigs 'Tw-ache' (2014) 4:19. D: Tom Beard and FKA twigs, P: Holly Restrieaux, DoP: Tim Sidell, Ch: FKA twigs and Aaron Sillis. PC: Partizan (Alexa). Commissioned by Jennifer Byrne for Dazed.

Peace 'Money' (2014) 3:46. D: Ninian Doff, P: Rik Green, DoP: Steve Annis, Ch: Supple Nam, Ed: Leo King @ Stich, Col: Julien Baird @ Finish, Post: Andy Copping. PC: Pulse Films. Commissioned by Lisa Foo for Sony Music.

Arcade Fire 'We Exist' (2014) 6:23. D: David Wilson, P: Jason Baum, DoP: Larkin Seiple, Ch: Ryan Heffington, Ed: Thomas Grove Carter, Col: Simon Bourne, Post: Munky. PC: The Directors Bureau.

Ed Sheeran 'Thinking Out Loud' (2014) 4:59. D: Emil Nava, P: Danyi Deats and Lanette Phillips, DoP: Daniel Pearl, Ch: Tabitha and Napoleon D'umo (Nappytabs), Ed: Anna Gerstenfeld, Col: Beau Leon. PC: London Alley (16mm). Commissioned by Dan Curwin for Atlantic Records (Asylum).

Jungle 'Julia' (2014) 3:19. D: Oliver Hadlee Pearch, P: Corin Taylor, DoP: Adam Scarth, Ch: Aaron Sillis, Ed: Max Windows, Col: Julien Biard @ Finish. PC: Colonel Blimp. Commissioned by Phil Lee for XL Recordings.

Gwilym Gold 'Triumph' (2015) 3:53. D: and Ch: Holly Blakey, P: Sarah Aranda-Garzon, DoP: Charlie Herranz, Ed: Sam Jones @ Cut+Run, Col: Jason Wallis at Electric Theatre Collective. PC: Knucklehead. Commissioned by Brille Records.

Hurts 'Lights' (2015) 6:57. D: Dawn Shadforth, P: Rachel Rumbold and Caroline Purkayastha, DoP: Robbie Ryan, Ch: Callum Powell, Ed: Dom Leung, Col: Simone at Time Based Arts, Post: Coffee and TV. PC: Sonny London (Alexa Mini). Commissioned by Laura Clayton.

Young Fathers 'Shame' (2015) 4:14. D: Jeremy Cole, P: James Payne, DoP: David Wright, Ch: Holly Blakey, Ed: Julian Fletcher, Col: J. P. Davidson. PC: Lemonade Money. Commissioned by Hannah Turnbull-Walter for Big Dada.

Salute 'Storm' (2016) 3:18. D: Raine Allen-Miller, P: Elly Camisa, EP: Hannah Turnbull-Walter, DoP: Deepa Keshvala, Ch: Enzinne Asinugo, Ed: Leila Gaabi, Col: Jack McGinity. PC: Somesuch.

The Chemical Brothers feat. Beck 'Wide Open' (2016) 4:38. D: Dom & Nic, P: John Madsen, DoP: Steve Chivers, Ch: Wayne McGregor, Ed: Ed Cheesman, Col: Dave Ludlum @ The Mill, Post: The Mill. PC: Outsider (Alexa Raw). Commissioned by Alisa Robertson.

Disc 4: Stories

1/ Love Stories

Ultravox 'Vienna' (1981) 5:05. D: Russell Mulcahy, P: Lexi Godfrey, DoP: Nic Knowland, Ed: Russell Mulcahy. PC: MGMM. Commissioned by Peter Wag at Chrysalis.

Human League 'Don't You Want Me' (1981) 3:56. D: Steve Barron, EP: Siobhan Barron, P: Siobhan Barron and Adam Whittaker, DoP: Oliver Stapleton, Ed: Pete Cornish. PC: Limelight (35mm). Commissioned by Tessa Watts for Virgin Records.

A-ha 'Take On Me' (1985) 3:47. D: Steve Barron, EP: Siobhan Barron, P: Siobhan Barron and Adam Whittaker, DoP: Oliver Stapleton, Ed: David Yardley. PC: Limelight (35mm). Commissioned by Jeff Airoff for A&M USA.

Sade 'Smooth Operator' (1984) 8:33. D: Julien Temple, P: Amanda Temple, DoP: Clive Tickner, Ed: Richard Bedford. PC: Nitrate Film (16mm).

Robbie Williams 'She's the One' (1999) 5:17. D: Dom & Nic, P: John Madsen, DoP: Dan Landin, Ed: Struan Clay, Col: Tareq Kubaisi @ VFX: VTR. PC: Oil Factory (35mm). Commissioned by Carrie Sutton.

Badly Drawn Boy 'Disillusion' (2000) 4:46. D: Garth Jennings, P: Nick Goldsmith, DoP: Jim Fealy, Ed: Dominic Leung, Col: Tareq Kubaisi @ VTR. PC: Hammer & Tongs (35mm). Commissioned by Richard Skinner.

Texas 'In Demand' (2000) 4:00. D: Vaughan Arnell, P: Jason Kremer, DoP: John Lynch, Col: Tareq Kubaisi @ VTR. PC: Godman. Commissioned by Tess Wight for Mercury Records.

Hiatus 'We Can Be Ghosts Now (Feat. Shura)' (2013) 4:19. D and P: Tom Jobbins, DoP: Matthias Pilz, Art: John Reynolds, Ed: Robert Mila, Col: Danny Atkinson. PC: Th1ng. Commissioned by Cyrus Shahrad.

2/ Heroes and Anti-Heroes

Kate Bush 'Cloudbusting' (1985) 7:00. D and Ed (film): Julian Doyle, Co-D: Kate Bush, Ed (video): David Yardley, DoP: Brian Herlihy. PC: PMI.

Radiohead 'Just' (1995) 4:35. D: Jamie Thraves, P: Niki Amos, DoP: Alex Melman, Ed: Tony Kearns, Col: Tareq Kubaisi @ VTR. PC: Oil Factory (S16mm). Commissioned by Dilly Gent for Parlophone.

The Chemical Brothers 'Elektrobank' (1997) 6:18. D: Spike Jonze, P: Vince Landay, DoP: Lance Accord, P(UK Post): Emily Caston, Ed: Adam Finch, Col: Tom Russell. PC: Satellite Films (35mm). Commissioned by Carole Burton-Fairbrother for Virgin Records.

UNKLE 'Rabbit in Your Headlights' (1998) 5:09. D: Jonathan Glazer, P: Nick Morris, DoP: John Mathieson, Col: Tareq Kubaisi @ VTR. PC: Academy. Commissioned by Robin Dean for A&M Records.

Travis 'Turn' (1999) 5:49. D: Ringan Ledwidge, P: Emily Caston, DoP: Andrzej Sekula, Ed: Rich Orrick, Col: Tareq Kubaisi @ VTR. PC: The End (35mm). Commissioned by Robin Dean for Independiente.

Robbie Williams 'Supreme' (2000) 4:34. D: Vaughan Arnell, P: Jason Kremer Godman, DoP: John Lynch, Ed: Gary Knight @ Final Cut, Col: Tareq Kubaisi @ VTR. PC: Godman. Commissioned by Carrie Sutton for EMI Records.

Coldplay 'The Scientist' (2002) 4:26. D: Jamie Thraves, P: Sally Llewellyn, DoP: Tat Radcliffe, Ed: Tony Kearns @ Swordfish, Col: Tareq Kubaisi @ VTR. PC: Oil Factory. Commissioned by Faith Holmes for Parlophone.

The Prodigy 'Warriors Dance' (2009) 3:26. D: Corin Hardy, P: Liz Kessler, DoP: Stuart Bentley, Puppetry: Dark Vast, Ed: Amanda James. PC: Academy. Commissioned by Rob Collins for Cooking Vinyl. GB4110900380.

Sigur Rós 'Ekki Múkk' (2012) 10:11. D: Nick Abrahams, P: Dhiraj Mahey, DoP: Martin Dohrn and Ole Birkeland, Ed: Adam Biskupski, Col: John Claude. Commissioned by Big Dipper.

The Shoes feat. Anthonin Ternant 'Time to Dance' (2012) 8:35. D: Daniel Wolfe, P: Lee Groombridge and Dougal Meese, DoP: Robbie Ryan, Ed:

Tom Lindsay, Col: Simon Bourne, Somesuch (35mm). Commissioned by Pierre Le Ny.

Jon Hopkins 'Open Eye Signal' (2013) 8:02. D: Aoife McArdle, P: Tamsin Glasson / Brian Welsh, DoP: Steve Annis, Ed: Dan Sherwen @ Final Cut, Col: James Tillett @ MPC. PC: Colonel Blimp / Good Company. Commissioned by Jonny Bradshaw for Domino Records.

Disclosure 'Grab Her!' (2014) 3:55. D: Emile Sornin, P: Jules de Chateleux, DoP: Nicolas Loir, Ed: Nicolas Larrouquere, Post: Mathematic. PC: Division. Commissioned by John Moule.

Massive Attack / Young Fathers 'Voodoo in My Blood' (2016) 5:26. D: Ringan Ledwidge, P: Ellie Fry, DoP: Franz Lustig, Ed: Rich Orrick, Col: Lewis Crossfield, Post: Electric Theatre Collective. PC: Rattling Stick (Alexa Mini). Commissioned by James Hackett for Virgin.

3/ Social Realism

UB40 'Red Red Wine' (1984) 3:24. D: Bernard Rose, P: Rob Small, DoP: Syd MacCartney, Ed: Peter Cornish. PC: Stagefright (16mm). Commissioned by Dep Records.

Oasis 'The Importance of Being Idle' (2005) 3:55. D: Dawn Shadforth, P: Sally Llewelyn, DoP: Peter Suschitzky, Ed: Amanda James, Col: Tareq Kubaisi @ VTR. Black Dog / RSA (35mm). Commissioned by Emma Greengrass for Ignition.

The Chemical Brothers 'Believe' (2005) 4:38. D: Dom & Nic, P: John Madsen, DoP: Dom & Nic, Ed: Tony Kearns, Col: Dave Ludlam @ Framestore, Post: Framestore. PC: Oil Factory (Mini DVCam to 35mm print). Commissioned by Carole Burton-Fairbrother for Virgin Records.

Doves 'Black and White Town' (2005) 4:30. D: Lynne Ramsay, P: Jane Harrison, DoP: Tom Townend, Ed: Offline Editing Co., Col: Tareq @ VTR. PC: Oil Factory. Commissioned by Dilly Gent.

Plan B 'Stay Too Long' (2009) 4:05. D: Daniel Wolfe, P: Tim Francis, DoP: Lol Crawley, Ed: Dominic Leung, Col: Simon Bourne @ Framestore. PC: Partizan. Commissioned by Tim Nash.

Plan B 'She Said' (2010) 3:47. D: Daniel Wolfe, P: Tim Francis, DoP: Lol Crawley, Ed: Tom Lindsay, Col: Simon Bourne @ Framestore. PC: Partizan. Commissioned by Tim Nash.

Plan B 'Prayin'' (2010) 6:07. D: Daniel Wolfe, P: Tim Francis, DoP: Robbie Ryan, Ed: Tom Lindsay, Col: Simon Bourne at Framestore. PC: Partizan. Commissioned by Tim Nash.

Coldplay 'Paradise' (2011) 4:44. D: Shynola, P: Lou Whiston, DoP: Richard Stewart, Ed: Julia Knight, Col: Tom Russell. PC: Black Dog / RSA. Commissioned by James Hackett and Naomi Gurdol for EMI.

Disc 5: Wit

1/ *Sex, Drugs & Rock'n'Royalty*

Happy Mondays 'Wrote for Luck' (1988) 3:23. D: The Bailey Brothers.

Flowered Up 'Weekender' (1992) 17:39. *Original Credits*: D: WIZ, P: Adam Dunlop and Nicci Power, DoP: Tim Maurice-Jones, Ed: Robert Wallace. PC: MediaLab (16mm). Commissioned by Jeff Barrett for Heavenly and Steve Hodges for Columbia Recordings. *Restoration Credits*: Film transfer: IDailies, Ed: Adam Dunlop, TK: Tom Russell @ Lipsync, Post: Time Based Arts, EPs: Emily Caston and Mike O'Keefe, P: Jamie Clark, Prod Manager: Louise Whiston.

The Shamen 'Ebenezer Goode' (1992) 3:50. D, DoP and Ed: Richard Heslop, P: Kim Mnguni. PC: Oil Factory (16mm). Commissioned by One Little Indian.

The Prodigy 'Smack My Bitch Up' (1997) 3:35. D: Jonas Åkerlund, P: Niki Amos, DoP: Henrik Halvarson, Ed: Petersson Åkerlund, Col: Tareq Kubaisi @ VTR. PC: Oil Factory. Commissioned by Nick Goldsmith for XL Recordings.

The Streets 'Blinded by the Lights' (2004) 5:11. D: Adam Smith, P: Matthew Fone, DoP: Tat Radcliffe, Ed: Joe Guest. PC: Colonel Blimp (16mm). Commissioned by John Hassay for 679 Recordings.

Basement Jaxx 'U Don't Know Me' (2005) 3:32. D: Mat Kirkby, P: Claire Oxley, DoP: Mat Kirkby, Ed: Dominic Leung. PC: Black Dog / RSA (Mini DVCam). Commissioned by Phil Lee for XL Recordings.

Oasis 'Falling Down' (2008) 5:08. D: WIZ, P: Benedict Cooper, EP: Paul Fennelly and Toby Hyde, DoP: Dan Landin, Ed: Tom Lindsay, Col: Tom Russell at VTR. PC: Factory Films (16mm) Commissioned by Emma Greengrass for Ignition Management and Big Brother Records.

Chase and Status feat. Liam Bailey 'Blind Faith' (2011) 9:14. D: Daniel Wolfe, P: Tim Francis, DoP: Lol Crawley, Ed: Dominic Leung. PC: Somesuch. Commissioned by Dan Curwin for Mercury.

2/ *Classic Comedy*

The Who 'Happy Jack' (1966) 2:07. D: Michael Lindsay-Hogg, DoP: Tony Mander (16mm).

Judas Priest 'Breaking the Law' (1983) 2:37. D: Julien Temple, DoP: Oliver Stapleton, Ed: Richard Bedford (16mm).

The Boomtown Rats 'I Don't Like Mondays' (1979) 3:42. D: David Mallet.

Aphex Twin 'Donkey Rhubarb' (1995) 3:54. D: David Slade, P: Robert Lloyd, DoP: Nigel Kinnings, Ed: Tim Hardy @ Lexington Post, Col: Adrian Seery @ Rushes. PC: Spidercom. Commissioned by Robert Mitchell for Warp Records.

Robbie Williams 'Millennium' (1998) 3:38. D: Vaughan Arnell, P: Amanda Tassie, DoP: John Lynch, Ed: Jake Wynne, PD: Robin Brown. PC: Godman (35mm and Super 8). Commissioned by Carrie Sutton for EMI / Chrysalis.

Gomez 'Bring It On' (1999) 4:14. D: Ringan Ledwidge, P: Emily Caston, DoP: Peter Thwaites, Ed: Rich Orrick, Col: Tareq Kubaisi @ VTR. PC: The End (35mm). Commissioned by Carole Burton-Fairbrother for Virgin.

Blur 'Coffee and TV' (1999) 6:21. D: Garth Jennings, P: Nick Goldsmith, DoP: Igor Jadue Lillo, Ed: Dominic Leung, Art and SFX: Dan and Ben at Cloch Stock and Barrel, Col: Tareq Kubaisi @ VTR, Post: Wes @ VTR. PC: Hammer & Tongs. Commissioned by Carrie Sutton for EMI / Parlophone.

Whale 'Crying at Airports' (1998) 4:14. D: Ringan Ledwidge, P: Emily Caston, DoP: John Mathieson, Ed: Rich Orrick, Col: Tareq Kubaisi @ VTR. PC: Harry Nash (35mm). Commissioned by Carole Burton-Fairbrother for Virgin.

Lily Allen 'Alfie' (2006) 2:54. D: Sarah Chatfield, P: Fiona Wright, DoP: Tom Townend, Ed: Amanda James, Col: Jamie Wilkinson @ MPC, Post: Pete Young at Prime Focus (16mm). Commissioned by Kirstin Cruickshank.

Roots Manuva 'Witness (1 Hope)' (2001) 4:40. D: Mat Kirkby, P: Jo Rudulphy, DoP: Mat Kirkby, Ed: James Bryce. PC: Battlecruiser / Harry Nash (Digital Video Camcorder). Commissioned by John Hassay for Big Dada.

Coldplay 'Life in Technicolor II' (2008) 4:26. D: Dougal Wilson, P: Matthew Fone, DoP: Bret Turnbull, Ed: Joe Guest, Puppets: Nonny Beakes, SFX: Artem, Col: Jean Clement-Soret. PC: Colonel Blimp (35mm). Commissioned by Kirstin Cruikshank for Parlophone.

3/ Pop Will Eat Itself

The Buggles 'Video Killed the Radio Star' (1979) 3:35. D: Russell Mulcahy, P: Lexi Godfrey. PC: MGMM (videotape).

Dire Straits 'Money for Nothing' (1985) 5:00. D: Steve Barron, EP: Siobhan Barron, P: Siobhan Barron and Adam Whittaker, DoP: Oliver Stapleton, Ed: David Yardley, Col and Post: Rushes. PC: Limelight (35mm). Commissioned by Ed Bicknell.

Thomas Dolby 'Close But No Cigar' (1992, remastered 2009) 4:22. D: Michel Gondry, P: Georges Bermann, DoP: Jean Poisson. PC: Partizan. Commissioned by Carole Burton-Fairbrother for Virgin.

Orbital 'The Box' (1996) 4:15. D: Luke Losey and Jez Benstock, P: Tracey Bass, DoP: Maxim Ford, Ed: Technobabble (35mm). Commissioned by Christian Tattersfield for London Records.

Aphex Twin 'Come to Daddy' (1997) 6:02. D: Chris Cunningham, P: Cindy Burnay, EP: Ted Thornton, DoP: Simon Chaudoir, Ed: Gary Knight. PC: Black Dog / RSA (35mm). Commissioned by Rob Mitchell for Warp Records.

Basement Jaxx 'Where's Your Head At' (2002) 4:10. D: Traktor, Ed: Rick Russell, Post: MPC. PC: Partizan. Commissioned by XL Recordings.

Wiley 'Numbers in Action' (2011) 3:06. D: Us (Chris Barrett and Luke Taylor), P: Liz Kessler, DoP: Marcus Domleo, Ed: Ed Cheeseman, Post: Jan Meyer. PC: Academy A+. Commissioned by Jamie Collinson.

One Direction 'Best Song Ever' (2013) 6:13. D: Ben Winston (Co-writer James Corden), P: Carly Shackleton and Luti Fagbenle, DoP: Maz Makhani, Ed: Claudia Wass. PC: Fulwell 73. Commissioned by Mike O'Keefe for Sony Music.

Noel Gallagher's High Flying Birds 'Ballad of the Mighty I' (2014) 6:11. D: John Hardwick, P: Shabana Mansuri, DoP: Sam Care, Ed: Ben Unwin. PC: My Accomplice. Commissioned by Carrie Sutton for Sour Mash Records.

4/ The State We're In

Paul Hardcastle '19' (1985) 3:40. D: Jonas McCord and Bill Couterie, Ed: Ken Grunbaum.

Manic Street Preachers 'A Design for Life' (1996) 4:45. D: Pedro Romhanyi, P: Steven Elliott, DoP: Joe Dyer, Ed: Tony Kearns, Col: Tareq Kubaisi @ VTR. PC: Oil Factory.

The Chemical Brothers 'Out of Control' (1999) 4:29. D: WIZ, P: Alison Newling, EP: Heidi Herzon, DoP: Christopher Soos, Ed: Bill Yukich, Col: Dave Hussey @ Company 3. PC: Oil Factory (35mm reversal). Commissioned by Carole Burton-Fairbrother and David Levine for Virgin.

Faithless 'We Come 1' (2001) 4:07. D: Dom & Nic, P: John Madsen, DoP: Simon Chaudoir, Ed: Struan Clay, Col: Tareq Kubaisi @ VTR, Post: Smoke and Mirrors. PC: Oil Factory (35mm). Commissioned by Mike O'Keefe for Sony Music.

Kasabian 'Club Foot' (2004) 3:53. D: WIZ, P: Jane Harrison, DoP: Tom Townend, Ed: Tom Lindsay @ Imagemakers, Col: Tareq Kubaisi @ VTR. PC: Oil Factory. Commissioned by Mike O'Keefe for BMG (MiniDV, transferred to 35mm).

Dizzee Rascal 'Sirens' (2007) 3:50. D: WIZ, P: Laura Kanerick, EP: Paul Fennelly and Toby Hyde, DoP: Tom Townend, Ed: Julia Knight @ Metropolis, Col: Tom Russell at VTR. PC: Factory Films (35mm). Commissioned by Phil Lee for XL.

M.I.A. 'Born Free' (2010) 8:57. D: Romain Gavras, P: Mourad Belkeddar, DoP: Andre Chemetoff. PC: El Niño. Commissioned by Interscope.

Paolo Nutini 'Iron Sky' (2014) 8:42 D: Daniel Wolfe, P: Lee Groombridge, DoP: Robbie Ryan, Ed: Tom Lindsay, Col: Simon Bourne. PC: Somesuch. Commissioned by Dan Curwin for Atlantic.

U2 'Every Breaking Wave' (2015) 13:16. D: Aoife McArdle, P: Nick Goldsmith and Chris Martin, DoP: Steve Annis, Ed: Dan Sherwen @ Final Cut, Col: Simon Bourne. PC: Somesuch. Commissioned by Jefferson Hack / MAD / Island Records.

M.I.A. 'Borders' (2015) 4:42. D and Ed: M.I.A., EP: Ramji Soma, DoP: Nirav Shah, Post: Electric Theatre Collective, EP (Post): Juliette Larthe @ Prettybird, Col: Houmam Abdallah, Post: Paul Wilmot. PC: Unique Studios. Commissioned by Interscope.

Disc 6: Portraits

1/ Femininities

Grace Jones 'I've Seen That Face Before (Libertango)' (1981) 4:56. D: Jean-Paul Goode.

Robert Palmer 'Addicted to Love' (1985) 3:56. D: Terence Donovan.

Neneh Cherry 'Buffalo Stance' (1988) 4:12. D: John Maybury.

Shakespears Sister 'Goodbye Cruel World' (1991) 5:06. D and Ed: Sophie Muller, P: Rob Small, DoP: Steve Chivers, Art: Alison Dominitz, Col: Tom Russell @ VTR. PC: Oil Factory (16mm). Commissioned by Pete Tong.

Sade 'No Ordinary Love' (1992) 4:10. D and Ed: Sophie Muller, P: Rob Small, DoP: Steve Chivers, Art: Alison Dominitz. PC: Oil Factory (35mm and 16mm).

Annie Lennox 'Why' (1992) 4:55. D and Ed: Sophie Muller, P: Rob Small, DoP: Steve Chivers, Col: Tom Russell @ VTR. PC: Oil Factory (35mm).

The Chemical Brothers 'Setting Sun' (1996) 4:08. D: Dom & Nic, P: John Madsen, DoP: Steve Chivers, Ed: Simon Hilton, Col: Tareq Kubaisi @ VTR. PC: Oil Factory (S16mm). Commissioned by Carole Burton-Fairbrother for Virgin.

All Saints 'Never Ever' (1997) 4:43. D: Sean Ellis, P: Roger W. Moore, DoP: Freddie Francis, Ed: Gary Knight. PC: Tsunami. Commissioned by Alan Parks for London Records.

Portishead 'Only You' (1998) 4:29. D: Chris Cunningham, P: Cindy Burnay, EP: Emily Caston, DoP: Simon Chaudoir, Ed: Gary Knight, Col: The Mill. PC: Black Dog / RSA (35mm). Commissioned by Cynthia Lole for GO! Beat.

Moloko 'Sing It Back' (1998) 4:09. D and Ed: Dawn Shadforth, P: Cindy Burnay, DoP: John Lynch, Col: Dom @ Rushes. Black Dog / RSA (35mm.)

Björk 'All Is Full of Love' (1999) 4:28. D: Chris Cunningham, P: Cindy Burnay, DoP: John Lynch, Ed: Gary Knight, Art: Chris Oddy, Col: Marcus @ The Mill, Post: Glassworks. PC: Black Dog / RSA (35mm). Commissioned by Paul McKee at One Little Indian.

PJ Harvey 'This Is Love' (2000) 3:48. D and Ed: Sophie Muller, P: Niki Amos, DoP: Dan Landin. PC: Oil Factory. Commissioned by Liz Kessler for Universal / Island.

Girls Aloud 'Sexy! No, No, No' (2007) 3:34. D: Trudy Bellinger, P: Fran Barnes, DoP: Tom Townend, Ed: Matthew MacKinnon @ Peep Show, Col: Mark Horrobin @ Smoke and Mirrors, Post: Fassa @ Golden Square. PC: Crossroads (16mm). Commissioned by Ross Anderson for Polydor.

M.I.A. 'Bad Girls' (2010) 4.13. D: Romain Gavras, P: Khalid Tahhar, EP: Mourad Belkeddar, DoP: Andre Chemetoff, Ed: Walter Mauriot, Post: Digital District. PC: Iconoclast. Commissioned by Michelle Ann for Interscope.

Florence and the Machine 'Dog Days Are Over' (2010) 3:47. D: Georgie Greville and Geremy Jasper, P: Malachy McAnenny, DoP: Adam Frisch, Ch: Mark Battershall, Ed: Paul Snyder, Post: Black Hole. PC: ROKKIT. Commissioned by Alisa Robertson.

Lily Allen 'Hard Out Here' (2013) 4:15. D: Chris Sweeney, P: Amalia Rosen-Rawlings, DoP: Rob Witt, Ed: Sam Neal, Col: James Bamford. PC: Good Egg. Commissioned by Sam Seager for Parlophone.

FKA twigs 'Pendulum' (2015) 5:00. D: FKA twigs, P: Morgan Clement, DoP: Ben Magahy, Ch: FKA twigs and Aaron Sillis, Ed: Thomas Grove-Carter @ Trim, Col: Julien Biard @ Finish. PC: Academy A+.

The Moonlandingz 'The Strangle of Anna' (2016/17) 3:41. D: Dawn Shadforth, P: Elly Camisa, EP: Hannah Turnbull-Walter, DoP: Robbie Ryan, Ed: Magdalena Plugowska @ Trim, Col: Jack McGinty @ Time Based Arts. PC: Somesuch (16mm). Commissioned by Moonlandingz.

2/ Masculinities

Sex Pistols 'My Way' (1978) 4:31. D: Julien Temple, P: Malcolm McLaren, Ed: Richard Bedford. PC: Glitterbest (35 mm).

Adam and the Ants 'Prince Charming' (1981) 3:22. D: Mike Mansfield.

Culture Club 'Karma Chameleon' (1983) 3:56. D: Peter Sinclair, P: Siobhan Barron.

Bronski Beat 'Smalltown Boy' (1984) 4:59. D: Bernard Rose, P: Tim Bevan and Luc Roeg, DoP: Dennis Crossan, Ed: Michael Pike. PC: Aldabra (16mm). Commissioned by London Records.

Queen 'I Want To Break Free' (1984) 4:21. D: David Mallet, P: Jacqui Byford.

George Michael 'Faith' (1987) 3:40. D: Andy Morahan, DoP: Peter MacKay. PC: Vivid (35mm). Commissioned by Steve Hodges.

Seal 'Killer' (1991) 3:52. D: Don Searll.

Supergrass 'Alright' (1995) 3:22. D: Dom & Nic, P: Louise Whiston, DoP: Dan Landin, Ed: Simon Hilton @ Metropolis, Col: Tareq Kubaisi @ VTR. PC: Oil Factory (S16mm). Commissioned by Dilly Gent for Parlophone.

Take That 'Back for Good' (1995) 4:01. D: Vaughan and Anthea, P: Sandy Watson, DoP: Steve Chivers, Ed: Rick Russell. PC: Lewis and Watson. Commissioned by Louise Hart for RCA.

The Prodigy 'Firestarter' (1996) 3:45. D: Walter Stern, P: John Payne, DoP: Billy Malone, Ed: Tony Kearns. PC: Academy. Commissioned by XL Recordings.

Jamiroquai 'Virtual Insanity' (1996) 3:57. D: Jonathan Glazer, P: Nick Morris, DoP: Stephen Keith-Roach, Ed: Nigel Smith. PC: Academy. Commissioned by Mike O'Keefe for Sony Music.

George Michael 'Outside' (1998) 5:36. D: Vaughan Arnell, P: Amanda Tassie, DoP: Georgio Scali, Ed: Rick Russell. PC: Godman. Commissioned by Andy Stephens for Epic.

Paul Weller 'The Changingman' (1998) 3:36. D: Pedro Romhanyi, P: Gareth Francis, Ed: Tony Kearns.

Robbie Williams 'Rock DJ' (2000) 4:24. D: Vaughan Arnell, P: Emma Clare, DoP: Joseph Yacoe, Ed: Gary Knight @ Final Cut, Col: Tareq Kubaisi @ VTR. PC: Godman. Commissioned by Carrie Sutton for Chrysalis.

James Blunt 'You're Beautiful' (2005) 3:20. D: Sam Brown, P: Kat Armour-Brown, DoP: Robbie Ryan, Ed: Amanda James @ Final Cut, Col: Tom Russell @ VTR. PC: Flynn Productions. Commissioned by Richard Skinner for Atlantic.

The Fat White Family 'Touch the Leather' (2016) 3:31. D, P, DoP and Ed: Roger Sargent.

BIBLIOGRAPHY

Abel, Richard, and Rick Altman (eds) (2001), *The Sounds of Early Cinema* (Bloomington: Indiana University Press).
Abrahams, Lynn (2010), *Oral History Theory* (Abingdon and New York: Routledge).
Abravanel, Genevieve (2012), *Americanizing Britain: The Rise of Modernism in the Age of the Entertainment Empire* (New York: Oxford University Press).
Adams, Ruth (2008), 'The Englishness of English Punk: Sex Pistols, Subcultures, and Nostalgia', *Popular Music and Society* 31.4: 469–88.
Adams, Ruth (2014), 'Who Says White Men Can't Dance? Deconstructing Racial Stereotypes in "Windowlicker"', *Unsettling Whiteness*, 11: 263–73.
Adegoke, Yomi (2018), 'RIP Channel U: the urban music champion that gave power to the people', *The Guardian*, 4 June, <https://www.theguardian.com/music/2018/jun/04/rip-channel-u-urban-music-grime-dizzee-rascal-skepta> (last accessed 24 January 2020).
Adler, Tim (2004), *The Producers: Money, Movies and Who Really Calls the Shots* (London: Methuen).
Adorno, Theodor, and Max Horkheimer ([1944] 1979), *Dialectic of Enlightenment* (London: Verso).
Aftab, Kaleem (2015), 'Daniel Wolfe: From Directing Music Promos to Feature Films', *The Independent*, 23 February, <http://www.independent.co.uk/arts-entertainment/films/features/daniel-wolfe-from-directing-music-promos-to-feature-films-10065868.html> (last accessed 24 January 2020).
Altitude Film (n.d.), 'Daniel Wolfe', <http://www.altitudefilment.com/directors/profile/14/daniel-wolfe> (last accessed 24 January 2020).
Altman, C. F. (1977), 'Towards a Theory of Genre Film', in B. Lawton and J. Staiger (eds), *Film Studies Annual: Part II: Film-Historical Speculations* (New York: Redgrave), pp. 31–43.

Altman, C. F. (1995), 'A Semantic / Syntactic Approach to Film Genre', in B. K. Grant (ed.), *Film Genre Reader II* (Austin: University of Texas), pp. 26–40.

Altman, Rick (1992), *Sound Theory Sound Practice* (London: Routledge).

Altman, Rick (2001), 'The Living Nickelodeon', in Richard Abel and Rick Altman (eds), *The Sounds of Early Cinema* (Bloomington: Indiana University Press), pp. 232–40.

Amin, Takiyah Nur (2011), 'A Terminology of Difference: Making the Case for Black Dance in the 21st Century and Beyond', *Journal of Pan African Studies*, 4.6: 7–15.

Amin, Takiyah Nur (2018), 'African American Dance Revisited: Undoing Master Narratives in the Studying and Teaching of Dance History', in Geraldine Morris and Larraine Nicholas (eds), *Rethinking Dance History: Issues and Methodologies*, 2nd edition (Abingdon: Routledge), pp. 44–55.

Anderson, Jack (1994), *Ballet and Modern Dance: A Concise History*, 2nd edition (Highstown, NC: Princeton Book Company).

Anderson, Peter, and David Saunders (eds) (1992), *Moral Rights Protection in a Copyright System* (Queensland: Institute for Cultural Policy Studies).

Anderson, Zoe (2008), 'British Choreographers Are Now Sought After the World Over; So What's Their Secret?', *The Independent*, <http://www.independent.co.uk/arts-entertainment/theatre-dance/features/british-choreographers-are-now-sought-after-the-world-over-ndash-so-whats-their-secret-806889.html> (last accessed 24 January 2020).

Apter, Jeff (2009), *Never Enough: The Story of The Cure* (London: Omnibus).

Arnold, Gina, Daniel Cookney, Kirsty Fairclough and Michael Goddard (eds) (2017), *Music/Video: Histories, Aesthetics, Media* (London: Bloomsbury Academic).

Aston, Martin (2014), *Facing the Other Way: The Story of 4AD* (London: HarperCollins).

Attias, Bernardo Alexander (2016), 'Authenticity and Artifice in Rock and Roll: "And I Guess That I Just Don't Care"', *Rock Music Studies* 3.2: 131–47.

Aufderheide, Pat (1986), 'Music Videos: The Look of the Sound', *Journal of Communication* 36.1: 57–78.

Auslander, Philip [1999] (2008), *Liveness: Performance in a Mediatized Culture* (Abingdon: Routledge).

Aust, Michael P., and Daniel Kothenschulte (2011), *The Art of the Pop Video* (Cologne: Distanz).

Austerlitz, Saul (2007), *Money for Nothing: A History of the Music Video from the Beatles to the White Stripes* (New York: Continuum).

Austerlitz, Saul (2010), 'Don't You Cry Tonight', in Henry Keazor and Thorsten Wübbena (eds), *Rewind, Play, Fast Forward: The Past, Present and Future of the Music Video* (Berlin: De Gruyter), pp. 35–40.

Balázs, Béla (1952), *Theory of the Film* (London: Dobson).

Balls, Richard (2014), *Be Stiff: The Stiff Records Story* (London: Soundcheck Books).

Banks, Jack (1996), *Monopoly Television: MTV's Quest to Control the Music* (Boulder, CO: Westview Press).

Banks, Mark, and Kate Oakley (2016), 'The Dance Goes On Forever? Art Schools, Class and UK Higher Education', *International Journal of Cultural Policy* 22.1: 41–57.

Bannister, Matthew (2006), *White Boys, White Noise: Masculinities and 1980s Indie Guitar Rock* (Abingdon: Routledge).
Bannister, Matthew (2017), '"Where are we going, Johnny?" Homosociality and the Early Beatles', in Stan Hawkins (ed.), *The Routledge Research Companion to Popular Music and Gender* (Abingdon and New York: Taylor & Francis), pp. 35–47.
Barker, Hugh, and Yuval Taylor (2007), *Faking It: The Quest for Authenticity in Popular Music* (London: Faber and Faber).
Barron, Steve (2014), *Egg n Chips & Billie Jean: A Trip Through the Eighties* (Scotts Valley, CA: Createspace Independent Publishing).
Batchelor, Bob, and Scott Stoddart (2007), *The 1980s* (Westport, CT: Greenwood), p. 125.
Battan, Carrie (2014), interview with FKA twigs, *Pitchfork*, <https://pitchfork.com/features/interview/9460-fka-twigs/> (last accessed 24 January 2020).
Baxter, R., C. De Riemer, A. Landini, L. Leslie and M. W. Singletary (1985), 'A Content Analysis of Music Videos', *Journal of Broadcasting and Electronic Media* 29: 333–40.
Bayton, Mavis (1997), 'Women and the Electric Guitar', in Sheila Whiteley (ed.), *Sexing the Groove: Popular Music and Gender* (New York: Routledge), pp. 37–40.
Beaven, Zuleika, Marcus O'Dair and Richard Osborne (eds) (2018), *Mute Records: Artists, Business, History* (New York: Bloomsbury Publishing USA).
Bechky, Beth A. (2006), 'Gaffers, Gofers, and Grips: Role-Based Coordination in Temporary Organizations', *Organization Science* 17.1: 3–12.
Beebe, Roger (2007), 'Paradoxes of Pastiche: Spike Jonze, Hype Williams, and the Race of the Postmodern Auteur', in Roger Beebe and Jason Middleton (eds), *Medium Cool: Music Videos from Soundies to Cellphones* (Durham, NC, and London: Duke University Press), pp. 303–28.
Beebe, Roger, and Jason Middleton (eds) (2007), *Medium Cool: Music Videos from Soundies to Cellphones* (Durham, NC, and London: Duke University Press).
Bennett, Andy, Barry Shank and Jason Toynbee (eds) (2006), *The Popular Music Studies Reader* (London: Routledge).
Bernstein, David (1986), 'The Television Commercial: An Essay', in Brian Henry (ed.), *British Television Advertising: The First 30 Years* (London: Century Benham), pp. 251–86.
Bernstein, Matthew (2008), 'The Producer as Auteur', in Barry K. Grant (ed.), *Auteurs and Authorship: A Film Reader* (Malden, MA: Blackwell), pp. 180–9.
Bessman, Jim (1985), 'Anti-War Clip Provokes Network Wrath', *Billboard* 97.22 (1 June), pp. 38–9.
Bey, William, and Thomas Bail (2012), *MicroBionic: Radical Electronic Music and Sound Art in the 21st Century* (London: Belsona Books Ltd).
BFI (2015), 'Seven Essential Films Shot by Robbie Ryan', <http://www.bfi.org.uk/news-opinion/news-bfi/lists/seven-essential-films-shot-robbie-ryan> (last accessed 24 January 2020).
Billman, Larry (2002), 'Music Video as Short Dance Film', in Judy Mitoma, Elizabeth Zimmer and Dale Ann Stieber (eds), *Envisioning Dance on Film and Video* (New York: Routledge), pp. 12–20.

Birringer, Johannes (2011), 'Dancing in the Museum', *PAJ: A Journal of Performance and Art* 33.3: 43–52.

Biskind, Peter (2004), *Down and Dirty Pictures: Miramax, Sundance and the Rise of Independent Film* (London: Bloomsbury).

Blackman, Shane (2004), *Chilling Out: The Cultural Politics of Substance Consumption, Youth and Drug Policy* (Maidenhead: Open University Press).

Blake, Andrew (2004), 'Americanisation and Popular Music in Britain', in Neil Campbell, Jude Davies and George McKay (eds), *Issues in Americanisation and Culture* (Edinburgh: Edinburgh University Press), pp. 147–62.

Blandford, James R. (2009), *PJ Harvey: Siren Rising* (London: Omnibus Press).

Bloginity (n.d.), 'Interview: Put On Your Dancing Shoes', <https://www.bloginity.com/2012/04/the-shoes-interview/> (last accessed 24 January 2020).

Bloore, Peter (2009), 'Re-defining the Independent Film Value Chain', UK Film Council, London, <https://www.bfi.org.uk/sites/bfi.org.uk/files/downloads/redefining-the-independent-film-value-chain.pdf> (last accessed 24 January 2020).

Bobo, Jacqueline (ed.) (2013), *Black Women Film and Video Artists* (Abingdon: Routledge).

Bolter, Jay David, and Richard Grusin (2000), *Remediation: Understanding New Media* (Cambridge, MA: MIT Press).

Booth, Gregory D. (2011), 'Preliminary Thoughts on Hindi Popular Music and Film Production: India's "Culture Industry (ies)", 1970–2000', *South Asian Popular Culture* 9.2 (2011): 215–21.

BOP Consulting (2014), *Soho: The World's Creative Hub*, <https://www.thecreativeindustries.co.uk/media/232461/soho-bop-report.pdf> (last accessed 2 March 2020).

Borelli, Melissa Blanco (ed.) (2014), *The Oxford Handbook of Dance and the Popular Screen* (Oxford: Oxford University Press).

Born, Georgina (2004), *Uncertain Vision: Birt, Dyke and the Reinvention of the BBC* (London: Secker & Warburg).

Born, Georgina (2010), 'The Social and the Aesthetic: For a Post-Bourdieuian Theory of Cultural Production', *Cultural Sociology* 4.2: 171–208.

Born, Georgina, and David Hesmondhalgh (eds) (2000), *Western Music and Its Others: Difference, Representation, and Appropriation in Music* (Oakland: University of California Press).

Bourdieu, Pierre (1977), *Outline of a Theory of Practice* (Cambridge: Cambridge University Press).

Bourdieu, Pierre (1980), *The Logic of Practice* (Stanford, CA: Stanford University Press).

Bourdieu, Pierre (1984), *Distinction: A Social Critique of the Judgement of Taste* (Cambridge, MA: Harvard University Press).

Bourdieu, Pierre (1988), *Homo Academicus* (Stanford, CA: Stanford University Press).

Bourdieu, Pierre (1990), *In Other Words: Essays Towards a Reflexive Sociology* (Stanford, CA: Stanford University Press).

Bourdieu, Pierre (1991), *Language and Symbolic Power* (Cambridge, MA: Harvard University Press).

Bourdieu, Pierre (1993), *The Field of Cultural Production: Essays on Art and Literature* (Cambridge: Polity).

Bourdieu, Pierre (1998), *Practical Reason: On the Theory of Action* (Stanford, CA: Stanford University Press).
Bowler, Dave, and Bryan Dray (1995), *Faith* (London: Sidgwick and Jackson).
Boyd, Jade (2004), 'Dance, Culture, and Popular Film', *Feminist Media Studies* 4.1: 67–83.
Braddock, J., and Stephen Hock (eds) (2001), *Directed by Allen Smithee* (Minneapolis: University of Minnesota Press).
Brannigan, Erin (2011), *Dance Film: Choreography and the Moving Image* (Oxford: Oxford University Press).
Branwyn, Gareth (1996), 'Never Mind the Broadcast: In Search of the Art of Music Video', *Popular Music and Society* 20.3: 95–117.
British Film Institute Oxera (2017), 'Impacts of Leaving the EU on the UK's Screen Sector', prepared for the Screen Sector Task Force, <https://www.bfi.org.uk/sites/bfi.org.uk/files/downloads/bfi-impact-leaving-eu-uk-screen-sector-2017-v1.pdf> (last accessed 24 January 2020).
Brown, Geoff (2000), 'Something for Everyone: British Film Culture in the 1990s', in Robert Murphy (ed.), *British Cinema of the 90s* (London: British Film Institute), pp. 27–36.
Brown, Jane D., and Kenneth Campbell (1986), 'Race and Gender in Music Videos: The Same Beat but a Different Drummer', *Journal of Communication* 36.1: 94–106.
Brown, Royal S. (1994), *Overtones and Undertones: Reading Film Music* (Berkeley, Los Angeles and London: University of California Press).
Brown, Simon, Sarah Street and Liz Watkins (2013), *Color and the Moving Image: History, Theory, Aesthetics, Archive* (Abingdon: Routledge).
Brozzoni, Vera (2017), 'Completing the Mystery of Her Flesh: Love, Eroticism, and Identity in Björk's Videos', in Gina Arnold, Daniel Cookney, Kirsty Fairclough and Michael Goddard (eds), *Music / Video: Histories, Aesthetics, Media* (New York: Bloomsbury Publishing USA), pp. 109–20.
Bruce, Graham (1997), *Bernard Herrmann: Film Music and Narrative* (Ann Arbor: University of Michigan).
Buckingham, David, Maria Pini and Rebekah Willett (2007), '"Take back the tube!": The Discursive Construction of Amateur Film and Video Making', *Journal of Media Practice* 8.2: 183–201.
Buckland, Theresa J., with Elizabeth Stewart (1993), 'Dance and Music Video', in Stephanie Jordan and Dave Allen (eds), *Parallel Lines: Media Representations of Dance* (London: John Libbey and the Arts Coucil of Britain), pp. 51–80.
Buhler, James, Caryl Flinn and David Neumeyer (eds) (2000), *Music and Cinema* (London and Hanover, NH: Wesleyan University Press).
Buhler, James, David Neumeyer and Rob Deemer (2010), *Hearing the Movies: Music and Sound in Film History* (Oxford: Oxford University Press).
Burgess, Jean (2008), '"All your chocolate rain are belong to us?" Viral Video, YouTube and the Dynamics of Participatory Culture', in Geert Lovink and Sabine Niederer (eds), *Video Vortex Reader: Responses to YouTube* (Amsterdam: Institute of Network Cultures), pp. 101–9.
Burgess, Jean, and Joshua Green (2009), *YouTube: Digital Media and Society Series* (Cambridge: Polity Press).

Burns, Gary, and Robert Thompson (1987), 'Music, Television, and Video: Historical and Aesthetic Considerations', *Popular Music and Society* 11.3: 11–25.

Burns, Lori, and Marc LaFrance (2017), 'Gender, Sexuality and the Politics of Looking in Beyoncé's "Video Phone" (featuring Lady Gaga)', in Stan Hawkins (ed.), *The Routledge Research Companion to Popular Music and Gender* (Abingdon and New York: Taylor & Francis), pp. 102–16.

Burns, Lori, and Stan Hawkins (eds) (2019), *The Bloomsbury Handbook of Popular Music Video Analysis* (New York: Bloomsbury Publishing USA).

Buscombe, Edward (1995), 'The Idea of Genre in the American Cinema', in B. K. Grant (ed.), *Film Genre Reader II* (Austin: University of Texas), pp. 11–25.

Butler, Ivan (1971), *To Encourage the Art of the Film* (London: Robert Hale).

Butler, Judith ([1990] 2002), *Gender Trouble* (Abingdon: Routledge).

Byrne, David (2013), *How Music Works* (Edinburgh: Canongate).

Cabitza, Mattia (2015), 'Listen: Kevin O'Hare on the UK Ballet Scene – "British Dance is Having a Renaissance"', Royal Opera House, <http://www.roh.org.uk/news/listen-kevin-ohare-on-the-uk-ballet-scene-british-dance-is-having-a-renaissance> (last accessed 24 January 2020).

Cagle, Van M. (1995), *Reconstructing Pop / Subculture: Art, Rock, and Andy Warhol* (Thousand Oaks, CA: Sage Publications).

Calavita, Marco (2007), '"MTV Aesthetics" at the Movies: Interrogating a Film Criticism Fallacy', *Journal of Film and Video* 59.3: 15–31.

Caldwell, John T. (2008), *Production Culture: Industrial Reflexivity and Critical Practice in Film and Television* (Durham, NC, and London: Duke University Press).

Caldwell, John T. (2009), '"Both sides of the fence": Blurred Distinctions in Scholarship and Production (a Portfolio of Interviews)', in Vicki Mayer, Miranda Banks and John T. Caldwell (eds), *Production Studies: Cultural Studies of Media Industries* (New York and London: Routledge), pp. 214–29.

Caldwell, John T. (2013), 'Authorship Below-the-Line', in Jonathan Gray and Derek Johnson (eds), *A Companion to Media Authorship* (Chichester: Wiley-Blackwell), pp. 349–69.

Campaign (2012), 'Why We're Loving . . . Director Daniel Wolfe, Somesuch and Co.', <http://www.campaignlive.co.uk/article/why-were-loving-daniel-wolfe-director-somesuch-co/1126387> (last accessed 24 January 2020).

Campbell, Neil, Jude Davies and George McKay (eds) (2004a), *Issues in Americanisation and Culture* (Edinburgh: Edinburgh University Press).

Campbell, Neil, Jude Davies and George McKay (2004b), 'Introduction: Issues in Americanisation and Culture', in Campbell, Davies and McKay (eds), *Issues in Americanisation and Culture* (Edinburgh: Edinburgh University Press), pp. 1–40.

Campbell, Neil, Jude Davies and George McKay (2004c), 'Conclusion: Globalisation, Americanisation and the "New World Order"', in Campbell, Davies and McKay (eds), *Issues in Americanisation and Culture* (Edinburgh: Edinburgh University Press), pp. 295–307.

Carlson, Marvin (1996), *Performance: A Critical Introduction* (Abingdon: Routledge).

Carroll, Noël (1998), *A Philosophy of Mass Art* (Oxford: Clarendon Press).

Carroll, Noël (2008), *The Philosophy of Motion Pictures* (Oxford: Blackwell).

Caston, Emily (2000), 'Directors' Rights in Music: Who Wrote the Script?', *Promo News*, September, pp. 12–13.

Caston, Emily (2012), '"Kick, Bollocks and Scramble": An Examination of Power and Creative Decision-Making in the Production Process During the Golden Era of British Music Videos 1995–2001', *Journal of British Cinema and Television* 9.1: 96–110.

Caston, Emily (2014), 'The Fine Art of Commercial Freedom: British Music Videos and Film Culture', *Scope: An Online Journal of Film and Television Studies*, 26: 1–18, <https://www.nottingham.ac.uk/scope/documents/2014/february/caston1.pdf> (last accessed 24 January 2020).

Caston, Emily (2015), 'Not Another Article on the Author! God and Auteurs in Moving Image Analysis: Last Call For a Long Overdue Paradigm Shift', *Music, Sound, and the Moving Image*, 9.2: 145–62.

Caston, Emily (2017a), 'The Dancing Eyes of the Director: Choreographers, Dance Cultures, and Film Genres in British Music Video 1979–2016', *Music, Sound, and the Moving Image* 11.1: 37–62.

Caston, Emily (2017b), '"The First Cut is the Deepest": Excerpts from a Focus Group on Editing Music Videos, with Explanatory Historical and Theoretical Notes', *Music, Sound, and the Moving Image* 11.1: 99–118.

Caston, Emily (2019a), 'Introduction: Hidden Screen Industries – British Music Video and Absent Bodies', *Journal of British Cinema and Television* 16.4: 484–91.

Caston, Emily (2019b), 'The Pioneers Get Shot: Music Video, Independent Production and Cultural Hierarchy in Britain', *Journal of British Cinema and Television* 16.4: 545–70.

Caston, Emily (2020a), 'Introduction: Curating Fifty Years of British Music Video', *Alphaville: Journal of Film and Screen Media*, Dossier, Summer (forthcoming).

Caston, Emily (2020b), 'Curating the Archives of British Music Video', *Alphaville: Journal of Film and Screen Media*, Dossier, Summer (forthcoming).

Caston, Emily, Nisha Parti, Nijico Walker and Carrie Sutton (2000), 'Report on the Music Video Industry in 1998 and 1999', *Promo*, May, pp. 6–7.

Caston, Emily, and Justin Smith (2017), 'Introduction', *Music, Sound, and the Moving Image*, Special Issue on the AHRC Funded Fifty Years of British Music Video, 11.1: 1–9.

Caston, Emily, and Justin Smith (2020), 'Dancing and Dreaming: Island Pictures and the Danza Contemporanea de Cuba', *Alphaville: Journal of Film and Screen Media*, Dossier, Summer (forthcoming).

Cateforis, Theo (2004), 'Performing the Avant-Garde Groove: Devo and the Whiteness of the New Wave', *American Music* 22.4 (2004): 564–88.

Cawood, Ian (2016), '"Don't let me go! Hold me down!": Inspiration, Voice and Image in Kate Bush's "Hounds of Love"', *Popular Music* 35.1: 41–63.

Chalaby, Jean K. (2002), 'Transnational Television in Europe: The Role of Pan-European Channels', *European Journal of Communication* 17.2: 183–203.

Chan, C. S. C. (2010), 'Housekeeper of Hong Kong Cinema: The Role of Producer in the System of Hong Kong Film Industry', *Wide Screen* 2.2.

Chapman, Ian (2015a), 'Authorship, Agency and Visual Analysis', in Eion Devereux, Aileen Dillane and Martin Power (eds), *David Bowie: Critical Perspectives* (New York and London: Routledge), pp. 196–214.

Chapman, Ian (2015b), *Experiencing David Bowie: A Listener's Companion* (Lanham, MD: Rowman and Littlefield).
Chilcott, Robert (2007), 'The Films of Peter Whitehead', *Vertigo* 8 (March), <https://www.closeupfilmcentre.com/vertigo_magazine/issue-8-march-2007/the-films-of-peter-whitehead/> (last accessed 24 January 2020).
Childed, Serg (2018), 'MTV and EMI did not appreciate the concept of Kate Bush's iconic Running Up That Hill', *Music Tales* <https://musictales.club/article/mtv-and-emi-did-not-appreciate-concept-kate-bushs-iconic-running-hill> (last accessed 24 January 2020).
Chion, Michael (1994), *Audio Vision: Sound on Screen* (New York: Columbia University Press).
Chion, Michael (2009), *Film: A Sound Art* (New York: Columbia University Press).
Chris, Cynthia, and David A. Gerstner (eds) (2013), *Media Authorship* (New York: Routledge).
Christensen, Jerome (2008), 'Studio Authorship, Corporate Art', in Barry K. Grant (ed.), *Auteurs and Authorship* (Oxford: Blackwell), pp. 167–79.
Clawson, Mary Ann (1999), 'Masculinity and Skill Acquisition in the Adolescent Rock Band', *Popular Music* 18.1: 99–114.
Cliff, Aimee (2016), 'This Video From Brighton Producer salute Will Truly Make You Proud To Be British', *The Fader*, 13 August <https://www.thefader.com/2016/08/03/salute-storm-video> (last accessed 24 January 2020).
Clifford, Hubert (1944), 'British Film Music', *Tempo* 3.08: 146–9.
Cloonan, Martin (1999), 'Pop and the Nation-State: Towards a Theorisation', *Popular Music* 18.2: 193–207.
Clover, Carol (2002), 'Dancin' in the Rain', in *Hollywood Musicals, the Film Reader* (Abingdon: Routledge), pp. 157–73.
Coates, Norma (1997), '(R)evolution Now? Rock and the Political Potential of Gender', in Sheila Whiteley (ed.), *Sexing the Groove: Popular Music and Gender* (New York: Routledge), pp. 50–64.
Coates, Norma (1998), 'Can't we just talk about music?: Rock and Gender on the Internet', in Thomas Swiss, John M. Sloop and Andrew Herman (eds), *Mapping the Beat: Popular Music and Contemporary Theory* (New York: Wiley), pp. 77–100.
Coates, Norma (2003), 'Teenyboppers, Groupies, and Other Grotesques: Girls and Women and Rock Culture in the 1960s and Early 1970s', *Journal of Popular Music Studies* 15.1: 65–94.
Coates, Norma (2010), 'Whose Tears Go By? Marianne Faithfull at the Dawn and Twilight of Rock Culture', in Laurie Stras (ed.), *She's So Fine: Reflections on Whiteness, Femininity, Adolescence and Class in 1960s Music* (Farnham: Ashgate), pp. 183–202.
Cobb, Shelley (2012), 'Film Authorship and Adaptation', in Deborah Cartnell (ed.), *A Companion to Literature, Film and Adaptation* (New York and Chichester: John Wiley and Sons), pp. 105–21.
Cobb, Shelley (2014), *Adaptation, Authorship, and Contemporary Women Filmmakers* (New York: Springer).
Cohan, Steven (ed.) (2002), *Hollywood Musicals: The Film Reader* (Abingdon: Routledge).

Cohan, Steve (ed.) (2004), *Movie Musicals: The Reader* (Abingdon: Routledge).
Collins, Michael (2018), *The Dave Clark Five: The 'Forgotten' Group of the British Invasion* (n.p.).
Comer, Stuart (2008), *Film and Video Art* (London: Tate Publishing).
Connell, Robert W. (2005), *Masculinities* (Cambridge: Polity).
Connell, Robert W., and James W. Messerschmidt (2005), 'Hegemonic Masculinity: Rethinking the Concept', *Gender & Society* 19.6: 829–59.
Conrich, Ian, and Estella Tincknell (eds) (2006), *Film's Musical Moments* (Edinburgh: Edinburgh University Press).
Constable, Catherine (2004), 'Postmodernism and Film', in Steven Connor (ed.), *The Cambridge Companion to Postmodernism* (Cambridge: Cambridge University Press), pp. 43–61.
Cooke, Mervyn (2008), *A History of Film Music* (Cambridge: Cambridge University Press).
Cooke, Mervyn (ed.) (2010), *The Hollywood Film Music Reader* (New York: Oxford University Press).
Cooper, David (2001), *Bernard Herrmann's Vertigo: A Film Score Handbook* (Westport, CT: Greenwood Press).
Cooper, David (2009), 'Trevor Jones's Score for *In the Name of the Father*', in Derek B. Scott (ed.), *The Ashgate Research Companion to Popular Musicology* (Aldershot: Ashgate), pp. 25–42.
Cooper, David, Christopher Fox and Ian Sapiro (2008), *Cinemusic? Constructing the Film Score* (Newcastle upon Tyne: Cambridge Scholars Press).
Copeland, Roger (1986), 'A Curmudgeonly View of the American Dance Boom', *Dance Theatre Journal* 4.1: 10–13.
Copeland, Roger (2004), *Merce Cunningham: The Modernizing of Modern Dance* (London: Routledge).
Corrigan, Timothy (1991), 'The Commerce of Auteurism – Coppola, Kluge, Ruiz', in Corrigan, *A Cinema Without Walls – Movies and Culture after Vietnam* (New Brunswick, NJ: Rutgers University Press).
Coulter, Bridget (2017), 'Singing from the heart': Notions of Gendered Authenticity in Pop Music', in Stan Hawkins (ed.), *The Routledge Research Companion to Popular Music and Gender* (Abingdon and New York: Taylor & Francis), pp. 267–80.
Cowan, Philip (2015), 'The Democracy of Colour', *Journal of Media Practice* 16.2: 139–54.
Craig, Mark (n.d.), 'Fat White Family, "Touch the Leather" (NSFW)', *Impose Magazine*, <https://www.imposemagazine.com/fat-white-family-touch-the-leather-nsfw/> (last accessed 24 January 2020).
Cubitt, Sean (1991), *Timeshift: On Video Culture* (London: Routledge).
Cubitt, Sean, and Stephen Partridge (eds) (2012), *REWIND: British Artists' Video in the 1970s and 1980s* (New Barnet: John Libbey).
Cummings, Alex Sayf (2013), *Music Piracy and the Remaking of American Copyright in the Twentieth Century: Democracy of Sound* (New York: Oxford University Press).
Cunningham, M. (1995), 'Roy Thomas Baker and Gary Langan: The Making of Queen's "Bohemian Rhapsody"', *Sound on Sound*.

Curtis, David (2006), *A History of Artists' Film and Video in Britain, 1897–2004* (London: BFI Publishing).

Cusic, Don (1996), *Music in the Market* (Bowling Green, OH: Bowling Green State University Popular Press).

D&AD (n.d.), 'Profile – Tom Lindsay', <https://www.dandad.org/profiles/person/36471/tom-lindsay/> (last accessed 24 January 2020).

Dalle Vacche, Angela, and Brian Price (2006), *Color, The Film Reader (In Focus: Routledge Film Readers)* (New York: Routledge).

Dancyger, Ken (2014), *The Technique of Film and Video Editing: History, Theory, and Practice* (Abingdon: Routledge).

Danino, Nina, and Michael Mazière (eds) (2002), *The Undercut Reader: Critical Writings on Artists' Film and Video* (London: Wallflower Press).

Darley, Andrew (2002), *Visual Digital Culture: Surface Play and Spectacle in New Media Genres* (Abingdon: Routledge).

Davies, Helen (2001), 'All Rock and Roll is Homosocial: The Representation of Women in the British Rock Music Press', *Popular Music* 20.3: 301–19.

Davies, Sam (2013), 'Eye Tunes', *Sight and Sound* 23.5 (May): 50–4.

Davison, Annette (2014), *Hollywood Theory, Non-Hollywood Practice: Cinema Soundtracks in the 1980s and 1990s* (Aldershot: Gower Publishing Ltd.).

Day, Amber (2018), 'Welcome to the Clickhole: The Economics of Internet Parody and Critique', in Nick Marx and Matt Sienkiewicz (eds), *The Comedy Studies Reader* (Austin: University of Texas Press), pp. 120–33.

Decherney, Peter (2012), *Hollywood's Copyright Wars: From Edison to the Internet* (New York: Columbia University Press).

Denisoff, R. Serge (1991), *Inside MTV* (New Brunswick: Transaction Publishers).

Denney, Alex (2015), 'The Story Behind Kate Bush's "Cloudbusting" Video', *Dazed*, 30 October, <https://www.dazeddigital.com/music/article/27217/1/the-story-behind-kate-bush-s-cloudbusting-video> (last accessed 24 January 2020).

Dibben, Nicola (1999), 'Representations of Femininity in Popular Music', *Popular Music* 18.3: 331–55.

Dibben, Nicola (2002), 'V. Constructions of Femininity in 1990s Girl-Group Music', *Feminism & Psychology* 12.2: 168–75.

Dibben, Nicola (2009), *Björk* (Indianapolis: Indiana University Press).

Dibben, Nicola (2014), 'Visualizing the App Album with Björk's *Biophilia*', in Carol Vernallis, Amy Herzog and John Richardson (eds), *The Oxford Handbook of Sound and Image in Digital Media* (Oxford: Oxford University Press), pp. 682–706.

Dickinson, Kay (ed.) (2003a), *Movie Music: The Film Reader* (London and New York: Routledge).

Dickinson, Kay (2003b), 'Pop, Speed, Teenagers and the "MTV aesthetic"', in Dickinson (ed.), *Movie Music: The Film Reader* (London and New York: Routledge), pp. 143–51.

Dickinson, Kay (2007), 'Music Video and Synaesthetic Possibility', in Roger Beebe and Jason Middleton (eds), *Medium Cool: Music Videos from Soundies to Cellphones* (Durham, NC, and London: Duke University Press), pp. 13–29.

Dickinson, Margaret (1999), *Rogue Reels: Oppositional Film in Britain 1945–90* (London: BFI Publishing).

DiCola, Peter (2013), 'Money from Music: Survey Evidence on Musicians' Revenue and Lessons about Copyright Incentives', *Arizona Law Review* 55: 301.

Dillane, Aileen, Eoin Devereux and Martin J. Power (2015), '3 Culminating Sounds and (En) visions', in Dillane, Devereux and Power (eds), *David Bowie: Critical Perspectives* (New York and London: Routledge), pp. 19–35.

Dmytryk, Edward (2012), *On Film Editing* (Waltham, MA: Focal Press).

Dodds, Sherril (2001), *Dance on Screen: Genres and Media from Hollywood to Experimental Art* (New York: Springer).

Dodds, Sherril (2004), *Dance on Screen: Genres and Media from Hollywood to Experimental Art* (Basingstoke: Palgrave Macmillan).

Dodds, Sherril (2009a), 'From Busby Berkeley to Madonna: Music Video and Popular Dance', in Julie Malnig (ed.), *Ballroom, Boogie, Shimmy Sham, Shake: A Social and Popular Dance Reader* (Urbana and Chicago: University of Illinois Press), pp. 247–60.

Dodds, Sherril (2009b), 'Dancing across Film, Television and the Digital Screen', *International Journal of Performance Arts and Digital Media* 5.2: 71–3.

Dodds, Sherril (2011), *Dancing on the Canon* (Basingstoke: Palgrave Macmillan).

Dodds, Sherril (2014), 'Values in Motion: Reflections on Popular Screen Dance', in Melissa Blanco Borelli (ed.), *The Oxford Handbook of Dance and the Popular Screen* (Oxford: Oxford University Press), pp. 445–54.

Dombal, Ryan (2005), 'Chris Cunningham', *Pitchfork*, 31 July, <https://pitchfork.com/features/interview/6103-chris-cunningham/> (last accessed 24 January 2020).

Donnelly, Kevin J. (ed.) (2001), *Film Music: Critical Approaches* (New York: Continuum International Publishing Group).

Donnelly, Kevin J. (2002a), 'Tracking British Television: Pop Music as Stock Soundtrack to the Small Screen', *Popular Music* 21.3: 331–43.

Donnelly, Kevin J. (2002b), *Pop Music in British Cinema* (London: BFI Publishing).

Donnelly, Kevin J. (2005), *The Spectre of Sound: Music in Film and Television* (London: BFI Publishing, and Oakland: University of California Press).

Donnelly, Kevin J. (2007a), *British Film Music and Film Musicals* (Basingstoke: Palgrave Macmillan).

Donnelly, Kevin J. (2007b), 'Experimental Music Video and Television', in Laura Mulvey and Jamie Sexton (eds), *Experimental British Television* (Manchester: Manchester University Press), pp. 166–79.

Doyle, Gillian ([2002] 2013), *Understanding Media Economics* (New York: SAGE Publications Ltd).

Drukman, Steven (1995), 'The Gay Gaze, or Why I Want My MTV', in Caroline Evans and Lorraine Gamman (eds), *A Queer Romance: Lesbians, Gay Men and Popular Culture* (Abingdon: Routledge), pp. 81–98.

Du Gay, Paul (ed.) (1997), *Production of Culture / Cultures of Production* (Milton Keynes: The Open University).

Duff, David (2000), *Modern Genre Theory* (London: Pearson).

Dupin, Christophe (2003), 'Early Days of Short Film Production at the British Film Institute: Origins and Evolution of the BFI Experimental Film Fund (1952–66)', *Journal of Media Practice* 4.2: 77–91.

Dutta, Kunal (2010), 'The Revolution that Killed Soho's Record Shops', *The Independent*, 12 May, <https://www.independent.co.uk/news/uk/this-britain/the-revolution-that-killed-sohos-record-shops-1971342.html> (last accessed 24 January 2020).
Dyer, Richard ([1977] 1981), 'Entertainment and Utopia', in Rick Altman (ed.), *Genre: The Musical* (Abingdon: Routledge).
Dyer, Richard (1982), 'Don't Look Now: The Male Pin-up', *Screen* 23.3–4: 61–73.
Dyer, Richard (1997), *White: Essays on Race and Culture* (Abingdon: Routledge).
Dyer, Richard ([1992] 2002), *Only Entertainment*, 2nd edition (Abingdon: Routledge).
Dyer, Richard (2013), *The Matter of Images: Essays on Representation* (Abingdon: Routledge).
Eastwood, Joel (2014), 'Recording Industry Earns More from Fan Videos Than from Official Music Videos', *The Star*, 18 March, n.p.
Edge, Kevin (1991), *The Art of Selling Songs: Graphics for the Music Business 1690–1900* (London: Futures).
Edmond, Maura (2014), 'Here We Go Again: Music Videos after YouTube', *Television and New Media* 15.4: 305–20.
Elsey, Eileen, and Andrew Kelly (2002), *In Short: A Guide to Short Film-making in the Digital Age* (London: British Film Institute).
Emerson, Rana A. (2002), '"Where my girls at?" Negotiating Black Womanhood in Music Videos', *Gender & Society* 16.1: 115–35.
English, James F. (2001), 'Afterword: Bastard Auteurism and Academic Auteurs: A Reflexive Reading of Smithee Studies', in Jeremy Braddock and Stephen Hock (eds), *Directed by Alan Smithee* (Minneapolis: University of Minnesota Press), pp. 269–88.
Evans, Caroline, and Lorraine Gamman (1995), 'The Gaze Revisited, or Reviewing Queer Viewing', in Evans and Gamman (eds), *A Queer Romance: Lesbians, Gay Men and Popular Culture* (Abingdon: Routledge), pp. 12–56.
Evans, Jeff (2016), *Rock and Pop on British Television* (London: Omnibus Press).
Evans, Mark, and Mary Fogarty (eds) (2016), *Movies, Moves and Music: The Sonic World of Dance Films* (Sheffield: Equinox Publishing).
Fabbri, Franco (1999), 'Browsing Music Spaces: Categories and the Musical Mind', paper delivered at IASPM (UK) conference.
Fact (2011), 'Sex, drugs and decay: Peter Care and Richard H. Kirk on the making – and re-making – of their Sheffield film noir' <https://www.factmag.com/2011/10/10/cabaret-voltaire-johnny-yesno-revisited-2/> (last accessed 24 January 2020).
Fagerjord, Anders (2009), 'After Convergence: YouTube and Remix Culture', in Jeremy Hunsinger, Lisbeth Klastrup and Matthew Allen (eds), *International Handbook of Internet Research* (Dordrecht: Springer), pp. 187–200.
Fairclough, K. (2017), 'Soundtrack Self: FKA twigs, Music Video and Celebrity Feminism', in Gina Arnold, Daniel Cookney, Kirsty Fairclough and Michael Goddard (eds), *Music/Video: Histories, Aesthetics, Media* (New York: Bloomsbury Publishing USA), pp. 121–32.
Faulkner, Robert R. (2013), *Hollywood Studio Musicians: Their Work and Careers in the Recording Industry* (Piscataway, NJ: Aldine Transaction).
Feldman-Barrett, Christine, and Andy Bennett (2016), '"All that glitters": Glam, Bricolage, and the History of Post-War Youth Culture', in Ian Chapman and Henry Johnson,

Global Glam and Popular Music: Style and Spectacle from the 1970s to the 2000s (Abingdon: Routledge), pp. 19–32.

Fenster, Mark (1993), 'Genre and Form: The Development of the Country Music Video', in Simon Frith, Andrew Goodwin and Lawrence Grossberg (eds), *Sound and Vision: The Music Video Reader* (Abingdon: Routledge), pp. 109–28.

Fetveit, A. (2011), 'Mutable Temporality in and beyond the Music Video: An Aesthetic of Post-Production', in Eivind Rossaak (ed.), *Between Stillness and Motion: Film, Photography, Algorithms* (Amsterdam: Amsterdam University Press), pp. 159–86.

Feuer, Jane (1982), *The Hollywood Musical* (London: British Film Institute).

Fine, Richard (2010), 'American Authorship and the Ghost of Moral Rights', *Book History* 13.1: 218–50.

Finney, Angus (1996), *Developing Films in Europe* (London: MBS-Routledge).

Fish, Mick (2002), *Industrial Evolution: Through the '80s with Cabaret Voltaire* (London: Poptomes).

Fisher, Clive (1984), *Music Video: A Specially Commissioned Report* (London: Oyez Longman Intelligence Reports, 1984).

Fletcher, Winston (2008), *Powers of Persuasion: The Inside Story of British Advertising 1951–2000* (Oxford: Oxford University Press).

Flinn, Caryl (1992), *Strains of Utopia: Gender, Nostalgia, and Hollywood Film Music* (Princeton, NJ: Princeton University Press).

Foege, Alec (1995), 'Out of Crass Commerce Arises the New Auteur', *The New York Times*, 27 August, <https://www.nytimes.com/1995/08/27/arts/pop-music-out-of-crass-commerce-arises-the-new-auteur.html> (last accessed 24 January 2020).

Foucault, Michel (1977), *Discipline and Punish: The Birth of the Prison* (London: Allen Lane).

Foucault, Michel (1980), *Power / Knowledge: Selected Interviews and Other Writings 1972–1977* (New York: Pantheon).

Fowler, William (2017), 'The Occult Roots of MTV: British Music Video and Underground Film-Making in the 1980s', *Music, Sound, and the Moving Image* 11.1: 63–77.

FRAME (2016), Music Video Panel at FRAME Film Festival, Rose Theatre, Kingston, London (transcription of audio recording), 11 June, University of Portsmouth.

Framestore (2012), 'The Shoes – Time to Dance' (last accessed 9 November 2015).

Framestore (n.d.), 'Simon Bourne', <https://www.framestore.com/work/simon-bourne> (last accessed 9 November 2015).

Fraser, Peter (1985), *Teaching Music Video* (London: BFI Publishing).

Frith, Simon (2019), '*Power to the People: British Music Videos 1966–2016*. Thunderbird Releasing, 2017. 900 minutes, 6 discs', *Popular Music* 38.2: 341–4.

Frith, Simon, Andrew Goodwin and Lawrence Grossberg (eds) (1993), *Sound and Vision: The Music Video Reader* (Abingdon: Routledge).

Frith, Simon, and Howard Horne (1987), *Art into Pop* (London: Methuen).

Frith, Simon, and L. Marshall (eds) (2009), *Music and Copyright*, 2nd edition (Edinburgh: Edinburgh University Press).

Fryer, Paul (1997), '"Everybody's on Top of the Pops": Popular Music on British Television 1960–1985', *Popular Music and Society* 21.3: 153–71.

Fuchs, Christian (2013), 'Class and Exploitation on the Internet', in Trebor Scholz (ed.), *Digital Labor: The Internet as Playground and Factory* (New York and London: Routledge), pp. 211–24.

Gabbard, Krin (1996), *Jammin' at the Margins: Jazz and the American Cinema* (Chicago and London: University of Chicago Press).

Gambetta, Diego (ed.) (1990), *Trust: Making and Breaking Cooperative Relations* (Oxford: Basil Blackwell).

Gambetta, Diego, and Heather Hamill (2005), *Streetwise: How Taxi Drivers Establish Customers' Trustworthiness* (New York: Russell Sage Foundation).

Gammage, Marquita Marie (2016), *Representations of Black Women in the Media: The Damnation of Black Womanhood* (Abingdon: Routledge).

Gamman, Lorraine, and Margaret Marshment (1988), 'Introduction: The Female Gaze', in Gamman and Marshment, *The Female Gaze: Women as Viewers of Popular Culture* (Seattle: Real Comet Press), pp. 1–12.

Gammons, H. (2011), *The Art of Music Publishing: An Entrepreneurial Guide to Publishing and Copyright for the Music, Film, and Media Industries* (Waltham, MA: Focal Press).

Gardner, Abigail (2016), *PJ Harvey and Music Video Performance* (Abingdon: Routledge).

Garrett, James (1986), 'Commercial Production', in Brian Henry (ed.), *British Television Advertising: The First 30 Years* (London: Century Benham), pp. 303–402.

Gaut, Berys (1997), 'Film Authorship and Collaboration', in Richard Allen and Murray Smith (eds), *Film Theory and Philosophy* (Oxford: Oxford University Press), pp. 149–73.

Geertz, Clifford (1973), *The Interpretation of Cultures* (New York: Basic Books).

Geertz, Clifford (1983), *Local Knowledge: Further Essays in Interpretive Sociology* (New York: Basic Books).

Genné, Beth (2018a), '"Dancin' in the street": Street Dancing on Film and Video from Fred Astaire to Michael Jackson', in Geraldine Morris and Larraine Nicholas (eds), *Rethinking Dance History: Issues and Methodologies*, 2nd edition (Abingdon: Routledge), pp. 186–96.

Genné, Beth (2018b), *Dance Me a Song: Astaire, Balanchine, Kelly, and the American Film Musical* (New York: Oxford University Press USA).

'George Michael – Making of "Faith" with Andy Morahan', short film, <http://imvdb.com/video/george-michael/faith> (last accessed 24 January 2020).

Giddens, Anthony (1983), 'Comments on the Theory of Structuration', *Journal for the Theory of Social Behaviour* 13.1 (March), pp. 75–80.

Gilbert, Pat ([2004] 2005), *Passion Is a Fashion: The Real Story of The Clash*, 4th edition (London: Aurum Press).

Gilbey, Ryan (2011), 'Jamie Thraves: Life is Bittersweet', *The Guardian*, 30 June, <http://www.theguardian.com/film/2011/jun/30/jamie-thraves-treacle-jr> (last accessed 24 January 2020).

Gill, Rosalind (2007), *Gender and the Media* (Cambridge: Polity).

Gillis, Stacy, and Rebecca Munford (2004), 'Genealogies and Generations: The Politics and Praxis of Third Wave Feminism', *Women's History Review* 13.2: 165–82.

Ginsberg, Jane (1992), 'Moral Rights in a Common Law System', in Peter Anderson and David Saunders (eds), *Moral Rights Protection in a Copyright System* (Queensland: Institute for Cultural Policy Studies), p. 35.
Glancy, Mark (2014), *Hollywood and the Americanization of Britain: From the 1920s to the Present* (London: I. B. Tauris).
Glynn, Stephen (2013), *The British Pop Music Film: The Beatles and Beyond* (Basingstoke: Palgrave Macmillan).
Goffman, Erving (1976), 'Gender Display', in Goffman, *Gender Advertisements* (London: Palgrave), pp. 1–9.
Goffman, Erving ([1959] 2002), *The Presentation of Self in Everyday Life* (Garden City, NY: Anchor).
Goldman, William (1985), 'Studio Executives' and 'Producers', in Goldman, *Adventures in the Screen Trade: A Personal View of Hollywood* (London: Abacus), pp. 39–58 and 60–72.
Goldmark, Daniel (2005), *Tunes For 'Toons: Music and the Hollywood Cartoon* (Berkeley and Los Angeles: University of California Press).
Goldmark, Daniel, Lawrence Kramer and Richard Leppert (eds) (2007), *Beyond the Soundtrack: Representing Music in Cinema* (Berkeley: University of California Press).
Goodridge, Peter (2011), *Film, Television and Radio, Books, Music and Art: UK Investment in Artistic Originals* (London: Imperial College Business School).
Goodwin, Andrew (1992), *Dancing in the Distraction Factory: Music Television and Popular Culture* (Minneapolis: University of Minnesota Press).
Goodwin, Andrew (1993), 'Fatal Distractions: MTV Meets Postmodern Theory', in Simon Frith, Andrew Goodwin and Lawrence Grossberg (eds), *Sound and Vision: The Music Video Reader* (Abingdon: Routledge), pp. 45–66.
Gorbman, Claudia (1987a), *Unheard Melodies: Narrative Film Music* (Indianapolis: Indiana University Press).
Gorbman, Claudia (1987b), 'Classical Hollywood Practice: The Model of Max Steiner', in Gorbman, *Unheard Melodies* (London: BFI Publishing, 1987), pp. 70–98.
Gorman, Paul (2008), *Reasons to be Cheerful: The Life and Work of Barney Bubbles* (Croydon: Adelita).
Gornostaeva, Galina (2007), 'Face-to-Face Interactions Along the Production Chain and Across Networks: A Study of Film and Television Industry in London', *International Journal of Knowledge, Culture and Change Management* 6.7: 45–54.
Gow, Joe (1992), 'Music Video as Communication: Popular Formulas and Emerging Genres', *The Journal of Popular Culture* 26.2: 41–70.
Gow, Joe (1996), 'Reconsidering Gender Roles on MTV: Depictions in the Most Popular Music Videos of the Early 1990s', *Communication Reports* 9: 151–61.
Graham, James (2017), 'Introduction: Collaborative Production in the Creative Industries', in James Graham and Alessandro Gandini (eds), *Collaborative Production in the Creative Industries* (London: University of Westminster Press), pp. 1–14.
Graham, James, and Alessandro Gandini (eds) (2017), *Collaborative Production in the Creative Industries* (London: University of Westminster Press).

Grantham, Bill (1999), *Some Big Bourgeois Brothel: Contexts for France's Culture Wars with Hollywood* (Luton: University of Luton Press).

Gray, Jonathan, and Derek Johnson (eds) (2013), *A Companion to Media Authorship* (Somerset, NJ: John Wiley and Sons).

Gray, Marcus (2009), *Route 19 Revisited: The Clash and London Calling* (London: Jonathan Cape).

Green, Dusin J. (2013), 'The Synthesizer: Modernist and Technological Transformations in Film Sound and Contemporary Music', BA thesis, Claremont McKenna College.

Greenfield, Amy (2002), 'The Kinesthetics of Avant-Garde Dance Film: Deren and Harris', in Judy Mitoma, Elizabeth Zimmer and Dale Ann Stieber (eds), *Envisioning Dance on Film and Video* (New York: Routledge).

Greenfield, Steve, and Guy Osborn (1998), *Contract and Control in the Entertainment Industry: Dancing on the Edge of Heaven* (Farnham: Ashgate Publishing Co).

Gregory, Georgina (2002), 'Masculinity, Sexuality and the Visual Culture of Glam Rock', *Culture and Communication* 5.2: 35–60.

Gregory, Georgina (2019), *Boy Bands and the Performance of Pop Masculinity* (Abingdon: Routledge).

Greig, Charlotte (1997), 'Female Identity and the Woman Songwriter', in Sheila Whiteley (ed.), *Sexing the Groove: Popular Music and Gender* (New York: Routledge), pp. 168–77.

Grice, Jeremy (2013), *Sorrow Might Come in the End: Legal Cases in the Music and Entertainment Industries* (Scotts Valley, CA: CreateSpace Independent Publishing).

Griffith, Richard (1976), 'Cycles and Genres', in Bill Nichols (ed.), *Movies and Methods*, vol. 1 (Berkeley: University of California Press), pp. 111–17.

Grossberg, Lawrence (1993), 'The Media Economy of Rock Culture: Cinema, Post-Modernity and Authenticity', in Simon Frith, Andrew Goodwin and Lawrence Grossberg (eds), *Sound and Vision: The Music Video Reader* (Abingdon: Routledge), pp. 185–209.

Guat, Berys (1997), 'Film Authorship and Collaboration', in Richard Allen and Murray Smith (eds), *Film Theory and Philosophy* (Oxford: Oxford University Press), pp. 149-173.

Gunkel, David J. (2012), 'What Does It Matter Who Is Speaking? Authorship, Authority, and the Mashup', *Popular Music and Society* 35.1: 71–91.

Gunning, Tom (1989), 'Primitive Cinema: A Frame-up? Or, The Trick's on Us', *Cinema Journal* 28.2: 3–12.

Gunning, Tom (1990a), 'The Cinema of Attractions: Early Film, Its Spectator and the Avant-Garde', in Thomas Elsaesser and Adam Barker (eds), *Early Cinema: Space Frame Narrative* (London: British Film Institute), pp. 56–62.

Gunning, Tom (1990b), 'Non Continuity, Continuity, Discontinuity: A Theory of Genres in Early Films', in Thomas Elsaesser and Adam Barker (eds), *Early Cinema: Space Frame Narrative* (London: British Film Institute), pp. 86–94.

Gunning, Tom (1990c), '"Primitive" Cinema: A Frame-Up? Or, The Trick's on Us', in Thomas Elsaesser and Adam Barker (eds), *Early Cinema: Space Frame Narrative* (London: British Film Institute), pp. 95–103.

Gunning, Tom (2003), 'Re-newing Old Technologies: Astonishment, Second Nature, and the Uncanny in Technology from the Previous Turn-of-the-Century', in David Thorburn and Henry Jenkins (eds), *Rethinking Media Change: The Aesthetics of Transition* (Cambridge, MA: MIT Press, 2003).
Haider, Arwa (2018), '"Don't tell the label": The Artists Reinventing the Music Video', *Financial Times*, 25 May, <https://www.ft.com/content/143148c2-5da9-11e8-ab47-8fd33f423c09> (last accessed 24 January 2020).
Hail the New Puritan, television film (Charles Atlas, Electronic Arts Intermix, UK, 1986).
Halliwell, Leslie, with Philip Purser (1986), *Halliwell's Television Companion* (London: Grafton).
Hamlyn, Nicky (2003), *Film Art Phenomena* (London: British Film Institute).
Hancox, Dan (2017), 'Attack the Block: How Grime's Visuals Went Pop', *The Guardian*, 20 April, <https://www.theguardian.com/music/2017/apr/20/attack-the-block-how-grimes-visuals-went-pop> (last accessed 24 January 2020).
Hanson, Matt (2006), *Reinventing Music Video: Next-Generation Directors, Their Inspiration and Work* (Houston: Gulf Professional Publishing).
Harper, Graeme, Ruth Doughty and Jochen Eisentraut (eds) (2014), *Sound and Music in Film and Visual Media: A Critical Overview* (New York: Bloomsbury Publishing USA).
Harper, Sue, and Justin Smith (2012), 'Cross-over', in Harper and Smith (eds), *Film Culture in the 1970s: The Boundaries of Pleasure* (Edinburgh: Edinburgh University Press), pp. 193–207.
Harries, Dan (2002), 'Film Parody and the Resuscitation of Genre', in Stephen Neale (ed.), *Genre and Contemporary Hollywood* (London: British Film Institute), pp. 281–93.
Harrison, Ann (2014), *Music: The Business*, 6th edition (London: Virgin Books).
Harrison, Ann (2017), *Music: The Business*, 7th edition (London: Virgin Books).
Hatcher, Jordan S. (2006), 'Are Auteurs Really All That Special? An Argument Against the Special Position of Film / Video Directors under UK Law', *Boston College Intellectual Property and Technology Forum*, 4, <http://bciptf.org/?p=204> (last accessed 24 January 2020).
Hawkins, Stan (1996), 'Perspectives in Popular Musicology: Music, Lennox, and Meaning in 1990s Pop 1', *Popular Music* 15.1: 17–36.
Hawkins, Stan (1997), 'The Pet Shop Boys: Musicology, Masculinity and Banality', in Sheila Whiteley (ed.), *Sexing the Groove: Popular Music and Gender* (New York: Routledge), pp. 118–35.
Hawkins, Stan (2013), 'On Male Queering in Mainstream Pop', in Sheila Whiteley and Jennifer Rycenga (eds), *Queering the Popular Pitch* (Abingdon: Routledge), pp. 280–95.
Hawkins, Stan (2015), *Queerness in Pop Music: Aesthetics, Gender Norms, and Temporality* (Abingdon: Routledge).
Hawkins, Stan (2017a), 'Introduction: Sensing Gender in Popular Music', in Hawkins (ed.), *The Routledge Research Companion to Popular Music and Gender* (Abingdon and New York: Taylor & Francis), n.p.
Hawkins, Stan (2017b), *The British Pop Dandy: Masculinity, Popular Music and Culture* (Abingdon: Routledge, 2017).

Hayward, Philip (1990), 'Industrial Light and Magic: Style, Technology and Special Effects in the Music Video and Music Television', in Hayward (ed.), *Culture, Technology and Creativity in the Late Twentieth Century* (Indianapolis: Indiana University Press), pp. 125–47.

Hearsum, Paula, and Ian Inglis (2013), 'The Emancipation of Music Video: YouTube and the Cultural Politics of Supply and Demand', in John Richardson, Claudia Gorbman and Carol Vernallis (eds), *The Oxford Handbook of New Audiovisual Aesthetics* (Oxford: Oxford University Press), pp. 483–500.

Hediger, Vinzenz, and Patrick Vonderau (2014), *Films that Work: Industrial Film and the Productivity of Media* (Amsterdam: Amsterdam University Press).

Herzog, Amy (2004), 'Discordant Visions: The Peculiar Musical Images of the Soundies Jukebox Film', *American Music* 22.1: 27–39.

Herzog, Amy (2007), 'Illustrating Music: The Impossible Embodiments of the Jukebox Film', in Roger Beebe and Jason Middleton (eds), *Medium Cool: Music Videos from Soundies to Cellphones* (Durham, NC, and London: Duke University Press), pp. 30–58.

Heslop, Richard (n.d.), 'Richard Heslop: Film Maker', Vimeo, <https://vimeo.com/user10208571/about> (last accessed 13 January 2017).

Hesmondhalgh, David (1998), 'The British Dance Music Industry: A Case Study of Independent Cultural Production', *British Journal of Sociology* 49.2: 234–51.

Hesmondhalgh, David (2005), 'Subcultures, Scenes or Tribes? None of the Above', *Journal of Youth Studies* 8.1: 21–40.

Hesse, Carla (1991), 'Enlightenment Epistemology and the Laws of Authorship in Revolutionary France, 1777–1793', in Robert Post (ed.), *Law and the Order of Culture* (Berkeley: University of California Press), pp. 109–37.

Hick, Darren Hudson (2014), 'Authorship, Co-Authorship, and Multiple Authorship', *The Journal of Aesthetics and Art Criticism* 72.2: 147–56.

Higson, Andrew (2003), *English Heritage, English Cinema: Costume Drama Since 1980* (Oxford: Oxford University Press).

Hilderbrand, Lucas (2007), 'YouTube: Where Cultural Memory and Copyright Converge', *Film Quarterly* 61.1: 48–57.

Hilderbrand, Lucas (2009), *Inherent Vice: Bootleg Histories of Videotape and Copyright* (Durham, NC: Duke University Press).

Hodkinson, Mark (2009), *Queen: The Early Years* (London: Omnibus Press).

Hoesterey, Ingeborg (2001), *Pastiche: Cultural Memory in Art, Film, Literature* (Bloomington and Indianapolis: Indiana University Press).

Holt, Fabian (2011), 'Is Music Becoming More Visual? Online Video Content in the Music Industry', *Visual Studies* 26.1: 50–61.

Hook, Peter (2013), *Unknown Pleasures: Inside Joy Division* (New York: Simon and Schuster).

Horn, Adrian (2009), *Juke Box Britain: Americanisation and Youth Culture 1945–1960* (Manchester: Manchester University Press).

Huygen, Annelies, Natali Helberger, Joost Poort, Paul Rutten and N. A. N. M. van Eijk (2009), 'Ups and Downs: Economic and Cultural Effects of File Sharing on Music, Film and Games', *TNO Information and Communication Technology Series*.

Inglis, Ian (2003), *Popular Music and Film* (London: Wallflower Press).

James, David E. (2016), *Rock'n'Film: Cinema's Dance With Popular Music* (Oxford: Oxford University Press).

Jameson, Fredric (1985), 'Postmodernism and Consumer Society', in Hal Foster (ed.), *Postmodern Culture* (London: Pluto Press), pp. 111–26.

Jenkins, Henry (1992), 'Layers of Meaning: Fan Music Video and the Poetics of Poaching', in Jenkins, *Textual Poachers: Television Fans and Participatory Culture* (New York and London: Routledge), pp. 223–49.

Jones, Steve, and Martin Sorger (2006), 'Covering Music: A Brief History and Analysis of Album Cover Design', *Journal of Popular Music Studies* 11.1: 68–102.

Jordan, Stephanie, and Dave Allen (1993), *Parallel Lines: Media Representations of Dance* (London: John Libbey).

Kael, Pauline (1963), 'Circles and Squares', *Film Quarterly* 16.3 (Spring): 12–26.

Kalinak, Kathryn (1992a), *Settling the Score: Music and the Classical Hollywood Film* (Madison, WI: University of Wisconsin Press).

Kalinak, Kathryn (1992b), 'The "Hysterical Cult of the Director"', in Kalinak, *Settling the Score: Music and the Classical Hollywood Film* (Madison, WI: University of Wisconsin Press), pp. 135–58.

Kalinak, Kathryn (2010), *Film Music: A Very Short Introduction* (Oxford: Oxford University Press).

Kaplan, E. Ann (1987), *Rocking Around the Clock: Music Television, Postmodernism, and Consumer Culture* (London and New York: Routledge).

Kaplan, E. Ann (1996), 'Feminism(s) / Postmodernism(s): MTV and Alternate Women's Videos and Performance Art', in Patrick Campbell (ed.), *Analysing Performance, a Critical Reader* (Manchester: Manchester University Press), pp. 82–104.

Karpovich, Angelina I. (2007), 'Reframing Fan Videos', in Jamie Sexton (ed.), *Music, Sound and Multimedia: From the Live to the Virtual* (Edinburgh: Edinburgh University Press), pp. 17–28.

Kaufman, Anthony (2001), 'Interview: Shooting the "Beast"; Jonathan Glazer Tames the Gangster Genre', *Indiewire*, <https://www.indiewire.com/2001/06/interview-shooting-the-beast-jonathan-glazer-tames-the-gangster-genre-80926/> (last accessed 24 January 2020).

Kaufman, Gil (2003), 'Lens Recap: The Story Behind Coldplay's "The Scientist"', MTV News, <http://www.mtv.com/news/1472164/lens-recap-the-story-behind-coldplays-the-scientist/> (last accessed 24 January 2020).

Keazor, Henry, and Thorsten Wübbena (eds) (2010), *Rewind, Play, Fast Forward: The Past, Present and Future of the Music Video* (Berlin: De Gruyter).

Kelley, Andrea (2015), '"A revolution in the atmosphere": The Dynamics of Site and Screen in 1940s Soundies', *Cinema Journal*, 54.2: 72–93.

Kelley, Andrea J. (2018), *Soundies: Jukebox Films and the Shift to Small Screen Culture* (New Brunswick, NJ: Rutgers University Press).

Kelly, Brenda (2018), '"Sometimes, Always": Erasure, Mute and the Value of Independence', in Zuleika Beaven, Marcus O'Dair and Richard Osborne (eds), *Mute Records: Artists, Business, History* (New York: Bloomsbury Publishing USA), p. 113.

Kennedy, Matthew (2014), *Road Show: The Fall of Film Musicals in the 1960s* (Oxford: Oxford University Press).

King, Martin (2016), *Men, Masculinity and the Beatles* (Abingdon: Routledge).
Kinsey, Rebecca (2014), *We Used to Wait: Music Videos and Creative Literacy* (London: MIT Press).
Kleiler, David (1997), *You Stand There: Making Music Video* (New York: Three Rivers Press).
Klein, Amanda Ann (2012), *American Film Cycles: Reframing Genres, Screening Social Problems, and Defining Subcultures* (Austin: University of Texas Press).
Klein, Bethany (2010), *As Heard on TV: Popular Music in Advertising* (Farnham: Ashgate).
Klinger, B. (1995), '"Cinema / Ideology / Criticism" Revisited: The Progressive Genre', in B. K. Grant (ed.), *Film Genre Reader II* (Austin: University of Texas), pp. 74–90.
Knight, Arthur (2002), *Disintegrating the Musical: Black Performance and American Musical Film* (Durham, NC: Duke University Press).
Knight, David (1995), 'Director's Ownership rights . . . a Preliminary Guide', *Promo* 10–11: 7–8.
Knight, David (1996a), 'Interview with Stéphane Sednaoui', *Promo*, November, pp. 14–15.
Knight, David (1996b), 'Editorial', *Promo*, November, p. 1.
Knight, David (1996c), 'MTV UK? Anything's Possible, Apparently', *Promo*, 13 December.
Knight, David (2013), 'Chris Sweeney on Making Lily Allen's "Hard Out Here" Video', *Promo News*, 26 November, <https://www.promonews.tv/interviews/chris-sweeney-making-lily-allens-hard-out-here-video/22981> (last accessed 24 January 2020).
Knight, David (2017), 'The Moonlandingz ft Rebecca Taylor "The Strangle Of Anna" by Dawn Shadforth', *Promonews*, 22 March, <https://www.promonews.tv/videos/2017/03/22/moonlandingz-ft-rebecca-taylor-strangle-anna-dawn-shadforth/46870> (last accessed 24 January 2020).
Knight, Julia, and Peter Thomas (2012), *Reaching Audiences: Distribution and Promotion of Alternative Moving Image* (Bristol: Intellect).
Korsgaard, Mathias Bonde (2013), 'Music Video Transformed', in John Richardson, Claudia Gorbman and Carol Vernallis (eds), *The Oxford Handbook of New Audiovisual Aesthetics* (Oxford: Oxford University Press), pp. 501–24.
Korsgaard, Mathias Bonde (2017), *Music Video after MTV: Audiovisual Studies, New Media, and Popular Music* (Abingdon: Routledge).
Kress, G., and T. Threadgold (1988), 'Towards a Social Theory of Genre', *Southern Review* 21.3: 215–43.
Kroes, Rob (1993), 'Americanisation: What Are We Talking About', in Rob Kroes, R. W. Rydell and D. E. J. Bosscher (eds), *Cultural Transmissions and Receptions: American Mass Culture in Europe* (Amsterdam: VU University Press).
Kruse, Holly (1988), 'Kate Bush: Enigmatic Chanteuse as Pop Pioneer', *Journal of Popular Music Studies* 1.1: 13–22.
Kuhn, Michael (2002), *One Hundred Films and a Funeral: The Life and Death of Polygram Films* (London: Thorogood).
Kuhn, Thomas S. (1962), *The Structure of Scientific Revolutions* (Chicago: University of Chicago Press).

Laing, Dave (1984), 'Music Video: Industrial Product, Cultural Form', *Screen* 26.2: 78–83.
Lannin, Steve, and Matthew Caley (eds) (2005), *Pop Fiction: The Song in Cinema* (Bristol: Intellect).
Lapedis, Hilary (1989), 'Popping the Question: The Function and Effect of Popular Music in Cinema', *Popular Music* 18.3, pp. 367–79.
Larthe, Juliette (2000), 'The Director's Lot', *Televisual*, May: 32.
Lawrence, Tim (2009), 'Beyond the Hustle: 1970s Social Dancing, Discotheque Culture, and the Emergence of the Contemporary Club Dancer', in Julie Malnig (ed.), *Ballroom, Boogie, Shimmy Sham, Shake: A Social and Popular Dance Reader* (Urbana and Chicago: University of Illinois Press), pp. 199–216.
Leach, Elizabeth Eva (2001), 'Vicars of "Wannabe": Authenticity and the Spice Girls', *Popular Music* 20.2: 143–67.
Leggott, James (2016), 'Come to Daddy? Claiming Chris Cunningham for British Art Cinema', *Journal of British Cinema and Television* 13.2: 243–61.
Lemish, Dafna (2003), 'Spice World: Constructing Femininity the Popular Way', *Popular Music and Society* 26.1: 17–29.
Lena, Jennifer C., and Richard A. Peterson (2008), 'Classification as Culture: Types and Trajectories of Music Genres', *American Sociological Review* 73.5: 697–718.
Leonard, Marion (2017), *Gender in the Music Industry: Rock, Discourse and Girl Power* (Abingdon: Routledge).
Letts, Don, and David Nobakht (2007), *Culture Clash: Dread Meets Punk Rockers* (London: SAF).
Lewis, Lisa A. (1990), *Gender Politics and MTV: Voicing the Difference* (Philadelphia: Temple University Press).
Lieb, Kristin J. (2013), *Gender, Branding, and the Modern Music Industry: The Social Construction of Female Popular Music Stars* (Abingdon: Routledge).
Livingston, Paisley (1997), 'Cinematic Authorship', in Richard Allen and Murray Smith (eds), *Film Theory and Philosophy* (Oxford: Oxford University Press), pp. 132–48.
Lockwood, Dean (2017), 'Blackened Puppets: Chris Cunningham's Weird Anatomies', in Gina Arnold, Daniel Cookney, Kirsty Fairclough and Michael Goddard (eds), *Music / Video: Histories, Aesthetics, Media* (New York: Bloomsbury Publishing USA), pp. 195–210.
Logie, John (2013), '1967: The Birth of "The Death of the Author"', *College English* 75.5: 493–512.
Logie, John (2014), 'Peeling the Layers of the Onion: Authorship in Mashup and Remix Cultures', in Eduardo Navas, Owen Gallagher and xtine burrough (eds), *The Routledge Companion to Remix Studies* (Abingdon: Routledge), pp. 306–19.
Losseff, Nicky (1999), 'Cathy's Homecoming and the Other World: Kate Bush's "Wuthering Heights"', *Popular Music* 18.2: 227–40.
Love, Emma (2010), 'It's Time for Women to Call the Music Video Shots', *The Independent*, 12 March, <https://www.independent.co.uk/arts-entertainment/music/features/its-time-for-women-to-call-the-music-video-shots-1920051.html> (last accessed 24 January 2020).

Lukow, Gregory (1991), 'The Antecedents of MTV: Soundies, Scopitones and Snaders, and the History of an Ahistorical Form', in Michael Nash (ed.), *Art of Music Video: Ten Years After* (Long Beach, CA: Long Beach Museum of Art), pp. 6–9.
Lundskaer-Nielsen, Miranda (2013), 'The Long Road to Recognition: New Musical Theatre Development in Britain', *Studies in Musical Theatre* 7.2: 157–73.
Lury, Karen (2001), *British Youth Television: Cynicism and Enchantment*, Oxford Television Studies (Oxford: Clarendon Press).
Macaulay, Alastair (ed.) (1999), *Matthew Bourne and His Adventures in Motion Pictures* (London: Faber and Faber).
McCormick, Neil (2010), 'George Michael's Image Will Outlast the Scandal', *The Telegraph*, 15 September <https://www.telegraph.co.uk/culture/music/rockand-popfeatures/8004149/George-Michaels-image-will-outlast-the-scandal.html> (last accessed 24 January 2020).
Macdonald, Laurence E. (2013), *The Invisible Art of Film Music: A Comprehensive History* (Lanham, MD: Scarecrow Press).
McDonald, Paul (1997), 'Romance, Dance and the Performing Male Body in the Take That Videos', in Sheila Whiteley (ed.), *Sexing the Groove: Popular Music and Gender* (New York: Routledge), pp. 277–94.
McGee, Kristin (2008), 'The Feminization of Mass Culture and the Novelty of All-Girl Bands: The Case of the Ingenues', *Popular Music and Society* 31.5: 629–62.
Mackrell, Judith (1992), *Out of Line: The Story of British New Dance* (London: Dance Books).
Mackrell, Judith (2013), *Flappers: Six Women of a Dangerous Generation* (London: Macmillan).
Macleay, Ian (2010), *Malcolm McLaren: The Sex Pistols, the Anarchy, the Art, the Genius: the Whole Amazing Legacy* (London: John Blake).
McRobbie, Angela (1984), 'Dance and Social Fantasy', in Angela McRobbie and Mica Nava (eds), *Gender and Generation (Youth Questions)* (Basingstoke: Palgrave Macmillan), pp. 130–61.
McRobbie, Angela (1999), *In the Culture Society: Art, Fashion and Popular Music* (London: Routledge).
McRobbie, Angela (2009), *The Aftermath of Feminism: Gender: Culture and Social Change* (London: Sage).
Malnig, Julie (ed.) (2009), *Ballroom, Boogie, Shimmy Sham, Shake: A Social and Popular Dance Reader* (Urbana and Chicago: University of Illinois Press).
Maltby, Richard (1995), *Hollywood Cinema: An Introduction* (Chichester: Wiley-Blackwell).
Marcuse, Herbert (1978), *The Aesthetic Dimension: Toward a Critique of Marxist Aesthetics*, trans. Erica Sherover (Boston: Beacon Press).
Marks, Craig, and Rob Tannenbaum (2012), *I Want My MTV: The Uncensored Story of the Music Video Revolution* (New York: Plume).
Marks, Martin Miller (1997), *Music and the Silent Film: Contexts and Case Studies, 1895–1924* (New York and Oxford: Oxford University Press).
Marshall, Stuart (1985), 'Video: From Art to Independence', *Screen* 26.2: 66–72.

Martin, Angela (2003), 'Refocusing Authorship in Women's Filmmaking', in Jacqueline Levitin, Judith Plessis and Valerie Raoul (eds), *Women Filmmakers: Refocusing* (Vancouver: University of British Columbia Press), pp. 29–37.
May, Brian, with Terry Gross on 'Fresh Air', NPR Radio Interview, 3 August 2010.
Maybury, John (2012), 'Culture Now: John Maybury', lunchtime talk at the ICA, 17 February, <https://archive.ica.art/whats-on/culture-now-john-maybury> (last accessed 2 March 2020).
Mayer, Vicki, Miranda J. Banks and John T. Caldwell (eds) (2009), *Production Studies: Cultural Studies of Media Industries* (New York: Routledge).
Meigh-Andrews, Chris (2006), *A History of Video Art: The Development of Form and Function* (London: Bloomsbury).
Mera, Miguel, and David Burnand (eds) (2006), *European Film Music* (Aldershot: Ashgate).
'Mexican Breakfast', item from *The Ed Sullivan Show*, television series (CBS, USA, 1 June 1969).
Middles, Mick (2009), *Factory: The Story of the Record Label* (London: Virgin Books).
Miller, Jeffrey S. (2000), *Something Completely Different: British Television and American Culture* (Minneapolis: University of Minnesota Press).
Miller, Zara (2010), 'Interview with Hammer & Tongs', *Little White Lies*, 25 November <http://www.littlewhitelies.co.uk> (last accessed 12 January 2014).
Minsker, Evan (2013), 'Watch: Jon Hopkins' "Open Eye Signal" Video Features a Skateboarding Odyssey', 24 April <https://pitchfork.com/news/50459-watch-jon-hopkins-open-eye-signal-video-features-a-skateboarding-odyssey/> (last accessed 24 January 2020).
Mitoma, Judy (ed.) (2002), *Envisioning Dance on Film and Video* (New York and London: Routledge).
MOMA (1985), 'Music Video: The Industry and its Fringes', press release.
Moore, Allan (2002), 'Authenticity as Authentication', *Popular Music* 21.2: 209–23.
Moorefield, Virgil (2010), *The Producer as Composer: Shaping the Sounds of Popular Music* (Cambridge, MA: MIT Press).
Morini, Massimiliano (2013), 'Towards a Musical Stylistics: Movement in Kate Bush's "Running Up That Hill"', *Language and Literature* 22.4: 283–97.
Morricone, Ennio (2013), *Composing for Cinema: The Theory and Praxis of Music in Film* (Lanham, MD: Scarecrow Press).
Morris, Gay (2009), 'Dance Studies / Cultural Studies', *Dance Research Journal* 41.1: 82–100.
Morris, Geraldine, and Larraine Nicholas (2018), *Rethinking Dance History: Issues and Methodologies*, 2nd edition (Abingdon: Routledge).
Moy, Ron (2006), 'A Daughter of Albion: Kate Bush and Mythologies of Englishness', *Popular Music Online*.
Moy, Ron (2007), *Kate Bush and Hounds of Love* (Farnham: Ashgate Publishing).
Moy, Ron (2015), *Authorship Roles in Popular Music: Issues and Debates* (New York: Routledge).
Muikku, Jari (1990), 'On the Role and Tasks of a Record Producer', *Popular Music and Society* 14.1: 25–33.

Muir, Anne Ross (1988), 'The Status of Women Working in Film and Television', in Lorraine Gamman and Margaret Marshment (eds), *The Female Gaze: Women as Viewers of Popular Culture* (Seattle: Real Comet Press), pp. 143–4.

Mulvey, Laura (1989), 'Visual Pleasure and Narrative Cinema', in Mulvey, *Visual and Other Pleasures* (London: Palgrave Macmillan), pp. 14–26.

Mundy, John (1999), *Popular Music on Screen: From Hollywood Musical to Music Video* (Manchester: Manchester University Press).

Mundy, John (2007), *The British Musical Film* (Manchester and New York: Manchester University Press).

Murch, Walter (1995), 'Sound Design: The Dancing Shadow', in John Boorman (ed.), *Projections 4: Film-makers on Film-making* (London: Faber and Faber), pp. 237–51.

Murch, Walter (2001), *In the Blink of an Eye: A Perspective on Film Editing*, 2nd edition (Los Angeles: Silman-James).

Murray, Virginia S. (2014), 'Collaborative Authorship in Film Production: Walter Murch and Film Editing', *International Journal of New Media, Technology and the Arts*, 8.2: 9–19.

Neal, Charles (1987), *Tape Delay: Confessions from the Eighties Underground* (Harrow: SAF Publishing).

Neale, Stephen (1995), 'Questions of Genre', in B. K. Grant (ed.), *Film Genre Reader II* (Austin: University of Texas), pp. 158–83.

Neale, Stephen (2000), *Genre and Hollywood* (New York and London: Routledge).

Neale, Stephen (ed.) (2002), *Genre and Contemporary Hollywood* (London: British Film Institute).

Neale, Stephen, and Murray Smith (eds) (1998), *Contemporary Hollywood Cinema* (London and New York: Routledge).

Negus, Keith (1992), *Producing Pop: Culture and Conflict in the Popular Music Industry* (New York: Oxford University Press).

Negus, Keith (1997), 'Sinéad O'Connor: Musical Mother', in Sheila Whiteley (ed.), *Sexing the Groove: Popular Music and Gender* (New York: Routledge), pp. 178–90.

Negus, Keith (1999), *Music Genres and Corporate Cultures* (London: Routledge).

Negus, Keith (2011), 'Authorship and the Popular Song', *Music and Letters* 92.4: 607–29.

Negus, Keith (2017), 'The Gendered Narratives of Nobodies and Somebodies in the Popular Music Economy', in Stan Hawkins (ed.), *The Routledge Research Companion to Popular Music and Gender* (Abingdon and New York: Taylor & Francis), pp. 152–65.

Negus, Keith, and Michael J. Pickering (2004), *Creativity, Communication and Cultural Value* (London: Sage).

Newman, Michael Z. (2014), *Video Revolutions* (New York: Columbia University Press).

Nixon, Sean (2013), *Hard Sell: Advertising Affluence and Transatlantic Relations* (Manchester: Manchester University Press).

Nott, James J. (2002), *Music for the People: Popular Music and Dance in Interwar Britain* (Oxford: Oxford University Press).

Nowness (2015), 'Gwilym Gold: Triumph' <https://www.nowness.com/story/gwilym-gold-triumph> (last accessed 24 January 2020).

Oasis: Time Flies 1994–2009, DVD music video compilation (UK, 2010).
O'Neill, Paul (2012), *The Culture of Curating and the Curating of Culture(s)* (Cambridge, MA: MIT Press).
Ogborn, Kate (2000), 'Pathways into the Industry', in Robert Murphy (ed.), *British Cinema of the 90s* (London: British Film Institute), pp. 60–7.
OnePointFour (2012), 'Gyllenhaal Murdering Hipsters in Dalston', <https://www.onepointfour.co/2012/04/04/gyllenhaal-murdering-hipsters-in-dalston/> (last accessed 24 January 2020).
Ortner, Sherry B. (2009), 'Studying Sideways: Ethnographic Access in Hollywood', in Vicki Mayer, Miranda J. Banks and John T. Caldwell (eds), *Production Studies: Cultural Studies of Media Industries* (New York and London: Routledge), pp. 175–89.
Ostrowska, Dorota (2010), 'Magic, Emotions and Film Producers: Unlocking the "Black Box" of Film Production', *Wide Screen* 2.2.
Pardo, Alejandro (2010), 'The Film Producer as a Creative Force', *Wide Screen* 2.2: 1–23.
Park, Alison, Caroline Bryson, Elizabeth Clery, John Curtice and Miranda Phillips (eds) (2013), *British Social Attitudes: the 30th Report* (London: NatCen Social Research), <https://www.bsa.natcen.ac.uk/media/38723/bsa30_full_report_final.pdf> (last accessed 24 January 2020).
Peake, Tony (1999), *Derek Jarman* (London: Little, Brown and Company).
Pearlman, Karen (2006), 'Editing as a Form of Choreography', in Jessica Vokoun (ed.), *Proceedings Screendance: State of the Art* (Durham, NC: American Dance Festival, Duke University Press), pp. 52–6.
Peeters, Heidi (2004), 'The Semiotics of Music Video: It Must Be Written in the Stars', *Image and Narrative: Online Magazine of the Visual Narrative*, May, <http://www.imageandnarrative.be/inarchive/issue08/heidipeeters.htm> (last accessed 24 January 2020).
Perone, James E. (2009), *Mods, Rockers, and the Music of the British Invasion* (London: Praegar).
Perrott, Lisa (2019), 'The Animated Music Videos of Radiohead, Chris Hopewell and Gaston Vinas: Fan Participation, Collaborative Authorship and Dialoguic Worldbuilding', in Lori Burns and Stan Hawkins (eds), *The Bloomsbury Handbook of Popular Music Video Analysis* (New York: Bloomsbury Publishing USA), pp. 47–68.
Petchers, Brian (2014), 'What to Expect From Music Videos in 2014', <http://www.forbes.com/sites/brianpetchers/2014/02/19/what-to-expect-from-music-videos-in-2014/> (last accessed 24 January 2020).
Philips, Julia (2002), *You'll Never Eat Lunch in This Town Again* (London: Faber and Faber).
Philo, Simon (2014), *British Invasion: The Crosscurrents of Musical Influence* (Lanham, MD: Rowman and Littlefield).
Philo, Simon, and Neil Campbell (2004), 'Biff! Bang! Pow! The Transatlantic Pop Aesthetic, 1956–66', in Neil Campbell, Jude Davies and George McKay (eds), *Issues in Americanisation and Culture* (Edinburgh: Edinburgh University Press), pp. 278–94.
Piggford, George (1997), '"Who's That Girl?": Annie Lennox, Woolf's *Orlando*, and Female Camp Androgyny', *Mosaic: A Journal for the Interdisciplinary Study of Literature* 30.3: 39–58.

Pini, Maria (1997a), 'Cyborgs, Nomads and the Raving Feminine', in Helen Thomas (ed.), *Dance in the City* (London: Palgrave Macmillan), pp. 111–29.
Pini, Maria (1997b), 'Women and the Early British Rave Scene', in Angela McRobbie (ed.), *Back to Reality? Social Experience and Cultural Studies* (Manchester: Manchester University Press), pp. 152–69.
Pini, Maria (2001), *Club Cultures and Female Subjectivity: The Move from Home to House* (Dordrecht: Springer).
Pitchfork, '100 Awesome Music Videos', <http://pitchfork.com/features/lists-and-guides/6364-100-awesome-music-videos/> (last accessed 24 January 2020).
Plantinga, Carl, and Greg M. Smith (eds) (1999), *Passionate Views: Film, Cognition, and Emotion* (Baltimore, MD: Johns Hopkins University Press).
Porter, Michael E. (1985), 'Technology and Competitive Advantage', *Journal of Business Strategy* 5.3: 60–78.
Porter, Michael E., and Victor E. Millar (1985), 'How Information Gives You Competitive Advantage', *Harvard Business Review*, July.
Powdermaker, Hortense (1950), *Hollywood, the Dream Factory: An Anthropologist Looks at the Movie-makers* (Boston: Little, Brown and Co.).
Powrie, Phil, and Robynn Stilwell (eds) (2006), *Changing Tunes: The Use of Pre-Existing Music in Film* (Aldershot: Ashgate).
Prato, Greg (2011), *MTV Ruled the World: The Early Years of Music Video* (n.l.: Greg Prato).
Pratt, Andy C., and Galina Gornostaeva (2009), 'The Governance of Innovation in the Film and Television Industry: A Case Study of London, UK', in Andy C. Pratt and Paul Jeffcutt (eds), *Creativity, Innovation and the Cultural Economy* (Abingdon: Routledge), pp. 119–36.
Preston, Hilary (2006), 'Choreographing the Frame: A Critical Investigation into How Dance for the Camera Extends the Conceptual and Artistic Boundaries of Dance 1', *Research in Dance Education* 7.1: 75–87.
Prior, Nick (2010), 'The Rise of the New Amateurs: Popular Music, Digital Technology and the Fate of Cultural Production', *Handbook of Cultural Sociology* (London: Routledge), pp. 398–407.
Promo (1998a), '"All Seeing I: The Beat Goes On" in Promo of the Month', April, pp. 4–5.
Promo (1998b), 'Walter Stern Massive Attack "Teardrop"', May, pp. 4–5.
Promo News TV (2015a), 'Is Feminism Changing Music Videos? Part 1 July 2015', <http://www.promonews.tv> (last accessed 12 August 2015).
Promo News TV (2015b), 'Feminism and Music Videos: Sexuality and Opportunity Part 2 July 2015', <http://www.promonews.tv> (last accessed 12 August 2015).
Putnam, David (1983), 'The Producer', in Jason E. Squire (ed.), *The Movie Business Book*, 3rd edition (New York: Simon & Schuster).
Pye, Ian (1986), 'Flying in the Face of Fear', *NME*, 13 December, pp. 12–13 and p. 42.
'Queen: Days of Our Lives' (2011), documentary, BBC2.
Railton, Diane, and Paul Watson (2005), 'Naughty Girls and Red Blooded Women: Representations of Female Heterosexuality in Music Video', *Feminist Media Studies* 5.1: 51–63.

Railton, Diane, and Paul Watson (2011), *Music Video and the Politics of Representation* (Edinburgh: Edinburgh University Press).
Ratcliff, Carter (1983), 'David Bowie's Survival', *Artforum* 21.5: n.p.
Reddington, Helen (2016), *The Lost Women of Rock Music: Female Musicians of the Punk Era* (Abingdon: Routledge).
Reed, S. Alexander (2013), *Assimilate: A Critical History of Industrial Music* (New York: Oxford University Press).
Rees, A. L. (1999), *A History of Experimental Film* (London: BFI).
Rees, A. L., David Curtis, Duncan White and Steven Ball (eds) (2011), *Expanded Cinema: Art, Performance and Film* (London: Tate Publishing).
Reiss, Steven, and Neil Feineman (2000), *Thirty Frames Per Second: The Visionary Art of the Music Video* (New York: Harry N. Abrams).
Reynolds, Simon (2008), *Energy Flash: A Journey through Rave Music and Dance Culture* (London: Picador).
Reynolds, Simon (2011), *Retromania: Pop Culture's Addiction to Its Own Past* (New York: Macmillan).
Richardson, John (2011), *An Eye for Music: Popular Music and the Audiovisual Surreal* (Oxford: Oxford University Press).
Richardson, John, Claudia Gorbman and Carol Vernallis (eds) (2013), *The Oxford Handbook of New Audiovisual Aesthetics* (Oxford: Oxford University Press).
Riordan, Ellen (2001), 'Commodified Agents and Empowered Girls: Consuming and Producing Feminism', *Journal of Communication Inquiry* 25.3: 279–97.
Robb, John (2009), *The North Will Rise Again: Manchester Music City 1976–1996* (London: Aurum).
Roberts, Mike (2019), *How Art Made Pop and Pop Became Art* (London: Tate Publishing).
Roberts, Robin (1996), *Ladies First: Women in Music Video* (Jackson: University Press of Mississippi).
Robins, Kevin (1997), 'What in the World's Going On?', in Paul du Gay (ed.), *Production of Culture, Cultures of Production* (London: Sage / Open University Press), pp. 11–67.
Rocks, Christopher (2017), *London's Creative Industries – 2017 Update*, GLAEconomics Working Paper 89 (London: Greater London Authority).
Rodger, Gillian (2004), 'Drag, Camp and Gender Subversion in the Music and Videos of Annie Lennox', *Popular Music* 23.1: 17–29.
Rogers, Holly (2013), *Sounding the Gallery: Video and the Rise of Art Music* (Oxford and New York: Oxford University Press).
Romney, Jonathan, and Adrian Wootton (eds) (1995), *Celluloid Jukebox: Popular Music and the Movies Since the '50s* (London: BFI).
Rose, Margaret A. (1993), *Parody: Ancient, Modern and Post-Modern* (Cambridge: Cambridge University Press).
Roseman, Jon (2010), *From Here to Obscurity* (Peterborough: Bambam Publishing).
Rush, M. (2007), *Video Art* (New York: Thames & Hudson).
Saed, Omnia (2016), 'Klein's Spoken Word Piece on Religion and Nigerian Upbringing Is a Must-Watch', *Okayafrica*, 29 July, <https://www.okayafrica.com/klein-interview-marks-of-worship/> (last accessed 24 January 2020).

Sanjek, Russell (1996), *Pennies from Heaven: The American Popular Music Business in the Twentieth Century* (Boston: Da Capo Press).

Saper, Craig (2001), 'Artifical Auteurism and the Political Economy of the Allen Smithee Case', in Jeremy Braddock and Stephen Hock (eds), *Directed by Alan Smithee* (Minneapolis: University of Minnesota Press), pp. 29–50.

Sarris, Andrew (1962), 'Auteur Theory and Film Evaluation', *Film Culture* 27.63: 1–8.

Sarris, Andrew (2001), 'Foreword: Allen Smithee Redux', in Jeremy Braddock and Stephen Hock (eds), *Directed by Alan Smithee* (Minneapolis: University of Minnesota Press), pp. vii–xvi.

Savage, Jon (2016), *1966: The Year the Decade Exploded* (London: Faber and Faber).

Schatz, Thomas (1977), 'New Directions in Film Genre Study: A Response to Charles F. Altman', in B. Lawton and J. Staiger (eds), *1977 Film Studies Annual: Part II: Film-Historical Speculations* (New York: Redgrave), pp. 44–52.

Schatz, Thomas (1981), *Hollywood Genres: Formulas, Filmmaking and the Studio System* (New York: Random House).

Schatz, Thomas (1989), *The Genius of the System: Hollywood Film-Making in the Studio Era* (London: Faber and Faber).

Schilt, Kristen (2003), '"A little too ironic": The Appropriation and Packaging of Riot Grrrl Politics by Mainstream Female Musicians', *Popular Music and Society* 26.1: 5–16.

Scholz, Trebor (ed.) (2013), *Digital Labor: The Internet as Playground and Factory* (New York: Routledge).

Schrader, Paul (2014), 'Game Changers: The Close-Up', *Film Comment*, September / October, n.p. <https://www.filmcomment.com/article/the-close-up-films-that-changed-filmmaking/> (last accessed 24 January 2020).

Schwartz, Lara M. (2007), *Making Music Videos: Everything You Need to Know from the Best in the Business* (New York: Billboard Books).

Seidman, S. A. (1992), 'An Investigation of Sex-Role Stereotyping in Music Videos', *Journal of Broadcasting and Electronic Media* 36: 209–16.

Sellors, C. Paul (2007), 'Collective Authorship in Film', *The Journal of Aesthetics and Art Criticism* 65.3: 263–71.

Sellors, C. Paul (2010), *Film Authorship: Auteurs and Other Myths* (London: Wallflower).

Sexton, Jamie, and Kevin J. Donnelly (2007), *Music, Sound and Multimedia: From the Live to the Virtual* (Edinburgh: Edinburgh University Press).

Sherman, Barry L., and Joseph R. Dominick (1986), 'Violence and Sex in Music Videos: TV and Rock'n'Roll', *Journal of Communication* 36.1: 79–93.

Shuker, Roy (2016), *Understanding Popular Music* (Abingdon: Routledge).

Signorielli, Nancy, Douglas McLeod and Elaine Healy (1994), 'Gender Stereotypes in MTV Commercials: The Beat Goes On', *Journal of Broadcasting and Electronic Media* 38: 91–101.

Simpson, David (2012), 'How We Made Ebeneezer Goode by the Shamen', *The Guardian*, 5 March <https://www.theguardian.com/culture/2012/mar/05/ebeneezer-goode-shamen> (last accessed 24 January 2020).

Simpson, Dave (2013), 'How We Made Killer', *The Guardian*, 11 March <https://www.theguardian.com/music/2013/mar/11/how-we-made-killer> (last accessed 24 January 2020).

Sky, Rick (1994), *The Show Must Go On: The Life of Freddie Mercury* (Secaucus, NJ: Carol Publishing Group).
Smart, Jackie (2001), 'The Disruptive Dialogue of Dance for the Camera', *Journal of Media Practice* 2.1: 37–47.
Smith, Anna Marie (1995), 'By Women, For Women, About Women Rules OK? The Impossibility of Visual Soliloquy', in Caroline Evans and Lorraine Gamman (eds), *A Queer Romance: Lesbians, Gay Men and Popular Culture* (Abingdon: Routledge), pp. 199–215.
Smith, Jeff (1998a), 'Did They Mention the Music? Toward a Theory of Popular Film Music', in Smith, *The Sounds of Commerce: Marketing Popular Film Music* (New York: Columbia University Press), pp. 1–22.
Smith, Jeff (1998b), *The Sounds of Commerce: Marketing Popular Film Music* (New York: Columbia University Press).
Smith, Justin (2017), '"Comparable to MTV – But Better": The Impact of *The Chart Show* on British Music Video Culture, 1986–1998', *Music, Sound, and the Moving Image* 11.1: 11–36.
Smith, Justin (2019), 'Absence and Presence: Top of the Pops and the Demand for Music Videos in the 1960s', *Journal of British Cinema and Television* 16.4: 492–544.
Smith, Marquita R. (2017), 'Beyoncé: Hip Hop Feminism and the Embodiment of Black Femininity', in Stan Hawkins (ed.), *The Routledge Research Companion to Popular Music and Gender* (Abingdon and New York: Taylor & Francis), p. 229.
Snyder, Allegra Fuller (1965), 'Three Kinds of Dance Film: A Welcome Clarification', *Dance Magazine* 39: 34–9.
Somesuch Stories (n.d.), 'White People's Vision', <https://somesuchstories.tumblr.com/post/44059213478/white-peoples-vision> (last accessed 24 January 2020).
Sommer, Sally (2009), 'C'mon to My House', in Julie Malnig (ed.), *Ballroom, Boogie, Shimmy Sham, Shake: A Social and Popular Dance Reader* (Urbana and Chicago: University of Illinois Press), pp. 285–301.
South of Watford (1986), ITV documentary series (London Weekend Television).
Southall, Mike (2009), *The Rise and Fall of EMI Records* (London: Omnibus Press).
Speiser, Peter (2017), *Soho: The Heart of Bohemian London* (London: British Library).
Spicer, Andrew (2004), 'The Production Line: Reflections on the Role of the Film Producer in British Cinema', *The Journal of British Cinema and Television* 1.2.
Spicer, Andrew (2010), 'The Precariousness of Production: Michael Klinger and the Role of the Film Producer in the British Film Industry during the 1970s', in Laurel Forster and Sue Harper (eds), *British Culture and Society in the 1970s: The Lost Decade* (Newcastle upon Tyne: Cambridge Scholars Press).
Stahl, Matthew (2002), 'Authentic Boy Bands on TV? Performers and Impresarios in *The Monkees* and *Making the Band*', *Popular Music* 21.3: 307–29.
Stahl, Matthew (2009), 'Privilege and Distinction in Production Worlds: Copyright, Collective Bargaining, and Working Conditions in Media Making', in Vicki Mayer, Miranda J. Banks and John T. Caldwell (eds), *Production Studies: Cultural Studies of Media Industries* (New York and London: Routledge), pp. 54–68.
Steimatsky, Noa (2017), *The Face on Film* (Oxford: Oxford University Press).
Stein, Gertrude (1935), *Lectures in America* (New York: Random House).

Stilwell, Robynn J. (1997). '"I just put a drone under him . . .": Collage and Subversion in the Score of *Die Hard*', *Music and Letters* 78: 551–80.

Stockdale, Nancy L. (2016), 'No Escape from Reality: The Postcolonial Glam of Freddie Mercury', in Ian Chapman and Henry Johnson, *Global Glam and Popular Music: Style and Spectacle from the 1970s to the 2000s* (Abingdon: Routledge), pp. 91–105.

Storr, Will (2011), 'The Truth about Life as a Background Dancer', *The Telegraph*, 5 June <http://www.telegraph.co.uk/culture/theatre/dance/8554651/the-truth-about-life-as-a-background-dancer.html> (last accessed 24 January 2020).

Strand, Joachim (2008), *The Cinesthetic Montage of Music-Video: Hearing the Image and Seeing the Sound* (Riga: VDM Verlag Dr Muller).

Strauven, Wanda (ed.) (2006), *The Cinema of Attractions Reloaded* (Amsterdam: Amsterdam University Press).

Street, Sarah (2012), *Colour Films in Britain: The Negotiation of Innovation 1900–1955* (London: BFI / Palgrave Macmillan).

Strøm, Gunnar (2007), 'The Two Golden Ages of Animated Music Video', *Animation* 2.

Sweeting, Adam (2008), 'Movie Soundtracks: Why British Composers Are Calling the Tune in Hollywood', *The Telegraph*, 31 January <http://www.telegraph.co.uk/culture/music/3670836/Movie-soundtracks-why-British-composers-are-calling-the-tune-in-Hollywood.html> (last accessed 24 January 2020).

Swynnoe, Jan G. (2002), *The Best Years of British Film Music, 1936–1958* (Woodbridge: Boydell & Brewer).

Tapper, John, Esther Thorson and David Black (1994), 'Profile: Variations in Music Videos as a Function of Their Musical Genre', *Journal of Broadcasting and Electronic Media* 38.1: 103–13.

Tate, Joseph (2005), *The Music and Art of Radiohead* (Farnham: Ashgate).

Taylor, Millie (2007), *British Pantomime Performance* (Bristol: Intellect Books).

Terranova, Tiziana (2000), 'Free Labor: Producing Culture for the Digital Economy', *Social Text* 63.18.2: 33–58.

Terry, Neil, John W. Cooley and Miles Zachary (2010), 'The Determinants of Foreign Box Office Revenue for English Language Movies', *Journal of International Business and Cultural Studies* 2.1: 12.

The Dave Clark Five and Beyond: Glad All Over (2014), BBC documentary.

The Flat Charleston Made Easy, short film (British Pathé, UK, 1927), <https://www.youtube.com/watch?v=CwtJMNeU1to> (last accessed 24 January 2020).

The Guardian (2004), 'Top of the Pops through the Decades', 29 November, <https://www.theguardian.com/music/2004/nov/29/popandrock.television> (last accessed 24 January 2020).

Thomas, Philippa (2014), 'Single Ladies, Plural: Racism, Scandal, and "Authenticity" within the Multiplication and Circulation of Online Dance Discourses', in Melissa Blanco Borelli (ed.), *The Oxford Handbook of Dance and the Popular Screen* (Oxford: Oxford University Press), pp. 289–304.

Thomson, Graeme (2012), *Under the Ivy: The Life and Music of Kate Bush*, revised and updated edition (London: Omnibus Press).

Thomson, Graeme (2014), '"This girl is very, very tough . . .": The Untold Story of Kate Bush's *Hounds of Love*', *Uncut*, August, <https://www.uncut.co.uk/features/

this-girl-is-very-very-tough-the-untold-story-of-kate-bush-s-hounds-of-love-4812/> (last accessed 24 January 2020).

Tierney, Luke, 'King Krule "A Lizard State" by Jamie-James Medina', *Promo News*, 10 January 2014 <https://www.promonews.tv/videos/2014/01/10/king-krule-lizard-state-jamie-james-medina/23522> (last accessed 4 November 2018).

Todorov, Tzvetan (1975), *The Fantastic: A Structural Approach to a Literary Genre*, trans. R. Howard (New York: Cornell University Press).

Todorov, Tzvetan (1981), *Introduction to Poetics*, trans. R. Howard (Brighton: Harvester).

Tsai, Addie (2016), 'Hybrid Texts, Assembled Bodies: Michel Gondry's Merging of Camera and Dancer in "Let Forever Be"', *The International Journal of Screendance* 6.

TV.com (n.d.), *Tiswas* episode guide <http://www.tv.com/shows/tiswas/episodes/all/> (last accessed 24 January 2020).

Vachon, Christine (2002), *Shooting To Kill: How an Independent Producer Blasts Through the Barriers To Make Movies that Matter* (New York: Quill).

Vaughan, David (2002), 'Merce Cunningham's Choreography for the Camera', in Judy Mitoma (ed.), *Envisioning Dance on Film and Video* (New York and London: Routledge), pp. 34–8.

Vernallis, Carol (2001), 'Kindest Cut: Screen Editing in Music Video', *Journal of Cultural Economics* 32.4: 243–59.

Vernallis, Carol (2002), 'The Functions of Lyrics in Music Video', *Journal of Popular Music Studies* 14.1: 11–31.

Vernallis, Carol (2004), *Experiencing Music Video: Aesthetics and Cultural Context* (New York: Columbia University Press).

Vernallis, Carol (2007), 'Strange People, Weird Objects: The Nature of Narrativity, Character, and Editing in Music Videos', in Roger Beebe and Jason Middleton (eds), *Medium Cool: Music Videos from Soundies to Cellphones* (Durham, NC, and London: Duke University Press), pp. 303–28.

Vernallis, Carol (2008), 'Music Video, Songs, Sound: Experience, Technique and Emotion in *Eternal Sunshine of the Spotless Mind*', *Screen* 49.3: 277–97.

Vernallis, Carol (2010), 'Music Video and YouTube: New Aesthetics and Generic Transformations', in Henry Keazor and Thorsten Wübbena (eds), *Rewind, Play, Fast Forward: The Past, Present and Future of the Music Video* (Berlin: De Gruyter), pp. 233–61.

Vernallis, Carol (2013a), *Unruly Media: YouTube, Music Video and the New Digital Cinema* (Oxford: Oxford University Press).

Vernallis, Carol (2013b), 'Music Video's Second Aesthetic?', in John Richardson, Claudia Gorbman and Carol Vernallis (eds), *The Oxford Handbook of New Audiovisual Aesthetics* (Oxford: Oxford University Press), pp. 437–65.

Vernallis, Carol, and Hannah Ueno (2013), 'Interview with Music Video Director and Auteur Floria Sigismondi', *Music, Sound, and the Moving Image* 7.2: 167–94.

Vincent, Richard C. (1989), 'Clio's Consciousness Raised? Portrayal of Women in Rock Videos Re-Examined', *Journalism Quarterly* 66: 155–60.

Vincent, Richard C., Dennis K. Davis and Lilly Ann Boruszkowski (1987), 'Sexism on MTV: The Portrayal of Women in Rock Videos', *Journalism Quarterly* 64.4: 750–941.

Vize, Lesley (2003), 'Music and the Body in Dance Film', in Ian Inglis (ed.), *Popular Music and Film* (London: Wallflower), pp. 22–38.

Waldrep, Shelton (2004), *The Aesthetics of Self-Invention: Oscar Wilde to David Bowie* (Minneapolis: University of Minnesota Press).

Waldrep, Shelton (2016), 'David Bowie and the Art of Performance', in Ian Chapman and Henry Johnson, *Global Glam and Popular Music: Style and Spectacle from the 1970s to the 2000s* (Abingdon: Routledge), pp. 50–62.

Wallis, Cara (2011), 'Performing Gender: A Content Analysis of Gender Display in Music Videos', *Sex Roles* 64.3–4: 160–72.

Wallis, Roger, and Krister Malm (1988), 'Push-Pull for the Video Clip: A Systems Approach to the Relationship between the Phonogram / Videogram Industry and Music Television', *Popular Music* 7.03: 267–84.

Ward, L. M. (2003), 'Understanding the Role of Entertainment Media in the Sexual Socialization of American Youth: A Review of Empirical Research', *Developmental Review* 23: 347–88.

Warwick, Jacqueline (2013), *Girl Groups, Girl Culture: Popular Music and Identity in the 1960s* (Abingdon: Routledge).

Weidhase, Nathalie (2015), '"Beyoncé feminism" and the Contestation of the Black Feminist Body', *Celebrity Studies* 6.1: 128–31.

Weis, Elizabeth, and John Belton (1985), *Film Sound: Theory and Practice* (Columbia: Columbia University Press).

Wells, Matt (2001), 'Wild Child takes on Gay Big Brother in Battle for Saturday Morning TV Ratings', *The Guardian*, 22 September <https://www.theguardian.com/media/2001/sep/22/uknews> (last accessed 24 January 2020).

Wener, Louise (2010), *Different for Girls: My True-life Adventures in Pop* (New York: Random House).

West, Candace, and Don H. Zimmerman (1987), 'Doing Gender', *Gender and Society* 1.2: 125–51.

Whiteley, Sheila (1997a), 'Seduced by the Sign', in Sheila Whiteley (ed.), *Sexing the Groove: Popular Music and Gender* (New York: Routledge), pp. 259–76.

Whiteley, Sheila (1997b), 'Little Red Rooster v. The Honkey Tonk Woman: Mick Jagger, Sexuality, Style and Image', in Sheila Whiteley (ed.), *Sexing the Groove: Popular Music and Gender* (New York: Routledge), pp. 67–99.

Whiteley, Sheila (2000), *Women and Popular Music: Sexuality, Identity and Subjectivity* (Abingdon: Routledge).

Whiteley, Sheila ([2007] 2013a), 'Which Freddie? Constructions of Masculinity in Freddie Mercury and Justin Hawkins', in Freya Jarman-Ivens (ed.), *Oh Boy!: Masculinities and Popular Music* (Abingdon: Routledge), pp. 29–46.

Whiteley, Sheila (2013b), *Women and Popular Music: Sexuality, Identity and Subjectivity* (Abingdon: Routledge).

Williams, Eliza (2014), 'Five Amazing Kate Bush Videos', *Creative Review*, 26 August, <https://www.creativereview.co.uk/cr-blog/2014/august/five-amazing-kate-bush-videos/> (last accessed 24 January 2020).

Winship, Lyndsey (2015), 'Meet the Man Behind FKA twigs' Experimental Performances', *Evening Standard*, 19 August, <https://www.standard.co.uk/lifestyle/london-life/meet-

the-man-behind-fka-twigs-experimental-performances-a2916976.html> (last accessed 24 January 2020).

Winters, Ben (2007), *Erich Wolfgang Korngold's The Adventures of Robin Hood: A Film Score Guide* (Lanham, MD: Scarecrow Press).

Wire (2012), 'William Burroughs's The Final Academy Resurrected in London', 20 September, <http://www.thewire.co.uk/news/19271/willliam-burroughs_s-the-final-academy-resurrected-in-london> (last accessed 24 January 2020).

Wojcik, Pamela Robertson, and Arthur Knight (eds) (2001), *Soundtrack Available: Essays on Film and Popular Music* (Durham, NC, and London).

Wollen, Peter (1986), 'Ways of Thinking about Music Video (and Post-Modernism)', *Critical Quarterly* 28.1: 167–70.

Woodall, Joanna (ed.), *Portraiture: Facing the Subject* (Manchester: Manchester University Press).

Wright, Julia Lobalzo (2017), 'The Boy Kept Swinging: David Bowie, Music Video and the Star Image', in Gina Arnold, Daniel Cookney, Kirsty Fairclough and Michael Goddard (eds), *Music / Video: Histories, Aesthetics, Media* (New York: Bloomsbury Publishing USA), pp. 67–78.

Xu, Haifeng, and Nadee Goonawardene (2014), 'Does Movie Soundtrack Matter? The Role of Soundtrack in Predicting Movie Revenue', *Proceedings of the 19th Pacific Asia Conference on Information Systems* (PACIS 2014) (Atlanta: Association for Information Systems).

Young, Rob (2005), *Warp: Labels Unlimited* (London: Black Dog).

INDEX

Academy, 100
Adam and the Ants
   'Stand and Deliver', 25
advertising industry
   music videos as advertising, 10, 11, 112, 130, 151
   online, 117, 153
   television advertising model, 10, 116, 130
Afrika Bambaata
   Afrika Shox', 120, 131, 134
Alan Smithee (pseudonym), 48–9
All Seeing I
   'The Beat Goes On', 68
Allen, Lily, 77
   'Hard Out Here', 101
The Animals
   pop promos, 5
   'When I Was Young', 22
animation
   in concept videos, 23–4
   DJ-led electronic music, 35, 36
anthropology, 13
Aphex Twins
   'Come to Daddy', 97, 133, 136
   'Windowlicker', 70–1, 130

appropriation
   African American dance, 62–4, 139
   ballet and dance film, 64–7
   club dance, 67–8
   music video as appropriation art, 18–19
   remediation in music videos, 147–8
   traits from Hollywood musicals, 58–61
Arcade Fire
   'We Exist', 60
Arctic Monkeys
   'Arabella', 36
   'Brianstorm', 70
   'The View from the Afternoon', 21
Arnell, Vaughan, 29, 44, 82, 86, 94, 136
Art of Noise
   'Close (to the Edit)', 21, 43, 142
artists
   acting skills of, 28–9
   as anti-heroes, 36, 136
   artist-as-authentic, 5, 6–7, 32–3, 88, 96, 124, 143
   artistic control of television performances, 107–8
   at British art schools, 128

INDEX

director-artist relationships, 5–6, 32–3, 88, 94–5, 103, 150–1
female rock artists, 75
moral rights of, 91, 130
audiences
   authentication of music videos by, 6, 7, 14
   loss of captive audiences, 115–16, 153
   for music videos, 3
   see also fans
authenticity
   artist-as-authentic, 5, 6–7, 32–3, 88, 96, 124, 143
   as an ascribed quality, 6–7, 14
   auteur producers, 100
   banned videos, 131
   in club dance videos, 67
   crisis of in America, 127
   in dance videos, 58, 70
   fan authentication, 3, 67, 101–3
   of genre works, 19
   grime videos, 111–12, 127
   mediatised videos and, 7, 32
   MTV Unplugged series, 7
   narratives of, 7
   objections to mimed performances, 107–8
authorship
   the artist as author, 101
   artist involvement, 94–6
   artistry-authenticity relationship, 88, 96
   auteur framework, 91–3
   British moral rights culture, 91, 130
   copyright regime, 90–1, 92, 149
   creative control, 6, 48–9
   director-artist relationships, 94–5, 103
   of directors, 4–5, 90
   fan authentication, 101–3
   fan-authored works, 149–50
   legal authorship, 90–1
   the studio as auteur, 97–8
   the video commissioner's influence, 98–9

Bananarama
   sales in America, 125
   'Venus', 57, 58
   'The Video Singles', 114–15
Barron, Siobhan, 109, 125
Barron, Steve, 9–10, 25, 92, 109, 125, 126, 130, 135
Basement Jaxx
   'Hush Baby', 59
   'Red Alert', 68
   'U Don't Know Me', 36, 136
   'Where's Your Head At', 135, 137
Basil, Toni, 57, 139
BBC, 9, 106; see also *Top of the Pops (TOTP)*
The Beatles
   American influences on, 138
   on European channels, 109
   gender performance, 73
   A Hard Day's Night, 20, 41, 139
   'I Should Have Known Better', 20
   in the States, 124
Beckett, Steve, 3, 97
Benassi, Benni
   'Satisfaction', 76–7
Benstock, Jez, 136
Bentley Rhythm Ace
   'Bentley's Gonna Sort You Out', 30
Berkeley, Busby, 58
Beyoncé
   artistic expression through videos, 140
   Lemonade, 121
   'Single Ladies', 62, 63–4
Bixler, Litza, 69
Björk
   as artist-composer, 155
   'Big Time Sensuality', 85
   'It's Oh So Quiet', 59
   Volumen, 115
Black Dog Films, 12, 125, 132
Blakey, Holly, 55, 67, 121
Blondie
   Eat to the Beat, 139
Blunt, Dean
   'Mersh', 116, 120, 142
Blunt, James
   'You're Beautiful', 82

213

Blur
  'Coffee and TV', 26
  'Music Is My Radar', 70
  'Parklife', 26, 94
  'Song 2', 31, 36, 76
Bowie, David
  artistic persona, 56, 79, 137
  'Ashes to Ashes', 79
  'John, I'm Only Dancing', 106–7
  mediatised videos, 7, 21, 32
  sales in America, 125
British, term, 7, 8
Bubbles, Barney, 133–4
the Buggles
  'Video Killed the Radio Star', 2, 106, 109, 135
Burton-Fairbrother, Carole, 71, 86–7, 99, 100, 131–2, 133, 136
Bush, Kate
  'Cloudbusting', 34, 84, 106
  The Hair of the Hound, 114
  The Line, The Cross and the Curse, 56
  'Running Up That Hill', 61, 65, 84, 106
  the self as work of art, 137
  The Whole Story, 114
  as woman artist–director, 83–4
  'Wuthering Heights', 74

Cabaret Voltaire, 113, 121
Cameron, Angus, 50–1
Channel 4, 110
The Chart Show, 2, 110–11, 157
The Chemical Brothers
  'Believe', 35, 134
  Born in the Echoes, 65
  'Elektrobank', 29
  'Let Forever Be', 58–9
  'Midnight Madness', 57
  'Out of Control', 135
  'Setting Sun', 85, 97
  video artistry of, 96–7
  'Wide Open', 65–6
Cherry, Neneh
  'Buffalo Stance', 62
choreography

African American dance, 62–4, 139
  by the artist, 59, 61
  ballet and dance film, 64–7
  in British music videos, 55–6
  casting of non-dancers, 69–70
  club dance videos, 67, 68
  the Hollywood musical, 58–61
  for interior mental states, 56
  movement direction and, 57–8
  in US dance videos, 59–60, 62, 69, 71
  see also dance videos
Christopherson, Peter, 12, 33–4, 80–1, 152
The Clash
  'London's Burning', 32
Coil
  'Tainted Love', 80–1
Coldcut
  'Timber', 21
Coldplay
  'Life in Technicolor II', 21
  'Place Your Hands Up', 21
commissioners
  artists' authenticity and, 143, 144
  differences in the British/US markets, 131–2
  genre concept and, 143
  influence of, 98–9
  open briefs, 133
  role of, 100, 145
  women as, 99
computer-generated imagery (CGI), 23–4, 36
COUM Transmissions, 80
Creation, 132
Crome, John, 23, 41
Culture Club, 125
Cunningham, Chris, 1, 70–1, 92, 93, 97, 120, 130, 132, 133, 134, 136
The Cure
  'Close to Me', 21, 42, 142
Curtis, Ian, 33
Curtis, Russell, 102
Cyrus, Miley, 77

dance videos
  African American dance, 62–4, 139
  authenticity in, 58, 70
  ballet and dance film, 64–7
  club dance, 67–8
  dance drama, 60
  Hollywood musicals and, 58–61
  movement direction, 56–8
  within the music video genre, 55–6
  scholarship on, 55, 56, 154
  star dancer performances, 61
  street casting in, 69–70
  'street dance' tradition, 62
  utopian redemption in, 60–1
  see also choreography

Dave Clark Five
  in America, 124, 139
  archives for, 156–7
  Catch Us If You Can, 124
  'Hits in Action', 124
  'Nineteen Days', 78, 124

Devo, 57, 120, 139
Dick, Nigel, 106, 132
Dire Straits
  'Money for Nothing', 40, 129, 135, 137

directors
  as auteurs, 5, 6, 32–3, 91–3, 143–4
  authorship of, 4–5, 90
  at British art schools, 128–9
  British directors in America, 125–6, 132–3
  careers as photographers, 26–7, 152
  director-artist relationships, 5–6, 32–3, 88, 94–5, 103, 150–1
  directors' cuts, 15
  independent film production (1966-76), 4–5
  moral rights, 91, 130
  music video as appropriation art, 18–19
  telecine process, 9
  track selection skills, 93–4
  use of editing, 44, 45–6
  women artist–directors, 83–4
  women directors, 83

The Directors' Label, 92–3
distribution
  in America, 108
  European television channels, 108–9
  internet, 115–22
  MTV's role, 105
  music videos as television programmes, 112–13
  television, 105–12, 115
  VHS distribution, 113–14
  video albums, 114–15

Dizzee Rascal
  Boy in da Corner, 111
  'Dream', 28, 37
  'Sirens', 135

DJ-led electronic music, 26, 34–5, 146
Dodds, Sherril, 56, 62, 119–20
Dolby, Thomas
  'Close But No Cigar', 135, 137
Dom & Nic, 16, 29, 65–6, 68, 85, 96–7, 100, 101, 134
Doves
  'Black and White Town', 48, 49
  Some Cities, 48–9
Doyle, Julian, 34
Drew, Ben, 26
Duran
  Arena (An Absurd Notion), 114
  MTV exposure, 125
  'The Wild Boys', 23, 114
DVD boxset (*Power to the People*), 14–15, 16–17

editing
  colour grading, 51–2
  concept videos, 42–4, 53
  directors' use of, 44, 45–6
  editors' role, 40, 145–6
  musicality and, 40–1, 44–5
  narrative videos, 48–50
  performance videos, 44–6
  process of, 41–2, 45–6, 53
  psychological realism, 50–1
  re-edited masters, 15
  scholarship on, 39, 40
  single-shot videos, 46–7
Egan, Nick, 18–19, 26–7, 132

Ellis Bextor, Sophie
   'Murder on the Dance Floor', 136
Eurythmics
   'Love is a Stranger', 74–5
   sales in America, 125
   Savage, 75
   Savage (video album), 114, 139
   'Sweet Dreams', 23, 75
   see also Lennox, Annie

Faithfull, Marianne, 148
   'Broken English', 73–4
Faithless
   'We Come One', 68
fans
   fan authentication, 3, 67, 101–3
   fan-authored works, 149–50
Fat White Family
   'Touch the Leather', 83, 120
Fatboy Slim
   'Praise You', 69, 116–17
   'Weapon of Choice', 59
filmmakers *see* directors
FKA twigs
   career as a dancer, 61, 67, 76
   'Cellophane', 61
   'Glass & Patron', 76
   'Video Girl', 76
   'Water Me', 76
   as woman artist–director, 83
A Flock of Seagulls
   A Flock of Seagulls, 109–10
Florence and the Machine
   'Drumming Song', 57
Flowered Up
   'Weekender', 102
Fosse, Bob, 56, 63, 64
4AD, 98
Frankfurt School, 19
Frankie Goes to Hollywood
   'Relax', 79–80, 107
   'Two Tribes', 80
Futureshock
   'Late At Night', 68

Gallagher, Noel, 37, 103, 132; *see also* Oasis

Gee, Grant, 27, 99
gender
   in Annie Lennox's work, 74–5
   in David Bowie's work, 79
   depictions of female sexuality, 72, 73–5, 85–7, 147
   and ethnicity, 76
   expressions of gender fluidity, 73, 141
   glam rock artists, 79, 81
   heteronormative masculinities, 77, 80–2
   hypersexualised male artists, 77–8, 82–3, 124
   parodies of sexist stereotyping, 76–7
   punk feminism, 73–4, 86
   woman artist–directors, 83–4
   women in the film industry, 83–5
genre
   artistic portraiture, 27
   concept videos, 22–6, 36, 42–4, 53, 95, 146
   cycles of, 29–30, 34, 143
   defined, 18, 143
   dramatic arcs, 21–2
   feature film genres, 28
   grime videos, 111–12, 127
   homage, 31, 37
   love story videos, 28
   metaphoric imagery, 21
   music genres and video genre, 34
   of music video, 19
   in music video, 26–8
   music video as appropriation art, 18–19, 62–4
   narrative videos, 24–6, 34, 48–50
   parodies/pastiche, 31, 36
   performance videos, 20–2, 27, 31, 32, 44–6
   references to British TV dramas, 27–8
   reverse narrative cycle, 30
   sports narratives, 29–30
   US/British mutual cultural influences, 138–41
   visual-led videos, 35–6
Gent, Dilly, 99, 101, 131
glam rock, 79, 137

Glazer, Jonathan, 24, 52, 61, 92, 96, 99, 100, 130, 156
Godley and Creme
　art school educations, 128
　'Cry', 27, 152
　'Rockit', 43–4
　'Two Tribes', 80
Gold, Gwilym
　'Triumph', 67
Gomez
　'Bring It On', 31
Gondry, Michel, 58–9, 92, 99, 135, 137
'Gorilla' advert, 117
Gowers, Bruce, 27, 125
Grant, Brian, 125, 126
grime videos, 111–12, 127, 140
Guns N' Roses
　'November Rain', 34, 126

Hancock, Herbie
　'Rockit', 43–4
Hardcastle, Paul
　'19', 35
Harvey, PJ, 128
　'Down By the Water', 24
　'This is Love', 85
　'This is Love', 75
Heslop, Richard, 43, 45, 100
Hexstatic, 21
High Flying Birds
　'Ballad of the Mighty I', 103, 135
hip-hop culture, 81–2
homophobia, 77, 80–1
Hook, Peter, 33
Hopkins, Jon
　'Open Eye Signal', 117–18
Horne, Trevor, 43, 77, 78, 98
Hot Chips
　'Over and Over', 116
Human League
　'Don't You Want Me', 25, 126
　sales in America, 125
Hunter, Paul, 63, 70, 127
Hurts
　'Lights', 60

Ifans, Rhys, 31
internet
　democratisation of production, 116–17
　digital music video, 147
　loss of the captive audience and, 115–16, 153
　lyric videos, 117, 120–1
　mobile platforms, 156
　music video consumption on, 118, 153
　novelty and spectacle, 116, 119
　remediation in music videos, 147, 148–9
　role of the visual, 117–18
　simplicity for, 120
　user-generated content (UGC), 149–50
　see also YouTube
Iron Maiden
　'Can I Play with Madness', 34

Jackson, Janet
　'Rhythm Nation', 59–60
Jackson, Michael
　'Billie Jean', 126
　'Thriller', 59–60, 62
Jagger, Mick, 20–1, 73, 74; see also Rolling Stones
Jamelia
　'Money', 70
James, Tony, 35
Jamiroquai
　'Virtual Insanity', 61
Jarman, Derek, 12, 73–4, 119, 128, 151
John, Elton
　Visions, 114
Jones, Grace
　'I've Seen That Face Before / Libertango', 76
Jonze, Spike, 1, 8, 29, 30, 59, 116, 133
Joy Division
　'Love Will Tear Us Apart', 33, 116
Judas Priest
　'Breaking the Law', 135
　British Steel, 135

Kasbian
  '*Club Foot*', 135
Kaye, Tony, 48–9
Kearns, Tony, 31, 40, 41, 46, 48
Kemp, Lindsay, 56
Kessler, Liz, 22, 30, 49, 100, 119, 120
Khan, Akram, 66–7, 94, 147
King Krule
  '*A Lizard State*', 37
The Kinks
  in British musical culture, 138
  '*Dead End Street*', 25, 31, 108, 124, 148
  promo clips, 4
Kirkby, Mat, 36, 136
Klein
  '*Marks of Worship*', 119
K-pop videos, 120
Kubaisi, Tareq, 9, 52

Ledwidge, Ringan, 29, 31, 42, 96
Leftfield
  Afrika Shox', 35, 120, 131, 134
Lennox, Annie
  Diva, 75, 84, 152
  Diva (video album), 114, 139
  gender performance, 74–5
  '*Little Bird*', 75
  mediatised videos, 21, 32
  Oil Factory, 100
  the self as work of art, 137
  '*Why*', 75, 84, 152
  see also Eurythmics
Lester, Richard, 20, 41, 139
Letts, Don, 32
Limelight, 125
Lindsay, Tom, 40
Lindsay-Hogg, Michael, 20–1
Losey, Luke, 136
love story videos, 28

McArdle, Aoife, 26, 83, 117–18, 121
McGregor, Wayne, 57, 66, 147
McLaren, Malcolm
  authenticity and, 107
  '*Buffalo Gals*', 62

Manfred Mann
  '*The Mighty Quinn*', 23, 41
  performance videos, 20
Manic Street Preachers
  '*Design for Life*', 94
  '*If You Tolerate This Your Children Will be Next*', 135
Massive Attack
  '*Karmacoma*', 24, 96
  '*Teardrop*', 23, 142
  '*Unfinished Sympathy*', 47, 116
  video artistry of, 95–6
Mathieson, John, 47
May, Brian, 28
mediatised videos
  artist/director tensions over, 32–3
  authenticity and, 7, 21, 32
  defined, 32
  '*It's Only Rock 'n Roll (But I Like It)*', 20–1
  performance videos, 32
Mercury, Freddie
  art school education, 128
  mediatised videos, 32
  the self as work of art, 137
  sexuality, 28, 81
  see also Queen
MGMM, 10, 125
M.I.A. (Maya Arulpragasam)
  art school education, 128
  '*Bad Girls*', 83, 135
  '*Born Free*', 135
  '*Boyz*', 134–5
  '*Double Bubble Trouble*', 135
Michael, George
  '*Faith*', 44, 51, 78
  '*I Want Your Sex*', 78
  '*Outside*', 86
Millaney, Scott, 41, 109
Minogue, Kylie
  '*Can't Get You Out of My Head*', 59, 60, 103
  Showgirl, 67
Mitchell Brothers
  '*Routine Check*', 112
Moby
  '*Body Rock*', 69

Moloko
  'Familiar Feeling', 68
Monkees, 108, 139
Moonlandingz
  'The Strangle of Anna', 72–3
Morahan, Andy, 1, 34, 44, 51, 78, 103, 126–7, 128, 132, 133
Morley, Paul, 43, 80, 98
Mount Kimbie, 142
  'Before I Move Off', 118, 142
Mr Benn, 137
Ms Dynamite
  'It Takes More', 102–3
MTV
  British content on, 109–10, 125
  consumption of music videos on, 120
  depictions of female sexuality, 72
  and the emergence of the music video form, 1, 146
  impact on music video production, 126–7
  MTV aesthetic, 39, 41, 45, 46
  TV-safe versions, 15
  in the UK, 110
  and US cultural imperialism, 1, 2
  as video distribution channel, 105
MTV Europe, 44, 110
MTV UK, 111
MTV Unplugged series, 7
Mulcahy, Russell, 25, 92, 114, 125
Muller, Sophie, 31, 44, 46, 59, 75, 76, 83–5, 94, 100, 103, 114, 121, 125, 128, 152
Mundy, John, 4, 55
Murch, Walter, 40
music videos
  as advertising, 10, 11, 112, 130, 151
  as an American format, 1–2, 146
  archives of, 14–16, 156–7
  audio/visual relationship, 142–3
  British culture of, 7–8
  British post-production industry, 129–30
  within the British screen industries sector, 11
  British style of, 131–8, 146
  as commercial film art, 3
  commercial value of, 1990s, 5
  film medium of, 9
  historical overview of, 3–5
  as an industrial product, 19, 149, 150, 151
  licensing deals for, 11
  parallels with album covers, 151–3
  as postmodern, 147–8
  remediation in, 148–9
  role of British art schools, 128–9, 146, 152
  as a route into commercial film, 5, 25–6, 29, 92, 130–1
  scholarship on, 1, 2–3, 10, 11–12, 142, 143–4, 154–7
  term, 9–10
Music Week, 9, 10, 13
musical shorts, 4–5
musicals, 2, 55
musicians *see* artists
Mute Records, 98
My Bloody Valentine
  'To Here Knows When', 50–1

Nash, Tim, 143
Nava, Emil, 133
Nava, Jake, 62, 63–4, 81–2, 85–6, 102–3, 133
New Order
  'True Faith', 64–5, 119–20
Nine Inch Nails (NIN), 137
  'March of the Pigs', 33–4

Oasis
  Definitely Maybe, 132
  'The Importance of Being Idle', 31
  intertextual referencing, 37
  'Morning Glory', 132
  What's the Story, Morning Glory? 132
O'Connor, Sinéad
  hair style, 75
  'Nothing Compares 2 U', 27, 46
  spat with Miley Cyrus, 77
Oil Factory, 100–1, 125
OK Go
  'Here It Goes Again', 117

O'Keefe, Mike, 117, 118, 120–1, 131, 150
One Direction
 'Best Song Ever', 118
Orbital
 'The Box', 136

Pet Shop Boys
 'West End Girls', 51–2
Pharcyde
 'Drop', 30
Pink Floyd
 'Arnold Lane', 128
 'Money', 15
 performance videos, 20
 pop promos, 5, 20
pluggers, 10, 106, 107, 131
Pope, Tim, 21, 42, 128, 142
post-production companies
 experimentation in, 136–7
 Rushes, 129
 Soho cluster effect, 7–8, 9, 40, 51, 53, 129, 131, 137, 145
 telecine process, 9
 in the UK, 129–30
Power to the People (DVD boxset), 14–15, 16–17
The Prodigy
 'Firestarter', 31, 45
 'Out of Space', 67–8, 102
 'Smack My Bitch Up', 131
production companies
 Academy, 100
 auteur *producers*, 100
 authorship claims, 90
 international culture of, 8
 Limelight, 125
 MGMM, 125
 Oil Factory, 100–1, 125
 partnership agreements, 125
 production culture, 6, 8
 production process, 88–90
 Soho cluster effect, 7–8, 9, 40, 51, 53, 129, 131, 137, 145
 in the States, 125
 value chains, 19
Promo News, 13

promotional clips (promos)
 authored art-school promotional clip, 124, 128
 on the BBC, 106
 concept of, 10
 Dave Clark Five, 124
 editing of, 41
 emergence of, 8–9, 146
 exported to America, 124, 137
 as an industrial product, 19
 1960s promos, 4–5, 20
Propaganda Films, 12, 125, 132
protest videos, 140–1
Prydz, Eric
 'Call on Me', 76–7
Pulp
 'Common People', 94, 95

Queen
 'Bohemian Rhapsody', 2, 27, 50, 107, 125, 137
 'I Want to Break Free', 28, 81

Radiohead
 'Just', 26, 30, 48
 'Meeting People Is Easy', 99
 'No Surprises', 27, 46, 99, 101, 116
 'Street Spirit (Fade Out)', 24, 50, 52, 137, 145
ramping, 52
Ramsay, Lynne, 48, 49
Ridley Scott Associates (RSA), 12, 125, 132
Rolling Stones
 American influences on, 138
 'It's Only Rock 'n Roll (But I Like It)', 20–1, 32
 Video Rewind, 114
 'We Love You', 148
Romhanyi, Pedro, 94–5, 100
Rooney, Michael, 59
Roots Manuva
 'Witness (1 Hope)', 36
 'Witness the Fitness', 136
Rose, Bernard, 134

Roseman, Jon, 125–6
Rushes, 129
Rybczyński, Zbigniew, 21, 43, 95

Sade
   'No Ordinary Love', 76, 85
   'Smooth Operator', 25–6
Salute
   'Storm', 69–70
Saoudi, Lias, 72, 83
Scott, Jake, 132
Seal
   'Killer', 82
Searll, Don, 82
Shadforth, Dawn, 31, 45–6, 56, 59, 60, 68, 72, 83, 85, 103
Shakespears Sister
   'Goodbye Cruel World', 31, 85
Shoes
   'Time to Dance', 49–50
Shynola, 23–4, 129
Sigue Sputnik
   'Love-Missile F1-11', 35–6
Sillis, Aaron, 55, 59, 61, 66, 67
Siouxsie and the Banshees, 86
   'Happy House', 74
Skepta, 111
   'It Ain't Safe', 112, 127
Skint Records, 8, 98
The Smiths, 150–1
So Solid Crew, 62–3
Soft Cell
   Non-Stop Erotic Cabaret, 114
   Non-Stop Exotic Video Show, 114
Soho, London, 7–8, 9, 40, 51, 53, 129, 131, 137, 145
The Specials
   'Ghost Town', 133–4, 147
Spice Girls
   depictions of femininity, 86–7
   'Say You'll Be There', 86
Stakker / Humanoid
   'Stakker Humanoid', 35
Stern, Walter, 23, 96, 100
Stewart, Dave, 100
Stewart, John, 100–1
Stiff Records, 80, 106, 132

Sutton, Carrie, 116–17, 119, 131, 132

Take That
   'Back for Good', 78
Talking Heads
   'Once in a Lifetime', 57, 120, 139
Taylor, Kris P., 109
techniques
   colour grading, 52
   early trick films, 154
   experimentation in, 50, 52, 129–30, 136–7, 147
   FX techniques for dance videos, 57
   the 'how did they do that?' factor, 23, 24, 40, 61, 116, 117
   innovative, 52
   intercutting techniques, 22–3
   motion capture, 68
   ramping, 52
   use of novelty effects, 137
telecine process, 9, 51–2
television
   advertising model, 10
   in America, 108, 126
   Channel U, 111–12
   The Chart Show, 2, 110–11, 157
   commercials, 112
   The Ed Sullivan Show, 124
   European television channels, 108–9
   Live and Kicking, 111
   loss of the captive audience, 115–16, 153
   Mr Benn, 137
   music videos on, 105–12
   TISWAS, 107
   TV-safe versions of videos, 15
   Video Jukebox, 108, 126
   see also MTV; Top of the Pops (TOTP)
Temple, Julien, 25, 135
Therapy?
   'Diane', 52
Thorgerson, Storm, 12, 128, 152
Thraves, Jamie, 26, 30, 44, 48, 93, 100, 121, 125, 128
3D (Robert Del Naja), 96

TISWAS, 107
Top of the Pops (TOTP)
  consumption of music videos on, 2
  mimed performances, 20, 106–7
  rules on music videos, 106–7, 134
  TV-safe versions, 15
Toy
  'Lose My Way', 22, 46, 142–3
Tricky
  '*Black Steel*', 50
23 Skidoo
  '7 Songs', 43

UB40
  '*Red Wine*', 107, 134, 147
Ultravox
  '*Vienna*', 25, 28
United States of America (USA)
  adoption of music video genre, 123, 125–7, 137
  African American dance, 62–4, 139
  artistic expression through videos, 140–1
  British directors in, 125–6, 132–3
  British invasions of, 2, 123–4, 125, 127
  British promos in, 124, 137
  crisis of authenticity, 127
  distribution in, 108
  The Ed Sullivan Show, 124
  music video as an American format, 1–2, 146
  mutual cultural influences, 138–41
  production companies in, 125–6, 127
  traits from Hollywood musicals, 58–61
  Video Jukebox, 108, 126
  see also MTV
UNKLE
  '*Guns Blazin*'', 23–4
Us, 100, 121, 135
user-generated content (UGC), 149–50

Vampire Weekend
  '*A-Punk*', 21–2
video albums, 114–15, 121, 139
Video Jukebox, 108

Warp Records, 3, 8, 97–8
Weait, Ollie, 98
Weller, Paul
  '*Changing Man*', 94–5
  Stanley Road, 95
Whale
  '*Crying at Airports feat. Bus*', 29
Whitehead, Peter, 5, 9, 20, 22, 106, 108, 119, 128, 148, 156
The Who
  '*Happy Jack*', 148
  pop promos, 20, 106
  Quadrophenia, 102
Wiley
  '*Cash in My Pocket*', 143
  as a main grime MC, 111, 112
  '*Numbers in Action*', 135, 137
  '*Wearing My Rolex*', 143
Williams, Hype, 1, 60, 63, 64, 70, 127
Williams, Robbie
  acting skills of, 28–9
  mediatised videos, 21, 32
  '*Rock DJ*', 29, 82
  '*She's the One*', 29
  '*Supreme*', 29, 136
Wilson, Dougal, 21, 27–8, 37
WIZ, 21, 26, 96, 100, 102, 121, 125, 135
Wolfe, Daniel, 26, 49, 121

Yardley, David, 40, 41
Young, Will
  '*Who Am I?*', 28
The Young Fathers
  '*Shame*', 70
YouTube
  consumption of music videos on, 120–1
  as a cultural archive, 14–15
  impact on music video genres, 116
  impact on music video production, 140
  low-fi model for, 116–17
  participatory culture of, 150

ZTT Records, 43, 80, 98

EU representative:
Easy Access System Europe
Mustamäe tee 50, 10621 Tallinn, Estonia
Gpsr.requests@easproject.com